CONTENTS

Helion & Company Limited
Unit 8 Amherst Business Centre
Budbrooke Road
Warwick
CV34 5WE
England
Tel. 01926 499 619
Email: info@helion.co.uk
Website: www.helion.co.uk
Twitter: @helionbooks
Visit our blog http://blog.helion.co.uk/

Text © Alexander Mladenov and Evgeni
Andonov 2020
Photographs © authors' collections unless
otherwise noted
Colour profiles ©Peter Penev 2020
Maps © Peter Penev 2020

Designed & typeset by Farr out Publications,
Wokingham, Berkshire
Cover design Paul Hewitt, Battlefield Design
(www.battlefield-design.co.uk)
Printed by Henry Ling Limited, Dorchester,
Dorset

ISBN 978-1-912866-91-5

British Library Cataloguing-in-Publication
Data
A catalogue record for this book is available
from the British Library

Bulgarian Air Force Military Ranks and their US Equivalents

Abbreviations   2

Introduction   3

1 Post-War Air Arm Reorganisations   5
2 New-style Air Arm in Construction and Expansion   9
3 Entering into the Jet Era   17
4 VVS enters the MiG-15 Era   24
5 Bulgarian Air Defences' Deepening Woes   31
6 Flight LY402 down   40
7 MiG-17 Era begins   65
8 Leitenant Solakov's Strange Escape to Italy   76
9 VVS in the Supersonic Era   80

Bibliography   86

Acknowledgements   88

About the Authors   88

Note: In order to simplify the use of this book, all names, locations and geographic designations are as provided in *The Times World Atlas*, or other traditionally accepted major sources of reference, as of the time of described events.

BULGARIAN AIR FORCE MILITARY RANKS AND THEIR US EQUIVALENTS

Bulgarian rank	US rank
Leitenant	2nd Lieutenant
Starshi Leitenant	1st Lieutenant
Capitan	Captain
Major	Major
Podpolkovnik	Lieutenant Colonel
Polkovnik	Colonel
General Major	Brigadier General (one-star)
General Leitenant	Major General (two-star)
General Polkovnik	Lieutenant General (three-star)
Armeyski General	General (four-star)

ABBREVIATIONS

ASCC   Air Standardisation Coordinating Committee

BAD   Bombardirovacha Aviatsionna Diviziya (Bomber Aviation Division)

BAP   Bombardirovachen Aviatsionen Polk (Bomber Aviation Regiment)

CO   Commanding Officer

IAP   Iztrebitelen Aviatsionen Polk (Fighter Aviation Regiment)

OIAP   Otdelen Iztrebitelen Aviatsionen Polk (Independent Fighter Aviation Regiment)

ORAE   Otdelna Razuznavatelna Escadrila (Independent Reconnaissance Squadron)

OPLAE   Otdelna Protivolodachna Eskadrila (Independent Anti-Submarine Warfare Squadron)

IAD   Iztrebitelna Aviatsionna Diviziya (Fighter Air Division)

IAE   Iztrebitelna Aviatsionna Eskadrila (Fighter Aviation Squadron)

IBAD   Iztrebitelno-Bombardirovachna Aviatsionna Diviziya (Fighter-Bomber Aviation Division)

IBAP   Iztrebitelno-Bombardirovachen Aviatsionen Polk (Fighter-Bomber Aviation Regiment)

IShAD   Iztrebitelno-Shturmova Aviatsionna Diviziya (Fighter-Attack Aviation Division)

NATO   North Atlantic Treaty Organisation

ShAD   Shturmova Aviatsionna Diviziya (Attack Aviation Division)

ShAP   Shturmovi Aviatsionen Polk (Attack Aviation Regiment)

SAC   Smesen Aviatsionen Corpus (Composite Aviation Corps)

TrAP   Transporten Aviatsionen Polk (Transport Aviation Regiment)

TrAE   Transportna Aviatsionna Escadrila (Transport Aviation Squadron)

MTAP   Minno-Torpeden Aviatsionen Polk (Mine-Torpedo Aviation Regiment)

MTAE   Minno-Torpedna Aviatsionna Escadrila (Mine-Torpedo Aviation Squadron)

NLBAD   Noshtna Lekobombardirovachna Aviatsionna Diviziya (Night Light Bomber Aviation Division)

UBAP   Uchebno-Boen Aviatsionen Polk (Training-Combat Aviation Regiment)

RAP   Razuznavatelen Aviatsionen Polk (Reconnaissance Aviation Regiment)

VE   Vodosamoletna Escadrila (Floatplane Squadron)

VV   Vazdushni Voiski (Air Troops)

VVS   Voennovazdushi Sili (Air Force)

VAP   Vertoleten Aviatsionen Polk (Helicopter Aviation Regiment)

INTRODUCTION

Soon after the end of the Second World War Bulgaria, a small country with population of seven million and an area of 111,000 sq km (42,860 sq miles), fell into total dependency on the Soviet Union as a direct result of the 1944 agreement of the 'spheres of influence' division of Europe between the victorious powers. The Bulgarian air arm, deeply-reformed in the Soviet style, was rapidly re-equipped with huge numbers of front-line aircraft, supplied by their new 'brother in arms' and thus emerged as one of the fastest growing air arms in the region on the eve of the Cold War. Upon the formation of the Warsaw Treaty Organisation in 1955, more commonly known as The Warsaw Pact, Bulgaria became a front-line state facing NATO's southern flank. The Bulgarian armed forces were modelled on the Soviet style and the country began receiving the most modern Soviet-made weapons available for export.

The rushed 'Sovetisation' of the country and its air arm eventually led to the change of the official title of the Bulgarian air arm in late 1949. The new name was identical to its Soviet counterpart – *Voennovazdushni Sily* (VVS) while its new organisational structure was also very similar to that of a Soviet front-line air army, comprising fighter, attack and bomber divisions. The national insignia applied on the Bulgarian military aircraft was also changed in the process of extensive 'Sovietisation' at the time. The existing white-and-red roundel with a horizontal green rectangle inset, introduced in 1945, was replaced by a Soviet-style five-pointed red star with the small national roundel inset.

The new wave of strengthening the Bulgarian air arm was initiated after 1948 as the Cold War in the Balkans gathered speed daily, and small incidents near the southern and western borders of the country began to occur with increased frequency. In this situation Soviet assistance in providing the VVS with modern combat aircraft and enhanced crew training grew considerably.

On 22 April 1951, the first Yakovlev Yak-23 'Flora' jet fighter made its first flight in Bulgarian airspace, taking off from the main fighter base at Graf Ignatievo, flown by a Bulgarian pilot, marking the beginning of the jet era in the history of the air arm. The biggest reorganisation of the decade was completed in late 1952 when the air arm had three fighter divisions with nine component regiments. Six of these regiments were fully equipped with the Yak-23, a total of 120 aircraft, plus 16 more Yak-17UTI two-seater jets used for conversion and continuation training. The famous swept-wing MiG-15 'Fagot' jet fighters followed in late 1951, equipping by late 1952 three fighter regiments. A total of 160 aircraft of three sub-versions were delivered up until 1955, plus 67 MiG-15UTI two-seaters. These were followed in 1955 and 1956 by 12 radar-equipped MiG-17PF 'Fresco' fighter-interceptors tailored for bad-weather and night operations, complemented between 1957 and 1961 by 62 more MiG-17Fs without radars, suitable for clear-weather intercepts and air combat. In turn, the sole bomber regiment took on strength Il-28 jet bombers in 1954.

In addition, large-scale efforts were initiated for the modernisation

In the early 1950s, the Bulgarian air arm began an accelerated training program for manning its rapidly expanded structure, comprising no fewer than ten fighter regiments in addition to six light bomber regiments, three bomber regiments, three attack regiments, one reconnaissance regiment and one transport regiment. This is a young pilot from the 15th IAP, a fighter regiment established in 1950 at Karlovo – Marino Pole. The regiment subsequently moved to Graf Ignatievo to be equipped with jet fighters in 1951 and then on to Bezmer in 1952. In 1953 the regiment moved again, now to the newly-built airfield at Ravnets near Bourgas on the Black Sea coast and stayed there, in one form or another until 2000, when it returned to Graf Ignatievo as a component squadron of the 3rd Fighter Air Base.

On the Cold War front in the Balkans, the Bulgarian MiG-15 fighters were involved in countering frequent airspace violations, which began in the late 1940s and occurred at a high-rate until 1955, while occasional intrusions into Bulgarian airspace continued to be reported until the early 1960s. The MiG-15s from the 18th IAP, stationed at Dobroslavtsi airfield near Sofia, were involved in shooting down an El Al Israel Airlines Lockheed L-149 Constellation airliner on 27 July 1955.

Servicing of the MiG-17's detachable armament platform by Bulgarian armament technicians. A very useful feature of both the MiG-15 and MiG-17, the platform contained two 23mm NR-23 cannons, each with 100 rounds of ammunition, in addition to one 37mm NR-37 cannon with 40 rounds. The common platform also contained the ammunition cases and the spent-cartridge collectors. For routine servicing, an easier loading of ammunition and inspection of the cannons it was able to be pulled down, thus shortening the pre-flight time between sorties.

The Yak-23 'Flora' is known as the definitive member of Yakovlev's first-generation, lightweight, jet-powered fighter family. It retained the so-called keel fuselage layout of the predecessor Yak-15 and Yak-17, combined with an increased-thrust engine for boosting up flight performance. As many as 120 aircraft, all of these second-hand examples, were delivered to Bulgaria in 1951 and 1952, with the last examples remaining in front-line use until 1958.

Soviet Union, or carrying out reconnaissance and dropping agitating leaflets against the Communist authorities ruling the country.

This rather tense situation at the beginning of the Cold War required the struggling air arm to maintain a constant high combat alert state, but the Bulgarian jet fighter force and anti-aircraft artillery proved largely unsuccessful in countering the frequent night intrusions. They were more successful, however, in gunning down high-altitude balloons, equipped with sophisticated photoreconnaissance equipment and launched by US intelligence from Western Europe in an effort to gather much-needed information about the countries behind the Iron Curtain.

In fact, the only occasion of the confirmed shooting down of foreign aircraft by the Bulgarian fighter force was El Al Flight LY402, a Lockheed L-149 Constellation four-engine airliner performing a regular passenger flight between London to Tel Aviv via Vienna and Istanbul. The ill-fated Israeli prop airliner is known as one of the biggest victims of the Cold War's poisonous atmosphere of tension, nervousness and distrust. Attacked by two MiG-15 fighters on 27 July 1955, after it had erroneously strayed off course into Bulgarian territory, the Constellation's remains fell in the south-western corner of Bulgaria, killing all 58 people onboard.

The formation of the Soviet-dominated Warsaw Pact Treaty Organisation on 14 May 1955 heralded the beginning of a bright new era in the air arm's development. As one of the most loyal Warsaw Pact member states, and the most important outpost on the Pact's southern flank, Bulgaria was readily supplied by the Soviet Union with huge numbers of new combat jets, anti-aircraft artillery, surface-to-air missile systems and early warning radars in an effort to boost the pact's southern flank defence.

of the ground infrastructure, including construction of concrete runways at each active military airfield and later-on a network of reserve airfields was set up, also equipped with runways with concrete or asphalt surfaces. The air defence capabilities were additionally strengthened by the mass deployment of large-calibre anti-aircraft artillery with radar fire control and long-range early warning radars.

Between 1951 and 1956, the Bulgarian air arm and air defence, existing at the time as separate services, had to endure difficult years, struggling to counter the frequent night overflights of Western aircraft ferrying sabotage teams parachuted into Bulgarian or Romanian territory, or sometimes even transported to the southern parts of the

According to the Soviet Supreme Command's plans, the wartime role of the beefed-up Bulgarian air arm was to provide air defence and air support to the national ground forces as well as air defence of the most important national industrial and urban areas pending the massed intervention of Soviet air and ground units from the Odessa

Military District in Ukraine as there were no permanently based Soviet military units in the country. The chief potential enemies were considered to be Bulgaria's two southern neighbours, Turkey and Greece, which by this time were already NATO members.

In the second half of the 1950s, only two years after the establishment of the Warsaw Pact Treaty Organisation, the Bulgarian air arm took on to its strength significant numbers of MiG-19S/P/PM 'Farmer' supersonic fighters and at last achieved its long-desired status of a reasonably potent air arm, maintaining a high state of combat readiness, able to provide air defence and air support in both defensive and offensive operations should the Cold War turn hot.

1
POST-WAR AIR ARM REORGANISATIONS

The 1947 Paris Peace Treaty set out the international status of Bulgaria, whose eight-month war effort with the Allies between September 1944 and May 1945 proved insufficient to overcome the serious damage incurred during its collaboration with the Third Reich between 1941 and 1944. In the event, the country was not recognised as a participant in the anti-Axis coalition and suffered from serious post-war sanctions and restrictions.

Signed on 10 February 1947 between Bulgaria and the victorious powers in the Second World War, the treaty called for the payment of hefty war reparations. Their total amount was US $70 million – $25 million of this going to Yugoslavia and the rest paid to Greece. The numerical strength of the country's armed forces was restricted to 65,500 troops – 55,000 in the Land Forces, 3,500 in the Navy, 1,800 in the Anti-Aircraft Artillery and 5,200 in the Air Force. The treaty was ratified by the country's parliament on 25 August and on 15 September 1947 it entered into force. A side effect was that Bulgaria was eventually left fully within the Soviet Union's sphere of influence.

The number of front-line aircraft was considerably restricted and the Vazdushni Voiski (VV, the Bulgarian Air Force) was denied any offensive aircraft types. The number of both the active and newly-trained pilots and navigators also came under severe restrictions. These, however, proved easy to circumvent using the services of Soviet advisors embedded in the Bulgarian military and the ready support provided by the Soviet, Romanian and Yugoslavian air arms. Some of the component units of the

5th Bombardirovachen Polk (bomber air division) were temporarily relocated to Yugoslavia and Romania, while the few bomber aircraft left for operations in Bulgaria — mostly twin-engine Pe-2s used for air reconnaissance purposes — were promptly stripped of their national insignias and serials. In addition, cadres of air and technical crews underwent their initial training in Yugoslavia while a large number of new pilots and navigators were also trained in Bulgaria under civilian

This Messerschmitt Bf 109G fighter from the 36th IAP, home-based at Karlovo – Marino Pole airfield in the central part of the country, is seen here adorned with new post-Second World War insignia of the Bulgarian air arm, popularly known as the OF-insignia.

A Bf 109G fighter of the Bulgarian air arm, seen overturned after an unsuccessful landing at its home airfield in the late 1940s. The type was used to equip the 36th IAP, a fighter regiment stationed at Karlovo – Marino Pole airfield until 1950, which had a mainly training role in the late 1940s, with the last flights reported in August 1950.

Bulgarian pilots and technicians seen here posing in front of one of the newly-delivered Yak-9M/Ds fighters. The picture was most likely taken at Bozhurishte airfield near Sofia in the second half of 1945 after the completion of the conversion-to-type training course of the 6th Fighter Polk pilots.

The first Soviet-made Yak-9M fighters were handed over to the Bulgarian air arm in the summer of 1945 and were used to complement the Bf 109Gs serving with the 6th Fighter Polk. The type remained in use with the front-line units until 1954, and its active use in the training role at the People's Air Force School also continued until the end of the same year. Here an aircraft is seen in 1945 or 1946, with the best Bulgarian Second World War pilot, Capitan Stoyan Stoyanov, sitting here to the left. Stoyanov was the leader of the Yak-9 conversion-to-type course in the summer of 1945 held at Balchik airfield.

promptly suspended and their leaders either killed or jailed. In July 1946 the communist-led government, headed by Prime Minister Georgy Dimitrov, took direct control of the armed forces, with Georgy Damyanov appointed as Defence Minister.

On 5 September the same year Bulgaria was proclaimed to be a People's Republic by the communist regime as the monarchy was abolished for good. Establishing full control over the armed forces was one of the most important aims of the Bulgarian communists and was implemented in cooperation with numerous Soviet military advisors, who came to Bulgaria together with the supplies of large numbers of Soviet-made heavy arms. The extensive purges of politically unreliable members of the armed forces involved the vast majority of the Second World War veteran officers — they were dismissed soon after and some of them were later jailed due to their anti-communist attitude and actions. Bulgaria also hosted a sizeable Soviet occupation corps which stayed in the country until 1947 to support the communist regime.

The process of a full and irreversible 'Sovietisation' of the Bulgarian armed forces, commencing at a rapid pace during early 1945, saw a successful completion four to five years later. By early 1949, a strong pro-Stalinist communist regime ruled the small Balkan country and it exercised a direct and total control over the country's military.

cover between 1948 and 1950. A significant number of the Pe-2 bombers and Yak-9 fighters 'hidden' in Yugoslavia were later inherited by the local air units there after Marshal Josip Broz Tito abruptly severed his relations with the Soviet Union and the other communist satellite states in 1948.

By that time Bulgaria was already in a state of total dependency on the Soviet Union. It called for the establishment of very strong Soviet political influence — immediately after the end of the war, 75 percent of the influence came from the Soviet Union and only 25 percent from Great Britain and the US, and not long after the British and US influence was reduced to zero.

Only two years after the war's end a hard-line communist regime assumed power in Sofia, with all pro-monarchist and liberal parties

The first large-scale reorganisation of the Bulgarian air arm took place in December 1944, initiated by a small group of Soviet-trained Bulgarian officers who actively participated in the war, serving with the Soviet Air Force. They were headed by General Major Zakhary Zakhariev, a Bulgarian pilot and commander, who emigrated to the Soviet Union in the 1930s and participated in the Spanish War where he had earned the extremely prestigious Hero of the Soviet Union award for his bravery in an extremely risky combat mission. He then served with the Red Army Air Force in a number of command positions, including CO of the Tambov Pilot School during the war.

The reformed Bulgarian air arm eventually emerged in January 1945 – now renamed VV (Vazdushni Voyski – Air Force), it had an organisational structure consisting of headquarters, two main air

Bulgarian emigrant and Red Army officer, General Major Zakhary Zakhariev was appointed in October 1944 as the Deputy Commander-in-Chief of the Bulgarian air arm and went on to became the Commander-in-Chief in 1948, serving in this position until 1954. Then he was again at the helm, commanding the Bulgarian air arm from 1957 to 1959. Zakhariev was subsequently promoted to General Leitenant (two-stars) and eventually to General Polkovnik (three-stars), serving until 1973.

commands and direct reporting services. General Major Gancho Manchev was appointed Commander-in-Chief and his deputy was General Major Zakhary Zakhariev.

The two main VV air commands were the Vazdushni Stroevi Chasti (Front-line Air Units) and the Vazdushni Uchebni Chasti (Air Training Units). The former, under the direct command of General Major Zakhariev, was comprised of four division-size combat units – the 1st Razuznavatelen (Reconnaissance) Polk, 2nd Shturmovi (Attack) Polk, 5th Bombardirovachen (Bomber) Polk and 6th Iztrebitelen (Fighter) Polk, in addition to independent liaison, floatplane and air transport yata (squadrons). The latter controlled the People's Air

Force School and the three advanced flying training schools, which were fighter/attack, instrumental (blind) flying and gunnery, as well as the communication and technical training schools. The Technical Air Service controlled the VV's three aircraft production and repair facilities at Lovech, Kazanlak and Karlovo.

By 1945 the general structure of the main front-line units remained close to that of the Second World War era. Each Polk (a structure, similar to the Soviet air division) controlled two or three Orlyaks (air wings or regiments), each based at its own airfield. The Orlyak itself comprised three yata (squadrons) of 12 fighters or nine bombers each in addition to a staff flight of three or four aircraft. In 1946, the Orlyaks were re-named as Royaks (Swarms).

The 16 March 1945 agreement between the Bulgarian and Soviet governments paved the way for the first large-scale supply of defence equipment to the small Balkan state now established in the Soviet sphere of influence. The VV took delivery of 120 Yakovlev Yak-9M/D/T fighters, 120 Ilyushin Il-2m3 attack aircraft, 98 Petlyakov Pe-2 dive bomber/recce aircraft plus 10 Yak-7V and 10 Il-2 two-seat conversion trainers. The majority of these new flying machines were delivered in the late spring and summer months of 1945 when the simultaneous conversion of all front-line units had commenced. In 1947, 36 units of the torpedo-bomber variant of the best Soviet-made piston-engined bomber — the Tupolev Tu-2T — entered service with the Balchik-based 25th MTAP (Mine-Torpedo Regiment).

Also in 1947, 59 Bulgarian Messerschmitt Bf 109Gs, together with 30 KB-11A reconnaissance aircraft and 10 DAR-9 trainers, were transferred to Yugoslavia in exchange for raw materials for aircraft production, metallic fuselages for the replacement of the wooden fuselages of the Il-2 attack aircraft and aero engines for the newly-designed Laz-7 single-engine training aircraft. The Bf 109 fighters continued serving with the Karlovo-based 36th IAP (Fighter Aviation Regiment), with the last flying operations conducted in August 1950.

The fate of about 40 surviving Dewoitine D.520s was much worse than that of the Bf 109 fleet. Immediately after the end of the war the French-made fighters, considered to be hopelessly obsolete at the time, were handed over from the combat units to the Fighter School where they saw some use in the training role before being finally retired and scrapped in 1948.

The first Yak-9s were delivered to the VV in the summer months of 1945 and transition training of the fighter pilots commenced at Balchik and later on continued at two other airfields, Karlovo and Bozhurishte, where the Orlyaks of the 6th Polk were permanently deployed. The final conversion of the air crews of the Orlyaks of the 6th Polk to the Soviet-made fighter was eventually completed by mid-1946.

The extensive purges of 'politically unreliable' VV officers, most of them still occupying important command positions within the Bulgarian air arm, began in late 1946. At the same time, however, the number of newly-graduated officers, most of them members of the Communist Party, was still insignificant. More than 400

This Yak-9M fighter, operated by the People's Air Force School between 1951 and 1954, sports the new Soviet-style Bulgarian insignia adopted in late 1949, a five pointed red star with the national roundel inset.

The Yak-9 was used for equipping a dedicated night-fighter squadron with the 14th OIAP at Karlovo – Marino Pole, which was used to provide QRA detachments, deployed to a network of auxiliary airfields alongside the Greek and the Turkish borders between 1951 and 1954, in order to counter the then frequent night low-level intrusions into the Bulgarian airspace.

officers, overwhelmingly Second World War combat veteran pilots, were abruptly dismissed in 1946 because they were considered too politically unreliable to serve on with the military any more. As a result, by early 1946 the total number of VV personnel fell to 8,351. As many as 1,324 officers, most if not all of them Second World War veterans, were eventually dismissed in 1946 and 1947. The number of newly-graduated pilots in the same period was only 77. As a consequence, the VV's numerical strength rapidly slumped to 47 percent below the required peacetime level.

The post-war period of air training featured extensive changes which eventually resulted in the setting up of a fast-track training system for large numbers of new aircrews badly needed for the rapidly expanding but still considerably undermanned air arm. In September 1946 the People's Air Force School was founded at Sofia-Vrazhdebna airfield, responsible for the training of officer pilots and technicians, with the first cadres graduating two years later. By that time the undermanned VV needed at least 600 new aircrews, but the Paris Peace Treaty prohibited any further expansion of the Bulgarian military flying training system at the time. The clever solution to the problem called for the prompt organisation of two basic flying training schools, masked as intended to satisfy the needs for the country's civil aviation. These so-called aeroclubs were formally controlled by the National Sports-Technical Union, based at the airfields in Gorna Oryakhovitsa and Graf Ignatievo, with their first output in 1948 numbering 281 newly-trained pilots. Upon graduation, they immediately began with the advanced flying training phase at the People's Air Force School, moved in June 1948 from Vrazhdebna to Dolna Mitropolya near the large city of Pleven. In 1950 the total number of students who commenced their flying training with the air school at Dolna Mitropolya and the two aeroclubs reached 400.

Full 'Sovietisation' of the Air Arm

By 1949 Bulgaria had emerged as one of the most loyal Soviet satellite countries in Eastern Europe, and particularly in the Balkans. Its main enemies were considered to be Greece and Turkey, then NATO candidate members; they became full-scale members in 1952. Another potential newly-emerging enemy was its former ally Yugoslavia because the Yugoslavian leader, Marshal Josip Broz Tito, had suddenly halted all relations with the Soviet Union and other communist counties in 1948, as he embarked on the independent development of the state, eventually turning towards the West for delivery of arms and establishing a broader industrial co-operation. Yugoslavia also inherited 55 ex-Bulgarian Yak-9 fighters, 48 Il-2 attack aircraft, 69 Pe-2 bombers, 30 KB-11 reconnaissance aircraft and 19

This is a group photo of the command personnel of the 6th IShAD, the fighter-attack aviation division with its HQ set up at Bozhurishte near Sofia, taken in 1947 or 1948. The division CO, Polkovnik Kiril Kirilov, is the second from the right in the first row. The fourth from the right is the Second World War veteran fighter pilot, Capitan Peter Manolev. Capitan Mikhail Grigorov, another Second World War veteran fighter pilot, is the first from the left in the third row.

Table No 1: VVS Order of battle, January 1949		
Unit	**Aircraft**	**Base**
Front-line units		
6th Fighter-Attack Division		**Bozhurishte**
16th IAP	Yak-9M/D	Bozhurishte/Vrazhdebna
36th IAP	Yak-9M/D	Karlovo
2nd ShAP	Il-2m3	Graf Ignatievo
25th Mine-Torpedo AP		**Balchik**
1st MTAE	Tu-2T, Fw 189, Fw 58	
2nd MTAE	Tu-2T, Fw 189, Fw 58	
15th Reconnaissance AP		**Gorna Oryakhovitsa**
1st RAE	Pe-2	
2nd RAE	Pe-2	
14th Transport AP		**Vrazhdebna**
1st TrAE	Ju 52, Fw 58, Bf 108, He 111, Fi 156, W 34	
2nd TrAE		
Training Units		
People's Air School		**Dolna Mitropolia**
2nd Eskadrila(basic training)	Ar 96, Yak-9M, Fw 58, Ju 52	Telish
3rd Eskadrila (advanced training)		

DAR-9 trainers, hidden on its territory in 1947 due to the restrictive clauses of the Paris Peace Treaty and waiting for better days when these restrictions would be removed. Then-friendly Yugoslavia had been considered as a suitable place in mid/late 1947, but the political upheaval committed by Tito in March 1948 eventually led to the confiscation of all Bulgarian military aircraft hidden in 1947 in Yugoslavia.

By the end of 1948 the two main VV front-line units – the fighter and attack Polks – had been renamed under the Soviet style as divisions — the 2nd Shturmova Divisiya (Attack Division) and the 6th Iztrebitelna Divisiya (Fighter Division) — each controlling two or three *aviopolks* (regiments). In turn, each aviopolk had three *escadrili* (squadrons), equipped with eight aircraft each. General Major Zakhary Zakhariev was appointed VV Commander-in-Chief in late 1948.

In early 1949, the strength of the main front-line units was considerably reduced. The existing attack and fighter divisions were merged into the 6th Iztrebitelno-Shturmova Divisiya (Fighter-Attack Division), controlling two fighter regiments (16th and 36th IAPs) and one attack regiment (2nd ShAP), with a total of nine combat squadrons. The other primary front-line units were the regiment-sized aviopolks (wings) – the 25th MTAP (mine-torpedo regiment), the 15th RAP (reconnaissance regiment), the 14th TRAP (transport regiment) as well as the 8th RVE (reconnaissance sailplane squadron). This temporary reduction measure in both the number and the inventory of the units was, in fact, unwanted and dictated by the insufficient number of pilots and technical personnel left after the extensive purges of the Second World War veteran officers between 1946 and 1948; in addition, the Paris Peace Treaty restrictions were still in force.

The extensive 'Sovietisation' of the Bulgarian air arm led to the eventual change of its official title in April 1949, becoming identical to its Soviet counterpart, the Voennovazdushni Sily (VVS). The VVS structure was similar to that of a Soviet front-line air army. The national insignia was also changed in an effort to be made more similar to that used by the Soviet Air Force. This Soviet-inspired insignia remained in use until September 1992 when a simplified large-size/high-visibility white-green-red national roundel was adopted by the yet again reformed Bulgarian air arm.

2

NEW-STYLE AIR ARM IN CONSTRUCTION AND EXPANSION

The VVS structure was expanded in July 1949 with the establishment of a night light bomber division, the 9th NLBAD, with the HQ and one of its regiments stationed at Yambol, while the other two regiments were based at Stara Zagora. In 1951, another night light bomber division, the 2nd NLBAD, was established with a HQ also at Stara Zagora. Both of these were equipped with the Bulgarian-made Laz-7 aircraft which was adopted for the bomber role due to the lack of any other suitable light aircraft. In this role the Laz-7 was armed with two wing-mounted and one turret-mounted machineguns and up to 120kg (265 lb) of bombs, either six 20kg (44 lb) or two 50kg (110 lb) bombs.

A total of 163 Laz-7s (including the prototypes) were produced at

The Bulgarian-made Laz-7 trainer was modified for front-line use and served with the newly-established night light bomber regiments, grouped into two night light bomber divisions, based at Stara Zagora and Yambol, each controlling three regiments. In its front-line role the prop-driven aircraft was armed with two wing-mounted and one turret-mounted 7.92mm machine-guns and up to 120kg (265lb) of bombs in either six 20kg or two 50kg loads.

This is the improved Laz-7M, also known as the ZAK-1, fielded in service with the regiments of the two short-lived night light bomber divisions in the early 1950s. By 1952, a total of six regiments were equipped with 108 aircraft, a mixed fleet of Laz-7s and Laz-7Ms, the last of which continued serving in the front-line role until 1957.

the air defence of the western part of the country, it controlled three newly-established fighter regiments, initially equipped with Bücker Bü 181 Bestmann trainers. The 18th IAP was stationed at Vrazhdebna airfield next to Sofia, while the other two regiments of the division, the 11th and 43rd IAPs were based at Karlovo and Bozhurishte respectively. Each of these comprised two or three component squadrons and a staff flight, and the 11th and 18th IAPs were slated to be equipped with Yak-9 fighters later in the same year. Then the 18th and the 43rd IAPs re-equipped with the Yak-23 and Yak-17UTI jet after their move in April 1952 to the newly-built Dobroslavtsi airfield near Sofia. The 11th IAP also received jet fighters and was initially based at Dobroslavtsi, moving in November that year to Gabrovnitsa, another newly-built airfield near the city of Mikhailovgrad and the border with Yugoslavia, some 70km (37nm) north of Sofia.

The VVS fighter fleet saw a significant reinforcement in late 1950, comprising 70 Yak-9Ps with all-metallic airframes, manufactured in the second half of the 1940s and supplied from the Soviet Union to equip the newly-formed 11th and 18th IAPs, while the 16th IAP was disbanded and its Yak-9M/Ds ferried to Karlovo to equip a newly-established regiment there. This move allowed the last Bf 109G survivors, serving with the 36th IAP at Karlovo and mostly used for training, to be withdrawn from use in the second half of 1950. Then the 36th IAP was disbanded.

The 14th OIAP, newly-formed in May 1950 and stationed at Karlovo – Marino Pole, was an independent fighter regiment reporting directly to the VVS HQ, and was essentially the successor of the 36th IAP, initially equipped with the survivors of Yak-9M/Ds delivered to Bulgaria back in 1945 (transferred from the disbanded 16th IAP). In the spring of 1952 it got all the Yak-9Ps, previously operated by 11th and 18th IAPs, as these two regiments had just completed their transition to the jet-powered Yak-23.

This way by January 1952, the 14th OIAP at Karlovo remained the only VVS front-line unit equipped with prop-driven fighters. There were also a number of single- and two-seaters — some of these locally-converted from single-seaters — operated by the People's Air Force School at Dolna Mitropolya in the period between 1951 and 1954. Initially the training was carried out at Polikraishte airfield in 1951, only for officer pilot training, and in 1952 it moved to Telish,

DSF-Lovech factory, re-named as Zavod-14, during 1949, followed by 150 more Laz-7Ms (ZAK-1), the last of which was handed over to the VVS in 1954.

The VVS's strike capabilities were further beefed up thanks to the establishment of the 5th ShAD (Attack Air Davison), based at Plovdiv airfield, controlling three attack regiments, the 17th, 20th and 23rd ShAPs. The first of these, the 23rd ShAP, was established on 14 November 1949 and its fleet comprised Il-2 attack aircraft, previously hidden in Romania, which were complemented and eventually replaced by the much-improved Il-10 armoured attack aircraft, with a total of 80 examples delivered in 1951, including six two-seaters for conversion and continuation training. The 25th MTAP at Balchik was used for the establishment of a bomber division, the 3rd BAD, with three component regiments, equipped with Tu-2T torpedo-bombers in addition to Focke Wulf Fw 189A-2s and Fw 58s used as continuation trainers.

A further organisational structure expansion was undertaken in November 1950, including the establishment of the 4th IAD (Fighter Aviation Division), headquartered at Bozhurishte. Responsible for where the Yak-9 was flown by student pilots in the last training phase before their graduation from the 3-year long theoretical and flight training course, also combined with officer training. Then Polikraishte and Brenitsa airfields continued to be used for dedicated summer training camps until 1954. By late 1952, the People's Air Force School had a fleet of 18 Yak-9 single-seaters in addition to no fewer than 11 two-seaters.

The 1st IAD was the second new fighter division to be equipped with jets, established in March 1951 at Graf Ignatievo, with three component fighter regiments — the 22nd, 25th and the 27th IAPs. The 10th IAD, also established in March 1951 at Graf Ignatievo, controlled three more fighter regiments — the existing 15th IAP and the newly-established 19th and 21st IAPs.

The 15th IAP was the first new regiment, established at Karlovo during May 1950, and a group of selected pilots from the new regiment was sent to the Soviet Union for jet fighter training, led by the regiment's CO, Major Vasil Velichkov. In the autumn of 1950, the regiment received five Yak-11 prop-trainers and was relocated to Graf Ignatievo. In February 1951, the 15th IAP got a large group of former Yak-9 pilots from the 14th OIAP who commenced training operations at Graf Ignatievo on the Yak-11 in anticipation of fielding into service the first jet fighters.

The Ilyushin Il-10 attack aircraft, taken on strength in 1951, equipped the three regiments in the 5th ShAD, stationed at Plovdiv airfield. Initially, the 17th ShAP, an attack regiment at Plovdiv, was equipped with the type, together with the 23rd ShAP at Gorna Oryakhovitsa. As many as 110 aircraft were eventually delivered to the Bulgarian air arm, which were maintained in active service until 1958, including 30 examples manufactured in Czechoslovakia, taken on strength in 1953 to replace the Il-2m3s in the fleet of the 20th ShAP stationed at Krumovo near Plovdiv.

The Yak-11, the first ten examples of which were delivered in 1950, was initially used as a training aircraft for pilots destined to convert to jet fighters in the newly-established jet fighter regiments of the 1st, 4th and 10th IADs in 1952-1952. In addition, the type was also fielded for initial pilot training with the People's Air Force School, flying at Telish airfield. As many as 45 Yak-11s were taken on strength by the Bulgarian air arm, with the last of these remaining in active use until 1965.

The eventual VVS development plan, outlined by the Ministry of People's Defence in January 1951, called for establishing the following organisational structure by April 1952: two fighter aviation divisions equipped with jet aircraft in addition to one fighter aviation division with prop-driven aircraft (in fact, only one regiment was established); one bomber aviation division; two light bomber aviation divisions; one attack aviation division; one composite aviation regiment; one reconnaissance aviation regiment and one sailplane naval squadron.

Each of the fighter, bomber and light bomber divisions had to be provided with a fleet of 62 aircraft, while the attack division was required to be equipped with as many as 90 examples. The fighter fleet's total numerical strength was set at 236 aircraft (including the fighters used for training at the People's Air Force School and the independent fighter regiment at Karlovo), of which 124 were to be jet-powered fighters and 112 prop-driven models. The bomber fleet's numerical strength was set at 68 examples, the attack fleet at 90, the

reconnaissance fleet at 29, the transport fleet at 20, the training fleet at 80, the combat-training fleet at 48, the liaison fleet at 48 and the medical evacuation fleet at 19, while the night light bombers were to number no fewer than 124 examples. The total VVS fleet was set to number 755 aircraft, including 547 combat examples, while the total number of personnel was set to reach 16,525, including 4,802 officers.

The Cold War begins

The Cold War for the Bulgarian air arm began in 1949 as the country had already been turned into a reliable Soviet satellite with a rather important front-line role in the Balkan Peninsula. The country became an active actor in the protracted running conflict between the superpowers of the USA and the Soviet Union lasting from 1945 to 1991, waged on wide political, economic, and propaganda fronts. A suitable Cold War definition that could be found in the Merriam-Webster Dictionary refers to it as a conflict over ideological differences carried on by methods short of sustained, overt military action, and

The Second World War-vintage Arado Ar 196A-3 floatplane was used by the VV until 1947. As many as nine aircraft were on strength in 1945. In 1947, the Floatplane Yato (squadron), based at Tchaika naval air station near Varna, was transferred to Bulgarian Navy control, but the unit was returned back to the VVS structure in 1951 while the Ar 196A-3 continued in military service until 1954. Here, Starshi Leitenant Simeov Angelov, a pilot from the squadron is seen preparing for a flight at Tchaika.

On 9 February 1948, two Turkish Air Force Supermarine Spitfire Mk V fighters were shot down by a Bulgarian small-calibre AAA battery near the Black Sea coastal town of Sozopol, some 60km (32nm) from the Bulgarian-Turkish border. Here Major Stoyan Stoyanov, a Second World War veteran pilot, is seen following a close inspection of the wreckage. The surviving Turkish pilot admitted that they got lost during a training sortie and strayed into Bulgarian airspace.

answer from the Western world. The Soviet Union's initiative to set up loyal, communist-dominated governments in its sphere of influence in Eastern Europe — including Poland, Hungary, Romania, Czechoslovakia and Bulgaria — resulted in the establishment of a fold of client countries situated behind the Iron Curtain. This latter term comes hand-in-hand with the Cold War and was pioneered by Winston Churchill in his speech on 5 March 1946 in Fulton, Missouri (USA).

Luckily, the Cold War never progressed into the next level — the so-called 'Hot War' — planned by both camps to be fought ruthlessly and with a mass deployment of nuclear weapons. In fact, the Cold War featured occasional hot moments of encounters in the air, continuing until its end, with these being more frequent in the early years of the conflict, in the 1950s and 1960s. Most of the hot encounters involved Western reconnaissance and transport aircraft falling under attack by Soviet or allied fighters while entering — intentionally or unintentionally — hostile airspace behind the Iron Curtain.

The Warsaw Pact Treaty Organisation, the Cold War's most emblematic by-product to be found behind the Iron Curtain, formed in 1955, was in fact, a mere formalisation of existing military co-operation agreements dating from the late 1940s between the Soviet Union and its satellite countries in Eastern Europe, including Bulgaria. The Pact was firmly dominated by the Soviet Union throughout its entire life, until 1991, with all other member states expected simply to follow the general policy set by Moscow in doctrine, training and procurement of new military equipment.

usually without breaking off diplomatic relations.

The winning wartime alliance in the Second World War between the Soviet Union and its Western allies proved to be too fragile, dissolving during late 1945 and early 1946 as the Western world gained a monopoly on nuclear weapons. In addition, a wide ideological gulf was claimed by the Soviet hard-line communist leader, Generalissimos Iosif Vissarionovich Stalin, to exist between Soviet communism — forcefully imposed on most of the states in Eastern Europe, with Bulgaria being among the most active and rapid adopters of the new ideology — and Western democracy, prompting him to impose a new increasingly hard-line policy that rapidly provoked a symmetric

The strengthening of the Bulgarian air arm became a high priority yet again after 1948 as the undeclared war in the Balkans gathered speed, and small incidents near the southern borders of the country began to occur with increasing frequency. The best-known of these occurred on 9 February 1948 when two Turkish Air Force Supermarine Spitfire fighters were shot down by small-calibre AAA over the Bulgarian coastal town of Sozopol, south of the big port city of Bourgas, after their pilots got lost in a training flight from Balikesir.

One of these crashed into the Black Sea, killing the pilot, while the wreckage of the other Spitfire Mk V fell on the ground some 3 km (1.7nm) from Sozopol and its pilot, Taliat Yunki Yud, was captured and later on returned to Turkey.

The Ar 196A-3 floatplane was used for clandestine reconnaissance missions in the Black Sea, entering into Turkish airspace in an effort to photograph warships and coastal infrastructure in and around the Turkish military port of Zonguldak.

The German-made Arado Ar 196A-3 Akula and Heinkel He 60 Tuylen floatplanes, inherited from the Second World War, remained in service with the Bulgarian air arm until 1947, serving in an independent floatplane yato (squadron-size unit). That year the unit was renamed as the 8th Floatplane Yato and transferred under Bulgarian Navy control. At that time the Navy strength was gradually expanded with the active assistance of the Soviet Union, supplying new combat ships; in a violation to the Peace Treaty it also clandestinely provided Bulgaria with torpedo boats and submarines. This process of strengthening the country's naval capabilities intensified the interest of, and the intelligence operations conducted by, the Turkish Navy in Bulgarian territorial waters. In response to these operations, the Bulgarian Navy began using its Ar 196A-3 fleet, comprising eight aircraft, to launch long-range reconnaissance patrols in the Black Sea. The strengthening of the Bulgarian air arm and the establishment of the 25th Mine-Torpedo Aviation Regiment at Balchik, equipped with torpedo-carrying Tu-2T bombers, intensified the anxiety in Ankara and led to the emergence of submarines and reconnaissance ships disguised as fishing vessels operating along the Bulgarian coast and the Navy floatplanes were also used for tracking their movements.

According to veterans from the 8th Floatplane Yato, a clandestine intelligence operation was organised around 1949-1950, to enter into Turkish airspace over the Black Sea and take photographs of ports and combat ships of interest. According to data provided by Soviet military intelligence, US Navy warships had entered the Black Sea, and selected aircrews from Tchaika naval air station were immediately tasked to fly to the Turkish port of Zonguldak to photograph these ships and track their movements around the Bosphorus straits. In case of counteraction by Turkish air defences, Yak-9 fighters were deployed to Sarafovo airfield near Bourgas, to provide aid. The depth of entry into the sea by the Ar 196A-3s was about 250 km (135 nm) and in order to extend the combat radius, the aircraft received auxiliary fuel tanks installed in the floats, replacing the smoke-generator unit.

The aircrews, made up of Second World War veterans, were sent on these missions in the early morning, one hour before sunset, or in the evening, one hour after sunset. They flew at 500m (1,600ft) altitude on the route to Zonguldak and after taking panoramic photos, the aircraft turned towards the Bosphorus, where the aircrews oriented themselves by using the coastal lighthouses and then headed back to Bourgas. As the veterans of these missions recall, US combat ships were never detected in or around Zonguldag. Following a crash during a water landing on Bourgas Lake in August 1950, a number of negative conclusions were drawn about the Navy's ability to operate its own aviation unit and from 1 April 1951, the unit, renamed as the

The Yak-9M fighter was used in the training role between 1952 and 1954 with the People's Air Force School. The first training course in 1952 had three female pilots, including Leitenant Dora Mochkova, pictured here to the right. The training of female pilots for the fighter branch began in the spring of 1951 but was a short-lived initiative, discontinued after a landing accident with Leitenant Maria Atanasova during the first course at Polikraishte in August 1952.

8th Floatplane Reconnaissance Aircraft Squadron, was returned back into the VVS structure, with a fleet of six Ar 196A-3s and one He 60. The number of personnel was 90, including 37 officers. The Ar 196A-3 continued in VVS service until April 1954.

Problematic Greek Border

The complicated and rather tense political situation in the late 1940s in the Balkans led to frequent border incidents, especially at the border with Greece. At that time, the border areas were subject to periodic aerial reconnaissance and intrusions into Bulgarian airspace. For example, in 1948, a total of 57 aircraft carried out 33 violations of Bulgarian airspace. In one of these daring intrusions, a Greek combat aircraft even mounted attacks on a Bulgarian border outpost near the village of Mochure.

With the launch of the decisive offensive of the Greek military for the liquidation of the pro-communist insurgency movement in 1949, the intrusions into Bulgarian airspace became even more frequent. Between January and September 1949, for instance, no fewer than 50 violations of the state border by a total of 107 aircraft were reported. Border Troop patrols duly registered the violations made by Greek aircraft on 28 October as well as on 6, 10, 13, 20, 28 and 29 November. More violations were reported on 3, 5, 24 and 26 December. On 3 January 1950, once again, Greek aircraft crossed the border with Bulgaria, apparently in a reconnaissance mission to search for the presence of insurgent camps set up on Bulgarian territory and taking photographs of border troop outposts.

In the autumn of 1950 the frequency of the air intrusions increased yet again. On the one hand, the reason for this was the seriously deteriorated relations with Yugoslavia, as well as the increased activity of the Greek Air Force in an attempt to end the assistance of communist Bulgaria furnished to the pro-communist insurgent forces in Greece.

Between 1945 and the early 1950s, in the wake of the political complications caused by the Paris Peace Treaty, the Bulgarian air arm refrained from flying reconnaissance missions over the territory of neighbouring countries with progressively deteriorating relations such as Yugoslavia, Turkey and Greece. However, there were some exceptions when an emergency response was required. With the escalation of the Greek Civil War, Bulgaria provided clandestine but otherwise limited assistance to the Democratic Army of Greece — the military branch of the Communist Party of Greece.

The civil war in Greece made Bulgaria cautious, so the support provided was generally limited to the provision of weapons and limited military assistance. However, the Greek communist insurgents, often pressed into their territory by regular Greek military units, were used to crossing the border and seeking shelter on Bulgarian territory. Such crossings, however, were deemed undesirable by the Bulgarian authorities but at the same time were also inevitable. Often, with their entry into Bulgarian territory, the communist insurgents were followed by Greek military units, leading to armed clashes with Bulgarian border posts.

Such border incidents saw the occasional use of the Pe-2 reconnaissance aircraft of the 15th RAP, dispatched to fly over the border line and often entering into Greek territory, in order to establish the situation and the location of the warring sides, so that the Bulgarian political leadership could make informed decisions. One such risky reconnaissance sortie flown by an aircrew from the 15th RAP was described in the memoirs of a General Polkovnik Zakhary Zahariev:

I remember sending the pilot Tonov [Capitan Atanas Tonov, Deputy CO of the 15th RAP — author's note] on a mission and I had no doubt that he would brilliantly accomplish it. He flew a Pe-2 aircraft with the task to investigate the border violation, committed by Greek military units in Capitan Andreevo area.

Since 1946, armed clashes along the Bulgarian-Greek border had been a frequent occurrence. Despite the end of the civil war in Greece, a peak in the border clashes was reported in 1952. The most serious of these was the unresolved dispute over the ownership of two large islands in the lower reaches of the Maritza river, near the point where the borders of Bulgaria, Greece and Turkey met. On 26 July, a Bulgarian border patrol near Capitan Andreevo discovered a two-person violation of what was believed to be a Bulgarian-held island. The border patrol took position on the island, well hidden in an ambush. About 30 Greek soldiers were sent to the island overnight and they were engaged by the Bulgarian patrol. The Greek offensive was repulsed by the Bulgarian side, which suffered from one wounded soldier. On the next night, the Greek attempt to occupy the island resumed. This time four border troops soldiers repelled another Greek offensive, killing an officer and eight soldiers. A particularly tense period followed, in which the Bulgarian territory and the positions of the border patrols were targeted by Greek mortar fire for days. This made it necessary for aerial reconnaissance to be carried out over the Bulgarian border in the area of Capitan Andreevo on 4 and 5 August. At the same time, more than 300 soldiers, armoured vehicles and artillery were concentrated near Petrich, just 50m (160ft) from the border line. In the area of Sultanitsa, a concentration of Greek troops was also spotted. Eight Greek aircraft were reported flying over Bulgarian villages near the border.

The situation continued to escalate on 7 August, with heavy mortar and machinegun fire opened at the Bulgarian positions around Maritsa river, near Capitan Andreevo. Five Greek tanks advanced from the riverside, unleashing more than 20 rounds, while a platoon of soldiers took positions on the other side of the river bank, at a distance of 100m (230ft) from the Bulgarian positions.

In order to avoid further complications, it was decided by the Bulgarian military authorities that the 5th ShAD (Attack Division) was to be held in Readiness State No.2 — with one four-aircraft flight, armed with 100kg bombs and ready to go in each of the three regiments. At the most tense times, and in the face of the threat of full-scale military action on the Bulgarian-Greek border, the 10th IAD (Fighter Division) was ordered to deploy a forward command post in the expected battle area. In turn, the 5th ShAD was tasked to provide an entire Il-2 or Il-10-equipped squadron in the air, fully armed and loitering in an area next to the combat zone, ready to provide immediate air support to ground forces in the escalating conflict.

After the escalation of tensions, talks began between the Bulgarian and Greek governments, under the auspices of the United Nations, and the conflict over the disputed islands in Maritsa river was finally resolved around early 1954.

Accordingly, the Greek secret services and the US CIA were keenly interested in what was happening in Bulgaria, and especially across the border. On 17 December 1950, the Minister of People's Defence, then General Leitenant Peter Panchevsky, reported to the Chairman of the Bulgarian Council of Ministers (Prime Minister), Valko Chervenkov: 'At 2:47, an enemy aircraft of unknown nationality, coming from Greek territory, entered our airspace near the village of Chorbadzhiisko and proceeded well inside the country...'

This particular aircraft went deep inside Bulgarian territory, reaching the city of Yambol and then dropping magnesium illuminating flares over the city of Harmanli, apparently in an attempt to take photographs of objects of interest on the ground. The country's Air Defence service, commanded at the time by Polkovnik Stefan Krastev, had failed to respond to the intrusion and the anti-aircraft artillery (AAA) batteries along the intruder's route stayed idle. On the letterhead of the Council of Ministers, Todor Zhivkov, the future long-

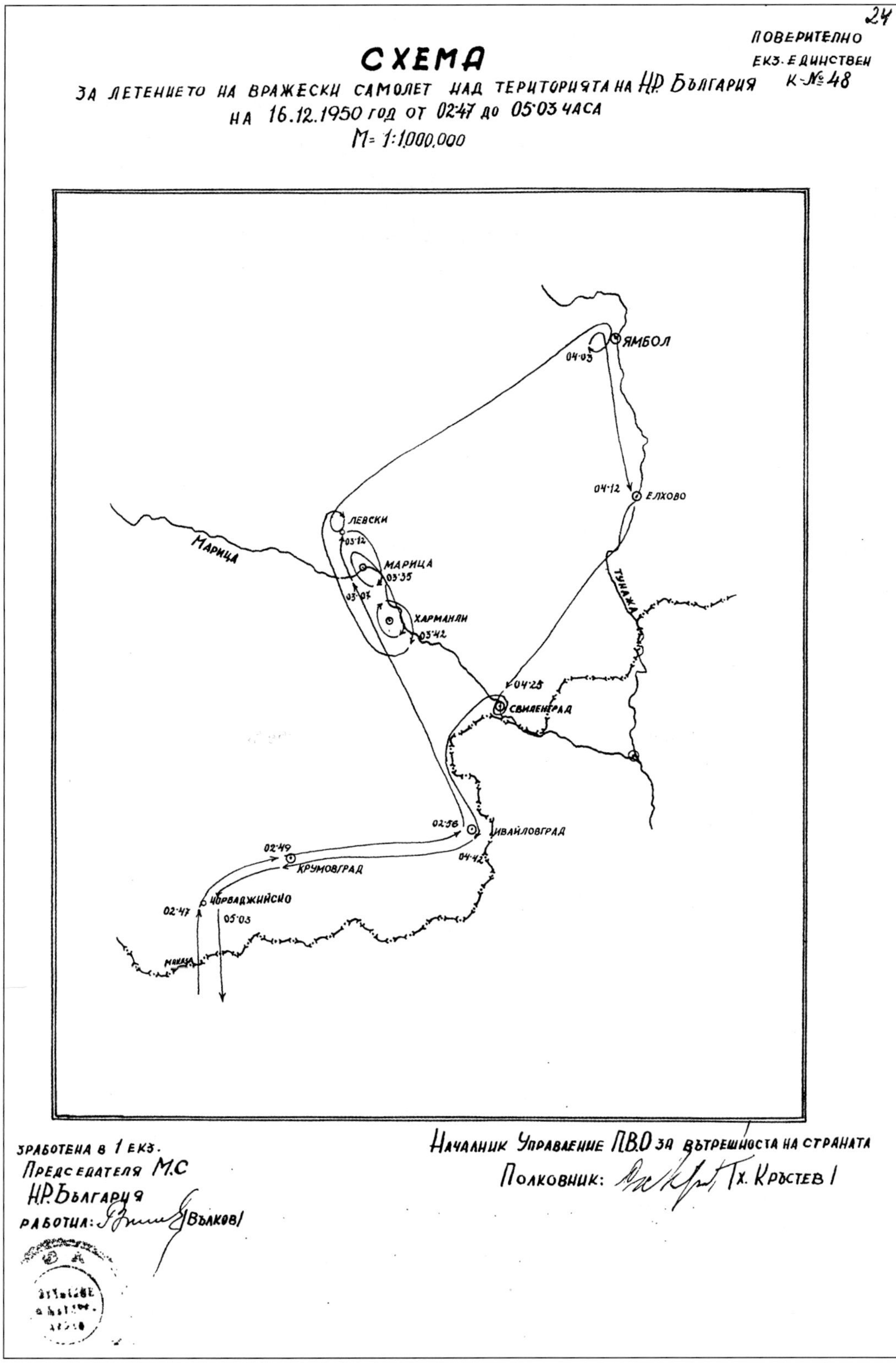

СХЕМА
ЗА ЛЕТЕНИЕТО НА ВРАЖЕСКИ САМОЛЕТ НАД ТЕРИТОРИЯТА НА НР. България
НА 16.12.1950 год ОТ 02:47 до 05:03 ЧАСА
М= 1:1.000.000

ПОВЕРИТЕЛНО
ЕКЗ. ЕДИНСТВЕН
К №48

A scheme of the deep violation of Bulgarian airspace committed on 16 December 1950, between 2:47 and 5:03, with the intruder aircraft entering into Bulgarian airspace at Chorbadjiisko village on the border with Greece and then flying over Krumovgrad, Ivailovgrad, Harmanli, Maritsa, Yambol, Elkhovo and Svilengrad, dropping agitation leaflets. Then it left Bulgarian territory at Chorbadjiisko again. The scheme, depicting the intruder's route, was specially produced for a presentation to the Bulgarian Prime Minister, Valko Chervenkov.

Relations with Yugoslavia were also very complex at the time. After the country's exclusion from the Soviet-led Cominform (the Information Bureau of the Communist and Workers' Parties, a centralised organisation of the international communist movement that existed between 1947 and 1956) and the sharp deterioration of relations between Josip Broz Tito and Stalin, the once brotherly Balkan state had turned almost overnight into a mortal enemy. At the same time Bulgaria granted shelter to a large number of young pro-Soviet communists from Yugoslavia who fled from Tito's 'renegade' regime.

Not long after, the active border crossing by sabotage teams and intelligence officers began — this was done on both sides at equal footing. Naturally, the Yugoslavian Communist leader Tito, who openly declared his independence from the Soviet Union, feared attacks being mounted by the countries that declared themselves after the war as loyal socialist allies of the Soviet Union. Hostile actions by Yugoslavian military aviation were aimed at reconnoitring the border areas in Bulgaria for possible signs of troop deployment in preparation of a Soviet-led invasion of Yugoslavia.

A Pe-2 downed by Friendly Fire

Unfortunately, the first victim of the nervousness accompanying the intercepts of unidentified aircraft flying in Bulgarian airspace was a friendly aircraft. A Pe-2 dive bomber, re-rolled as a reconnaissance aircraft, performing a training photoreconnaissance mission, stripped of the national insignia — due to the clandestine nature

time Communist Party leader and head of state (1956-1989), then a senior party functionary, wrote: 'The same explanations while the foreign aircraft continue to fly with impunity.' The Interior Minister, Anton Yugov, for his part, noted: 'The air defence in Dimitrovgrad area proved to be completely helpless ... it is interesting that even their phone line was not working right then...'. As a consequence, Yugov called for very strict disciplinary measures to be taken.

of the operations of the Bulgarian bomber, reconnaissance and attack assets otherwise banned by the 1947 Paris Peace Treaty — flew a training mission over the western part of the country, taking-off from Graf Ignatievo. Flying at 6,000m (19,680ft) altitude to the west of Sofia on 6 May 1949, it was intercepted by two Yak-9Ms from the 16th IAP, launched from Bozhurishte airfield. The fighters, held on QRA duty, were scrambled due to a mistake committed by the duty

The two-seat Yak-9Vs (known also as the Yak-9Us in Bulgarian service) were in high demand for training at the Fighter School of the People's Air Force School, flying at Polikraishte and Telish. This is fighter pilot Krum Popov, pictured in 1948 siting in a Yak-9V while serving with the Fighter School at Telish.

officer in the 6th IShAD's command post (CP) at Bozhurishte. A wire had been sent notifying the CP about the scheduled Pe-2 training mission in the area but he was not able to find it on the table in the duty room because it was hidden in a messy pile of documents. The fighter pilots then reportedly failed to identify the anonymous-looking Pe-2 as a friendly aircraft and went on to shoot it down — the attack was mounted only nine minutes after take-off. The unlucky Pe-2, flown by Capitan Georgi Chobanov, was erroneously assumed to be a Yugoslavian aircraft undertaking a reconnaissance mission deep in Bulgarian airspace and an order was immediately issued for it to be shot down without warning — this order is known to have been personally issued by the 6th IShAD CO, Polkovnik Kiril Kirilov. The pilot and the gunner managed to bail out, but the navigator stayed in the aircraft and was killed when the burning Pe-2 hit the ground near the city of Pernik, some 30km (15nm) to the west of Sofia.

On 20 October 1950, during a training sortie from Plovdiv airfield, an Il-2 from the 20th ShAP (Attack Regiment), flown by Leitenant Khristo Peshev, became lost and the pilot found himself in the area of Dimitrovgrad. An AAA battery in position next to Dimitrovgrad opened fire against the unidentified aircraft and the Il-2 took hits. The pilot had to perform an emergency landing with the damaged aircraft, without lowering the landing gear. As a consequence, the aircraft was destroyed and the radio operator killed in the crash landing, while the pilot survived the incident.

To counter the increasing number of night intrusions, in January 1951 the Ministry of People's Defence ordered the VVS to provide two squadrons with air crews trained for night-intercept operations in clear weather conditions in each of the fighter divisions until May of that year. In 1952, the VVS main unit held on quick reaction alert (QRA) was the 4th IAD, with its 18th and 11th IAPs stationed at Vrazhdebna and Karlovo until April 1952, and armed with Yak-9P fighters; in the same year the regiments began their re-equipment with the Yak-23 jet fighters. In fact, the Yak-9Ps were kept on QRA duty at night at Dobroslavtsi until the end of 1954. Compared to the older Yak-9M/Ds, the Yak-9P was a newer version with a much better instrumentation suite for night operations, allowing it to be safely

operated in this very demanding mission, where its pilots had to intercept intruders at low level following a visual search, with little or no assistance from the ground.

The establishment of an all-new network of command posts at various levels for the command and control of the rapidly expanding fighter aviation branch began in early 1952, together with the establishment of the command posts of the ground-based air surveillance, warning and communication (VNOS) branch. It was a dense network of visual observation posts deployed across the whole of Bulgarian territory. The airfields where the fighter regiments were based began to be equipped with early warning radars operated by dedicated radio-technical companies.

The first joint exercise between the fighter divisions and the VNOS system was carried out in the spring of 1952. Then this kind of practice began to be carried out in a systematic manner, with missions of the Tu-2 bombers and Li-2 transports, flown twice a month in order to simulate enemy aircraft intruding into Bulgarian airspace. The aircraft had to be visually detected and tracked by the VNOS network, reported to the respective CPs and then the VVS control-and-command-system scrambled the QRA fighters to perform practice intercepts.

Air Warning System Developments

In 1950, the air surveillance, warning and communication structure of the Bulgarian air defence system was represented by the 58th PolkVNOS, a regiment established in August 1948 on the basis of the existing Duzhina unit. It had two component units and in April 1951 was reformed into three independent VNOS battalions, stationed in Sofia, Stara Zagora and Varna. Also in 1950, dedicated visual observation posts were established at each of the VVS primary and secondary airfields – Bozhurishte, Vrazhdebna, Plovdiv, Graf Ignatievo, Stara Zagora, Yambol, Karlovo, Telish, Dolna Mitropolia, Lovech, Gorna Oryakhovitsa, Polikraishte, Tobukhin and Balchik.

The Radar Surveillance Troops (officially called Radio-Technical Troops) branch of the Air Defence service (PVO) was formally established in March 1953, comprising three air warning regiments set up on the base of the existing three independent VNOS battalions. The first regiment (1st PVNOS) had its HQ in Sofia and was responsible for the radar surveillance and visual observation of the airspace in the western part of Bulgaria. 2nd PVNOS, initially headquartered in Stara Zagora and then moved to Graf Ignatievo, was responsible for the central part of the country. 3rd PVNOS had its HQ in Yambol and was responsible for the eastern part of the country. Each of these regiments had four component companies fielding between 60 and 65 visual observation posts in addition to two radar companies each equipped with two radars, and two to five more radar companies each equipped with a single radar. At that time, the radar companies were equipped with newly-delivered Soviet-made P-3A, P-8 and P-20 radars. Before that the air warning was undertaken with German-made Freya radars, inherited from the Second World War-era.

The P-3A (NATO reporting name 'Dumbo'), named 'Milka' in Bulgarian service, was an outdated type, working in the metric wavelength, with a maximum detection range at high altitude of 150km (81nm). The P-8 (NATO 'Knife Rest A'), named 'Sokol', was a much more modern radar, equipped with the NRZ-1 Identification Friend or Foe (IFF) interrogator of the 'Kremnii-1' system, used by all Eastern Bloc countries, with a maximum detection range against high-altitude targets of 150km (81nm); when using a 30m (99ft) mast to elevate the antenna assembly, its range extended up to 250km (108 to 135nm). The P-20 (NATO 'Bar Lock'), named 'Khristo', was the most modern radar in Bulgarian service, also provided with the NRZ-1 IFF interrogator. A semi mobile system, mounted on eight trucks, it featured a decametric wavelength, had a 3D detection capability (range, azimuth and height), and its maximum range against high-altitude targets was 250km (135nm).

By 1952, the Bulgarian early warning network, fielded by the Air Defence service, included a total of 16 sites with early warning radars: Kichevo (north of Varna, on the Black Sea coast), Vetren (next to Bourgas, on the Black Sea coast), Indje Voivoda (south of Bourgas, on the Black Sea coast), Lyubimets (south of Khaskovo, in proximity to the borders with Greece and Turkey), Chamkovo (near Smolyan, in proximity to the border with Greece), Igralishte (near Sandanski, in proximity to the borders with Greece and Yugoslavia), Studeno Buche (near Mikhailovgrad, in proximity to the borders with Yugoslavia and Romania), Radishevo (near Pleven, in proximity to the border with Romania), Veliko Tarnovo (in the central part of the country), Razgrad (in the north-eastern part of the country, in proximity to the border with Romania), Graf Ignatievo (near Plovdiv in the central part of the country), Gotse Delchev (in proximity to the border with Greece), Bozhurishte (west of Sofia, in proximity to the border with Yugoslavia) and Yambol (in proximity to the border with Turkey).

The radar sites were tasked with continuous surveillance of Bulgarian airspace and the adjacent airspace in the neighbouring countries, supplying information to the Air Defence service's command posts.

The VNOS system, using a network of visual observation posts, was eventually disbanded in 1957, and the three existing air warning regiments were re-organised into radio-technical regiments, relying on the use of early warning radars only.

In 1957-1962, the radar early warning network was strengthened with new high-performance Soviet-made radars — such as the P-10, P-12, P-15, P-30 and PRV-10 — used for beefing-up the coverage of Bulgarian airspace and further improving the command-and-control facilities of the fighter branch.

3
ENTERING INTO THE JET ERA

The VVS officially entered the jet era in April 1951, as another decisive step for the strengthening of the service's combat capability was gathering speed daily, especially after the establishment of NATO and the eventual removal of the limitations on the Bulgarian armed forces development imposed by the Paris Peace Treaty.

The Yak-23 (NATO reporting name 'Flora') was the first combat jet of the Bulgarian air arm, with the first group of pilots of the newly-established 15th IAP at Karlovo – Marino Pole airfield, selected for conversion training in late 1949. It was a very careful selection of politically-reliable candidates as all the air crews and even their families underwent exhaustive background checks to prove their political loyalty. Each of the pilots was then personally approved by the Politbureau, the main executive body of the Bulgarian Communist Party, and a decree of the Council of Ministers was then issued to list the names of those officer pilots eventually selected for the first jet fighter training course in the Soviet Union.

In early spring of 1950 the first jet fighter regiment existed in a paper form only, fully equipped with aircrews, but many of them had no idea what was planned in the near term. Major Vasil Velichkov

was appointed as CO of the first VVS jet regiment, Captain Dimo Karaangelov was his Deputy and Capitan Jordan Milanov was the Chief of Staff. Some of the pilots selected for the jet conversion course had some prior experience of flying the Yak-9 and Bf 109G fighters in the two existing front-line regiments (16th and 36th IAP), but there were also many young and inexperienced aviators who had never flown combat aircraft before.

In May 1950 the group was gathered at Bozhurishte airfield to travel by train to Bagai Baranovka airfield near the big city of Saratov in the Soviet Union, where the 8th IAP of the Soviet Air Force was stationed.

The Yak-23 provided a successful transition of the Bulgarian air arm to the jet era, which proved both efficient and safe. This aircraft is from the fleet of the 43rd IAP, seen here during night training operations at Dobroslavtsi airfield near Sofia in the second half of the 1950s.

The Bulgarian pilots who flew the Yak-23 loved this rather primitive jet fighter thanks to its reliability, ease of handling and high agility.

Bulgarian technicians of the Yak-23-equipped 43rd IAP at Dobroslavtsi.

by the regiment's CO. As a result, on 1 July 1950, Major Velichkov flew the Yak-23 for the first time, followed by other Bulgarian pilots soon afterwards, in accordance with the seniority list.

By the end of the conversion training course, only two Bulgarian pilots showed poor results and eventually failed to convert to the jet fighters; upon their return to Bulgaria they were re-assigned to fly piston-powered aircraft. The jet conversion courses also included gunnery training, with the pilots strafing ground targets with the Yak-23's two 23mm guns. In these practice strafing sorties each of the guns was loaded with two rounds only, enough for a single 'hot' firing pass.

Upon completion of the conversion course at the end of the summer, each of the Bulgarian pilots logged 10 to 15 flight hours on the Yak-11 piston trainer and 20 to 25 more on both the Yak-23 and Yak-17UTI jets. The last flying day saw an original exam where the Bulgarian group at Bagai Baranovka was given four aircraft to be flown and serviced by Bulgarian crews only, with the Soviet personnel performing only supervisory functions.

The regiment returned to Bulgaria in September 1950 but then its pilots had to wait for a while for the arrival of the first jet fighters. It was stationed at Graf Ignatievo airfield near the big city of Plovdiv, which at the time was one of the only two in Bulgaria to be provided with a concrete runway. The regiment continued its training on four Bücker Bü 181 Bestmann trainers, temporary transferred to Graf Ignatievo from the flying school at Dolna Mitropolya.

The first Yak-23s arrived in Bulgaria in crates in the winter months of 1950 and by early 1951 as many as 40 examples were delivered by railway in disassembled form, together with five Yak-17UTIs.

First-Generation, Straight-Wing Jet

The Yak-23, built at the GAZ-31 plant in Tbilisi, was the definitive member of Yakovlev's first-generation, lightweight, jet-powered fighter family, retaining the keel fuselage design layout of its predecessors Yak-15 and Yak-17, but powered by an increased-thrust turbojet engine for better performance. It featured straight wings — inherited from the piston-engined Yak-3 — as it was intended to further develop the Yakovlev's 'trademark' concept of a lightweight,

Divided into several groups, initially the Bulgarian pilots underwent a theoretical training course for a month, and then the flying training phase followed. Its first stage was carried out on Yakovlev Yak-11 piston-engined trainers, said to be generally similar in its handling characteristics to the German-made Arado Ar 96 on which they were trained in Bulgaria.

The Bulgarian pilots were divided into two groups, each numbering 20 people and began a very intense flying training with Soviet flight instructors, starting with navigation sorties for area familiarisation. After completion of this stage each pilot was checked to assess the level of his flying skills before transition to the jet training stage. The check flight included take-offs, landings, circuits and aerobatics.

The second stage began with flying the Yak-17UTI (NATO reporting name 'Magnet') twin-seat jet fighter. There were a few of the younger pilots who were ready for their solo flying even earlier than the regimental CO and his deputies, but the Soviet training system strictly followed the rule that the first solo flight should be performed fast, well-armed and highly-agile fighter to perfection. The RD-500 jet engine was a direct copy of the Rolls-Royce Drewent Mk.V, rated at 15.94 kN (3,582lb st. or 1,625kgf). The pilot was accommodated in unpressurised cockpit in order to save weight and avoid adding the complex equipment needed for pressurisation and had a Yakovlev-designed ejection seat. The protection from projectiles and high-speed fragments included a 57mm-thick armoured windshield complemented by an 8mm-thick steel plate built into the seat's backrest. The cockpit had only a basic instrumentation, allowing for limited night and bad weather operations.

The aircraft had a mid-mounted and modestly tapered straight wing featuring wingtip mounts for the installation of external fuel tanks, while the empennage was of a cruciform type. The tricycle-type landing gear used a forward-retracting nose undercarriage unit with a non-steerable wheel, while the main undercarriage units folded into the fuselage. The armament consisted of two NR-23 23mm cannons with 90 rounds each, installed in the lower part of the nose.

In order to achieve as high a performance as possible, the Yak-23 had a bare minimum

In 1952, Bulgaria began building a strong air defence force, with an air component consisting of no fewer than nine jet fighter regiments, each equipped with 28 combat aircraft in three component squadrons. Six of these regiments were eventually equipped with the Yak-23, seen here, controlling a total of 18 squadrons with 120 aircraft, in addition to three more regiments flying the much more potent MiG-15, serving with a total of seven to nine squadrons at the time.

This represents a typical propaganda photo set up from the mid-1950s, showing Yak-23 pilots from the 43rd IAP checking their gun camera tapes.

of armour protection for the cockpit and the systems. As a result, its empty weight was only 1,902 kg (4,192 lb). In addition, the installation of all major systems near the aircraft's centre of gravity provided a welcome effect on the manoeuvrability performance.

Its landing speed was pretty low — only 157km/h (87kt) — a feature, which was welcomed by the front-line pilots. The rate of climb at sea level was very good too, reaching 41m/s (8,068fpm), and time to 5,000m (16,400ft) was 2.3 minutes. The practical ceiling was 15,000m (49,200ft) but due to the non-pressurised cockpit, the flights were restricted to 12,000m (39,360ft) only. The level speed at sea level was 925km/h (499kt), and at high level it reduced to 910km/h (491kt). The fighter had a maximum endurance of one hour and fifty minutes.

The Yak-23 entered into serial production for the Soviet Air Force in late 1948 as a lightweight fighter for front-line use, launched at the aviation factory in Tbilisi in the Georgian Soviet Socialistic Republic, known at the time as the GAZ-31 (State Aviation Plant No. 31). The first production-standard aircraft were rolled out in early 1949 and the total production at GAZ-31 accounted for 310 Yak-23s. After a short service stint with the Soviet Air Force most of these pretty basic jets were transferred to a number of Soviet satellite countries in Eastern

Europe such as Bulgaria, Poland, Czechoslovakia and Romania.

The Yak-23s were followed in 1951 by the first batch of four Yak-17U two-seat fighters intended to be used for conversion and continuation training. Also built at GAZ-31, the two-seater had the same design layout as that of the Yak-23, but was powered by an improved RD-10A turbojet, rated at 9.81kN (2,205lb st. or 1,000kgf), providing a maximum speed of 748km/h (403kt). It was a very short-legged jet aircraft, with only 375km (202nm) range, while the flight endurance was less than 30 minutes.

Jet Flying in Bulgaria

After assembly of the initial three Yak-23s, the first jet flight in Bulgaria was planned for 22 April 1951. The Yak-23 serialled '30', was flown by Major Velichkov. The flight at the landing circuit at 500m (1,600ft) altitude went well until the beginning of the final turn to land, soon after the undercarriage extension. The engine had suddenly started to run with interruptions and not long after it had flamed out completely. The pilot reacted immediately by retracting the undercarriage and lowering the flaps in an effort to perform an emergency belly landing in the field. The aircraft touched down on the ground in a level position

The first Yak-23 flight on Bulgarian soil, with a Bulgarian pilot on the controls, undertaken on 22 April 1951, proved to be a troublesome experience, with engine failure on landing approach. The pilot, Major Vasil Velichkov, CO of the first Bulgarian jet fighter regiment, had managed to perform a successful belly landing at Graf Ignatievo, without causing damage to the aircraft.

The Yak-17UTI 'Magnet' two-seat jet trainer, 16 of which were delivered second-hand to Bulgaria between 1951 and 1953, saw extensive use in the conversion and continuation role in the fighter and training regiments equipped with the single-seat Yak-23 fighters. The type had a very basic design but its safety of flight in Bulgarian service proved to be pretty good, with only one aircraft lost, due to a pilot error.

flying activity with the newly-delivered jets. The first pair of two-seat Yak-17UTIs were taken on strength in mid-May and two more followed in early June. Meanwhile, most of the pilots from the regiments of the two newly-established fighter divisions continued their training on the 20 available Yak-11s in anticipation of the beginning of their jet training course.

The Yak-17UTI two-seaters made it possible for the regiment to launch the jet conversion training of the first group of young pilots in Bulgaria. Grouped in a training squadron at Graf Ignatievo, their instructors were pilots from the first Soviet jet training course – Capitans Khristo Boichev and Dragan Draganov, and Starshi Leitenants Ivan Stankov, Lazar Belukhov, Kiril Apostolov, Tanyu Kaludov and Dimitar Banov. Each of them got three to four students, who initially trained on the Yak-11 before progressed onto the Yak-17UTI and then soloing on the Yak-23. After the completion of their basic jet conversion course, the young pilots continued improving their flying skills in the front-line squadrons. Their initial combat training goal called for gaining the necessary skills and experience for flying air combat missions in a four-ship flight. The first solo flights on the Yak-23 of the newly-converted jet pilots at Graf Ignatievo were made on 23 June 1952.

The available 40 Yak-23s and four Yak-17UTIs were used for training in Bulgaria of aircrews sufficient to equip three jet fighter regiments, together with the pilots who returned from the first jet training course in the Soviet Union. Later on in 1952 the Yak-23 fleet grew to 120 examples, while the Yak-17UTIs eventually numbered 16 examples, the last of which delivered in 1953.

Meanwhile, the VVS sent the second group to the Soviet Union for jet training in the autumn of 1950. This time it comprised only young and inexperienced lieutenants fresh from graduating from the air force school. They were trained at Razboishtina airfield near Saratov, in the structure of the Soviet Air Force 4th Fighter Aviation Training Centre, which also controlled the Bagai Baranovka-based 8th IAP.

These pilots had, however, much less flying experience than their colleagues from the first group and therefore had to be trained considerably longer on the Yak-11 in order to get to a level acceptable for beginning their jet conversion course. Their basic training was completed around mid-1951, but at that time it had been already decided that Bulgaria would be supplied with the MiG-15 in large numbers. As a result, a proportion of the pilots were soon sent to Bagai Baranovka to convert to the new fighter jet, while the rest returned to Bulgaria to continue flying the Yak-23 in the newly-established fighter regiments at Graf Ignatievo.

The newly-acquired jets were shown to the public for the first time during the 9 September 1951 military parade in Sofia. The group selected for the parade included the regiment's CO, Major Vasil Velichkov, in addition to Georgi Kolev, Atanas Atanasov, Simeon Simeonov, Dragan Draganov, Stefan Angelov, Khristo Ivanov, Emanuil Atanasov and Tanyu Kaludov. The Yak-23s were ferried from Graf Ignatievo to Vrazhdebna airfield next to Sofia, which was the first in

and after dragging for some 70m (220ft) came to a halt without any serious damage. The following investigation discovered a faulty seal of the fuel pump which had caused stoppage the fuel flow, leading to the subsequent engine flame out.

The jet flying operations at Graf Ignatievo continued on the next day, when Major Velichkov flight-checked the other two already assembled aircraft. Soon afterwards, the regiment began regular

Bulgaria to be equipped with a concrete runway. The parade set up to fly over the centre of Sofia included three three-ship Yak-23 flights, together with a mixed formation of Yak-9 fighters and Il-10 attack aircraft.

In March 1951, the first jet fighter regiment, the 15th IAP, was used as the base for establishing two new fighter aviation divisions, the 1st IAD and the 10th IAD, with each of these set to eventually include three fighter regiments (IAPs), which were formed by the year-end. In turn, each of the fighter regiments was designed to comprise three eight-aircraft fighter squadrons (IAEs).

The 1st IAD was placed under command of Major Vasil Velichkov, while the 10th IAD's CO was Major Simeon Simeonov. Initially, it was planned that the 1st IAD would remain at Graf Ignatievo in central Bulgaria while the 10th IAD was ordered to relocate to the newly-built airfield in Tolbukhin (now Dobrich) in the north-eastern corner of the country in October 1951. Major Simeonov, however, suggested that the divisions should switch their basing and the superior command authorities eventually agreed with this.

The Yak-23 had a relatively brief service in Bulgaria, accounting for seven years only, but the type proved reliable enough and was loved by the Bulgarian pilots and technicians.

A group of pilots from the 43rd IAP, based at Dobroslavtsi near Sofia, posing in front of a Yak-23. This was the last fighter regiment where it flew in the front-line until 1958, and then the faithful type was replaced by the MiG-15, which served for two years only, before the unit's disbandment in 1960.

As result, the 1st IAD was fully equipped with Yak-23s and Yak-17UTIs and relocated to Tolbukin in a prompt manner, while the 10th IAD began taking on strength the more modern MiG-15 and eventually remained stationed at Graf Ignatievo, with its HQ located in Plovdiv.

The 1st IAD had three component jet fighter regiments in its structure — 22nd, 25th and 27th IAPs, established by October 1951. These were manned by a mixture of pilots who undertook their jet conversion training in the Soviet Union, complemented by others trained locally in Bulgaria. All the Yak-23s were ferried from Graf Ignatievo to Tolbukhin in October and November without any major issues. The ferry flight of the Yak-17UTIs however, proved to be a rather problematic undertaking due to their short range and typical flight endurance of 20 to 25 minutes, while the maximum endurance extended to about 30 minutes. The short-legged two-seaters had to be ferried to Tolbukhin with a refuelling stop at Bezmer airfield, where a concrete runway was still under construction at the time. The four aircraft were ferried in two waves by 1st IAD pilots, Philip Penev and Ivan Stankov.

Immediately after their establishment, the regiments commenced their regular training activity, in order to be able to provide in a compressed timeframe pairs of aircraft on the QRA duty for day and night counter-air operations, and attain readiness for formation operations in pairs, four-ship flights and whole squadrons. The first training year on jet fighters was set to conclude in September 1952 with a large formation mission flown by each regiment with all of its aircraft in a bid to demonstrate the newly-gained operational capability.

The first fatal Yak-23 crash in Bulgaria happened on 19 May 1952 when two aircraft, flown by Leitenants Serafim Begov and Ivan Stefanov, collided in mid-air and their wreckages fell to the ground near Stozher village; Serafim Begov was killed in the crash. The next fatal crash involving a Yak-23 followed on 29 May the same year — during a training sortie another two aircraft collided in mid-air again. This time only the leader's aircraft, flown by Major Georgi Kolev, was seriously damaged after the wingman, Leitenant Todor Mitev, rammed it, damaging the fin and snapping the wire antenna. The pilot decided not to eject but to bail out with a parachute, exiting the aircraft, stepping on the wing and jumping. During the jump, however, the loose end of the wire antenna caught the parachute, which failed to open as required, and the pilot was killed from the impact forces when he hit the ground.

Another accident, this time non-fatal, happened when pilot, Leitenant Pasho Markov, failed to open the valve to feed the main fuel tanks with fuel from the wing tanks in a formation flight. As a result the main tanks were emptied and the engine flamed out soon after the formation break above the airfield, during the final turn. The pilot was able to get to the ground, cross the runway between the other landing aircraft and continue the landing roll in the field until hitting a pit. The nose undercarriage leg went into the pit, the aircraft overturned and the full wingtip fuel tanks caused the separation of both wings. The pilot was intact, rescued by troops working on a nearby construction site who retrieved him from the cockpit. Leitenant Markov, despite being trapped in the cockpit, started shouting at them to turn back because it was a secret airplane.

Yak-23 aircrews undertook air-to-air strafing practice against sleeve targets towed initially by Il-2 attack aircraft and later on by Yak-11 trainers. The shells used different colours for each pilot in order to assess their accuracy by the coloured traces left on the sleeve.

The night-time flying training with the Yak-23 began in January 1952, initially by the 10th IAD's command section at Graf Ignatievo, and later on in the same year it was also initiated by the three regiments of the 1st IAD.

Major Sodev's Fatal QRA Scramble

The end of 1952 saw an increased number of air violations at night, with unidentified aircraft entering from Greece and Turkey to perform missions over Bulgaria or continuing north to Romania and even to the southern territories of the Soviet Union, to deliver agents, supplies to local resistance groups or drop agitation leaflets. To counter the night overflights in the eastern part of Bulgaria, the 25th IAP was ordered to train its pilots in night flying, followed soon afterwards by the 22nd and 27th IAPs.

In the winter months the 25th IAP QRA pilots were on annual leave and in early March 1952 they began practicing night operations set to re-gain the currency needed for the night QRA duty. On 13 March the two pilots for the night QRA shift, Leitenants Tomov and Rashkov, flew refresher missions in the Yak-17UTI two–seater, with their instructors being the 25th IAP CO, Major Spas Sodev and his deputy, Capitan Ivan Stankov. The weather was rapidly deteriorating, with the cloud base at 2,500 to 3,000m (8,200 to 9,840ft) and expected heavy snowfall soon as a huge weather front was rapidly approaching Tolbukhin from the northeast, promising to bring a violent snow storm.

Tomov and Rashkov also flew two solo sorties in the Yak-23 and then began their QRA nigh shift. While the training flights at Tolbukhin were still underway, a scramble command was issued by the Sofia-based Central Command Post (CCP), ordering the QRA pilots to go to the Readiness No.1 state — sitting in the cockpit, ready for immediate take-off upon a further command. Both Sodev and Stankov were still flying as instructors in Yak-17UTIs, but after landing both of them rushed to the QRA aircraft, ordering the pilots to exit the cockpit. Sodev entered into the cockpit of Rashkov's aircraft while Stankov climbed in the cockpit of Tomov's Yak-23. In fact, at that moment Stankov was considered as being better-prepared to fly the difficult bad weather night intercept mission as he had more night flying experience on instruments; that is why he had asked Sodev to launch the first. Sodev, however, was the 25th's CO and instead ordered his deputy to go to the airfield's command post (CP) and monitor the sortie from there. Soon afterwards a red flare was launched from the CP, calling for the launch of the QRA fighter, flown by Major Sodev.

Immediately following take-off Sodev was ordered to maintain a north-westerly heading, flying towards the city of Rousse. He asked the divisional CP why they were directing him to Rousse, covered at that moment by a snow storm, threating to soon cause the loss of radio communication (in such conditions the Yak-23's radio transmitter had a range not exceeding 100km [54nm]) but nobody answered.

Major Spas Sodev, 25th IAP CO, was killed in a crash on 13 March 1952 during a QRA scramble from Tolbukhin at night in extremely bad weather conditions. He was ordered to launch and intercept an intruder in the Bulgarian airspace, detected to be flying near the city of Rousse on the border with Romania.

Ivan Stankov, on his own responsibility, issued an instruction to Sodev to return home by initiating a left-hand U-turn. The 10th IAD CP facility, however, issued an order for the pilot to continue the mission and maintain north-westerly heading. Soon afterward Major Sodev was directed northwards, to the city of Tutrakan on the Danube river but on his way the pilot had hit the ravaging snowstorm and lost contact with ground control. The pilot failed to return from the real-word combat mission.

The aircraft wreckage and the remains of the pilot were found a few days later due to the thick snow cover in the crash area which delayed the search effort. The crash site of Major Sodev was near Stefan Karadjovo village, not far away from Tutrakan. During the large-scale search operation, Bulgarian troops also found the remains of a Soviet fighter aircraft launched from an airfield in Romania that night, most likely tasked to intercept the same intruder. The fighter controller in the divisional GCI facility was discharged despite that fact that he had not controlled the intercept by his own initiative and instead simply retranslated the commands issued by the CCP in Sofia.

In March 1953, the 27th IAP relocated to the newly-built Bezmer airfield in south-eastern Bulgaria, near the big city of Yambol and continued flying the Yak-23 for two more years. Later on, Bezmer airfield also housed the 22nd IAP, commanded by Capitan Emanuil Atanasov, which relocated from Tolbukhin in March 1955 and began converting to the MiG-15.

In September 1955, the 25th IAP's CO, Major Ivan Stankov, got a wire from the VVS HQ, ordering him to place the regiment's Yak-23s in long-term storage at Tolbukhih and move the personnel by railway to Graf Ignatievo. In turn, the 27th IAP's CO also received a similar wire, ordering him to move the regimental personnel from Bezmer to

Balchik airfield on the northern part of the Bulgarian Black Sea coast, not far away from Tolbukhin.

Right in the middle of the move to Graf Ignatievo, the train transporting the 25th IAP was stopped and its CO received a new order to return back to Tolbukhin. It, however, proved impossible, as the railway movements were very slow and the food was near the end. In the event, the train got to Graf Ignatievo where it turned out that the wires to the 25th and 27th IAPs had been due to an

In 1955, the Yak-11 was introduced for training with the People Air Force School, used for training students destined to convert to the jet-powered Yak-17UTI and Yak-23.

error made by a radio communications operator. The original intent was the 25th IAP to move to nearby Balchik, while the 27th IAP from Bezmer was to relocate to Graf Ignatievo, which was also just a short trip. General Major Simeon Simeonov intervened in a prompt manner yet again in an effort to preserve the status quo, and the VVS HQ agreed with the current situation, swapping the planned new bases of these regiments. The relocation of the 25th and 27th IAPs had also brought to an end the Yak-23's operations with the 1st IAD, as the type was superseded by the MiG-15 and MiG-15bis, later on complemented by the MiG-17F/PF. In September 1955, the 25th IAP was included in the 10th IAD's structure.

The Yak-23 was also inducted in service in April 1952 with the 4th IAD – the 18th and 43rd IAPs were home-based at Dobroslavtsi near Sofia while the 11th IAP moved to Gabrovnitsa seven months later. Then 18th IAP converted to the MiG-15 in February 1955, while 11th IAP got its first MiG-15s in 1953; the 43rd IAP continued to fly the faithful Yak-23 until 1958.

The 27th IAP reported one fatal accident with the type, on 21 April 1954, when a Yak-23, flown by Starshi Leitenant Stoits Stoitsev, crashed near the village of Krushary northwest of Yambol. In total, the 18th IAP had two Yak-23 crashes with two pilots killed, while the 11th IAP lost two aircraft and one pilot during the type's three years of service with these regiments, operating a total of six squadrons. In turn, the 43rd also lost two aircraft and two pilots in six years of service.

In the 11th IAP, the first loss happened on 21 March 1953, when Starshi Leitenant Yordan Shishmanov was blinded by a landing searchlight and collided with the ground on landing approach. A Yak-17UTI from the same regiment was lost on 17 August 1955, when Starshi Leitenant Vasil Vutov became lost near Kyustendil during a ferry flight between Gabrovnitsa and Dobroslavtsi and upon burning all the fuel ejected successfully from the short-legged training jet.

The 18th IAP lost its first pilot flying the Yak-23 on 7 September 1954, when Starshi Leitenant Asen Dobrev entered into a spin and failed to recover, hitting the ground. Then, on 8 October that year Major Todor Todorov crashed at Dobroslavtsi due to a handling mistake.

In the 43rd IAP, the first crash happened on 5 June 1956, when Starshi Leitenant Peter Trizlov was killed in an unintentional ejection. The ejection sequence was triggered by negative-G-force during manoeuvring causing activation of the pyro cartridge, but the canopy failed to jettison. The second crash in the 43rd IAP happened on 12 July 1958, killing Leitenant Ivan Mishev, apparently due to health problems caused by the high-G force during aggressive manoeuvring and the following collision with the ground.

During the Yak-23's brief service with the 20th ShAP (Attack Regiment) at Krumovo near Plovdiv — between mid-1956 and mid-1958 — one crash was reported. It happened on 14 February 1958, with the pilot, Capitan Georgy Yordanov, killed in a collision with terrain during low-level manoeuvring.

In 1955 the Yak-23 and the Yak-17U were also taken on strength by the People's Air Force School — serving with the newly-established 1st UBAE (combat-training aviation squadron), which in 1956 was enlarged into the 2nd UBAP, a training-combat aviation regiment with two component squadrons, one of which was home-based at the newly-built Kamenets airfield east of Pleven, together with the regiment's HQ. There the Yak-17UTI and Yak-23 were used for advanced pilot training until the end of 1956. In fact, the first group of 20 student pilots, together with a group of instructors from the People's Air Force School, were cycled through their jet training course already during the second half of 1954 after having amassed 70 hours on prop-driven Laz-7 trainers. This training campaign took place at Bezmer airfield as Kamenets was still under construction and was completed around mid-1955.

The first flights for the instructors at Kamenets airfield with the Yak-17U were reported in March 1955. The students for the VVS fighter branch, graduating in 1955 were trained first on the Yak-11 and then continued with their advanced training phase on the jet aircraft. They graduated from the People's Air Force School rated to fly solo on the Yak-23 but were then required to practice combat manoeuvring and combat employment after their posting to the front-line regiments.

Then a second group of students, previously trained on the prop-driven Yak-11, began its jet training at Kamenets in 1956. The 2nd UBAP's jet fleet, used for the student training at the time, comprised of ten Yak-23s and six Yak-17UTIs, complemented by a dozen Yak-11 prop trainers. The Yak jets remained in use by the 2nd UBAP until the end of 1956, when the MiG-15 was introduced into service with the jet training squadron of the 2nd UBAP.

4

VVS ENTERS THE MIG-15 ERA

The MiG-15 (NATO reporting name 'Fagot'), often titled in Bulgaria as the 'aircraft-soldier', was de facto the Soviet Union's first operational swept-wing jet fighter, widely exported to satellite states in the early 1950s. Built in mass, it was affordable and capable. In fact, it was fairly advanced for its time and soon became the standard fighter of the Bulgarian air arm. The first MiG-15 deliveries to Bulgaria were made in November and December 1951, earmarked to equip the 19th and 21st IAPs — a total of 23 aircraft arrived in crated form, in addition to three more MiG-15UTI two-seaters for conversion and continuation training. Thirty four more MiG-15s and three MiG-15UTIs followed in 1952, while 1953 deliveries comprised six MiG-15s, 20 MiG-15bis and eight MiG-15UTIs in addition to 30 more MiG-15s manufactured by AERO in the Czechoslovakian Republic.

The MiG-15 was powered by one VK-45F turbojet (a non-licensed Rolls Royce Nene II derivative), delivering 2,225kN (2,200kgf or 4,928lb st.) of thrust. It featured a maximum speed of 1,031km/h (554.5kt) at 5,000m (16,400ft) altitude, 1,031 km/h (557kt) at sea level. The climb rate reached 42m/s (8,266fpm) and the time for climb to 5,000 m (16,400ft) was 2.3 minutes. Range on internal fuel was 1,335km (721nm), extending to 1,920km (1,037nm) when using two external tanks suspended under the wings.

The pilot was accommodated in a pressurised cockpit, with a canopy providing a very good view forward and rearward, and he sat on an ejection seat that granted a reliable bailout in high-speed flight. The canopy was made of two parts — a fixed forward with an armoured windshield and a section that was movable to the rear, opening by sliding aft.

The armament comprised a battery of three cannons – one 37mm N-37D (provided with 40 rounds) and two 23mm NR-23s (each provided with 100 rounds) mounted in the lower forward fuselage, with muzzles protruding under the starboard (N-37D) and port side of the nose (both NR-23s). All the three cannons were installed onto a common platform, together with the ammunition cases and the spent-cartridge collectors. The armament platform was made detachable and able to be pulled down for easing the servicing of the weapons and loading ammunition. The cockpit featured an ASP-3N gun-sight and an S-13 gun-camera.

The aircraft was capable of using improved shape external tanks, for 300 litres of kerosene, in order to allow the MiG-15's maximum speed with external fuel tanks to be increased to 900km/h (485kt) — equating to Mach 0.9 at high altitude —

The mass introduction of jet fighters by the Bulgarian air arm took place between 1951 and 1953, initially fielding the straight-wing Yak-23. The type served with no fewer than six fighter regiments, followed by the real game-changer, the swept-wing MiG-15 (shown here), which initially equipped the 10th IAD's three regiments. The 15th IAP was based at Bezmer and then moved to Ravnets near Bourgas in 1953, while the 19th IAP remained at Graf Ignatievo and the 21st IAP went on to Uzundzhovo near Khaskovo, also in 1953.

The MiG-15 was more difficult to master, especially by inexperienced pilots, compared to the Yak-23 but had much higher combat potential. It was also more complex for maintenance and required larger and better runways and taxiways.

while the manoeuvring limit was set at 5-G with full external tanks and 6.5-G with empty ones.

The MiG-15UTI 'Midget' two-seat training version used the basic airframe and powerplant of the single-seater, with a second cockpit (occupied by the instructor) inserted in the place of the fuel tanks, thus reducing the internal fuel tankage. The new design of the canopy included a sideways-hinging movable part for the front cockpit and an aft-sliding part for the rear one. The ejection seats were the same as those used on the single-seater, and the ejection sequence called for bailing out first the instructor pilot in the rear cockpit and then the student in the front. The pilots and armament were protected by two 10mm armoured plates installed in the nose, while both ejection seats were provided with armoured headrests. The two-seater's armament comprised of one YakB-E 12.7mm machinegun with 150 rounds.

The first MiG-15s were assembled from kits at Graf Ignatievo airfield in January 1952 and at the end of the month the new fighters were flight-checked by Soviet military advisers assigned to the 10th IAD. All of these aircraft were subsequently handed over to the 10th IAD, initially equipping the

The first MiG-15s arrived in Bulgaria, in crated form, in November 1951, a batch comprising 18 single-seat aircraft, set to eventually equip the regiments of the 10th IAD in late 1952. The improved MiG-15bis, seen here followed suit in August 1953, again first fielded with the regiments of the 10th IAD, the first of which was the 19th IAP at Graf Ignatievo.

The MiG-15 family became the backbone of the VVS fighter fleet until the late 1950s: as many 160 single seaters were eventually taken on strength by the Bulgarian air arm. This is an aircraft from the 11th IAP at Gabrovnitsa, pictured with a P-20 'Khristo' early warning radar in the background in the late 1950s.

19th IAP and the 15th IAP (replacing in the later the Yak-23), and not long after the 21st IAP. The aircraft were initially flown by the pilots who undertook their jet conversion course in the Soviet Union on the MiG-15, some of them also receiving instructor qualification. Most of the pilots trained on the MiG-15 in the Soviet Union were grouped into one of the squadrons of the 21st IAP, commanded at the time by Starshi Leitenant Sava Netsov.

A total of 18 new pilots were included in the first MiG-15 jet conversion course to be held in Bulgaria, with each of these required to amass 60 hours on the MiG-15, reaching the qualification to perform aerobatic manoeuvring. The training course also included gunnery practice against ground targets at the Tsertelevo shooting range, with strafing passes mounted with dive angles of 45° and 60°. By the end of the summer, the MiG-15 aircrews from the 19th and 21st IAPs began aerial gunnery practice against sleeve targets towed by Il-2 attack aircraft.

On 1 May 1952 the new fighters were shown for the first time to the public in the air parade over Sofia with a formation comprising of three three-aircraft flights.

In the summer of 1952, the 19th IAP pilots, flying the MiG-15, were also required to begin night training, initially flying the Polikarpov Po-2 biplanes and then on the Yak-11, before being sufficiently skilled to commence flying jet fighters at night.

In April 1952, the 15th IAP, equipped with MiG-15s, moved to its new base at Bezmer, followed one year later by the 21st IAP, which went to the newly-built Uzundzhovo airfield in April 1953. At its new base, the 21st IAP held its first QRA duty shift on 5 December that year.

The 19th IAP began its intensified training for night counter-air operations in May 1952 in order for the regiment to be able to provide QRA duty forces at night. By that time, the night QRA duty for the entire Bulgarian territory was rendered by the 14th OIAP, an independent fighter regiment, equipped with Yak-9M/P prop-driven fighters stationed at Karlovo and directly reporting to the VVS HQ. The regiment still had a good pool of experienced pilots, some of them Second World War veterans, such as Major Stefan Konzov.

The first QRA duty at the 19th IAP, held in daylight-only in the beginning, was reported on 5 May, involving the flights of Capitans

As many as 93 single-seat MiG-15s, manufactured in the Soviet Union and Czechoslovakia, were delivered between 1951 and 1953, together with 61 more MiG-15UTI two-seaters (seen here), the last of which was taken on strength in 1960.

The two-seat MiG-15UTI had a simplified armament, comprising only one YakB-E 12.7mm machine-gun with 150 rounds, used for gunnery practice. The two pylons under the wings were made capable of carrying one 50kg (110lb) or 100kg (220lb) bomb each on BD2-48 bomb racks. The front cockpit was equipped with an ASP-3N gun sight and also had a S-13 gun camera. The initial two-seaters in Bulgarian service wore single-digit serials while the follow-on examples received three- and four-digit serials.

sleeve, included spin recovery practice, carried out in two-seat MiG-15UTIs only.

The first jet night training sorties in the 19th IAP were reported on 25 July 1952, initially on MiG-15UTI two-seaters, and the single-seaters were flown for the first time at night on 30 July, with the night training course declared as completed by the 1/19 IAE and the regiment's command section in early September. The first night QRA duty was carried out on 4 September 1952. In October, the MiG-15 pilots began practicing strafing on air targets at night, lit and tracked by ground-based searchlights. Also in 1952, the airfield was equipped with navigation aids for bad weather operations, including an UHF direction finder, inner and outer radio beacons/radio markers and lightning systems for the approach and the runway contours. The new equipment at the airfield also included the RSP-5 ground-controlled approach (GSA) radar system to facilitate bad weather landing approaches at the weather minimum visibility conditions, with voice commands issued to the pilots to follow the glideslope by a dedicated air traffic controller using the GSA radar.

The airfield also got a P-20 surveillance radar and the 10th IAD also set up three new auxiliary CPs at Gorna Oryakhovitsa, Lyubimets and Chepelare, to be used for the control of intercept operations in the division's area of responsibility, equipped with radars and manned by combat control officers.

Tanyu Kaludov and Dimitar Banov. In July 1952, the 19th IAP pilots placed on the QRA carried their first practice scrambles, to intercept an Li-2 transport simulating an enemy aircraft. The operation was undertaken together with the VVS central command post (CCP) and the 19th IAP's own CP at Graf Ignatievo. The result from the exercise was negative as the 19th IAP's CP proved ill-suited to provide combat control to the scrambled aircrews, due to the interrupted communications between the command posts involved in the operation. Later on, the practices to scramble the QRA pair against simulated air intruders were carried out on a regular basis in order to hone the coordination between the combat control officers in the various CPs and the pilots performing the intercept.

The other new qualifications mastered by the 19th and 21st IAP aircrews, in addition to shooting at ground targets and at a towed air

In May 1952, the first MiG-15 crash in Bulgaria claimed the life of Starshi Leitenant Stefan Petkov from the 15th IAP, during a night training sortie, apparently due to pilot disorientation that led to a controlled flight into terrain. This happened during training operations from Graf Ignatievo, shortly before the completion of the regiment's relocation to Bezmer.

The spin recovery training on the two-seat MiG-15UTI began in mid-1952, using Soviet Air Force instructors who trained the first cadre of Bulgarian pilots, set to serve as instructors for the remaining aircrews in the 10th IAD. The spin recovery training was interrupted for some time after the crash of a MiG-15UTI from the 15th IAP at Bezmer. The crew, trainee Starshi Leitenant Dimitar Pavlov and instructor Major Stefan Angelov, the 15th IAP's CO, failed to recover the aircraft from a spin during a dedicated training sortie and were killed when the aircraft hit the ground at Bezmer on 31 October. This accident led to a ban of the spin recovery practice in the VVS for a prolonged period and it was not resumed before 1954, again using Soviet instructors at Graf Ignatievo.

The third MiG-15 loss in Bulgaria was also reported in October. During an exercise, the leader of a pair from the 19th IAP, Leitenant Grigor Ignatov, collided mid-air with an Il-10 attack aircraft near Ikhtiman. This happened in a dive attack on an Il-10 formation at low level, due to a late pull out. The MiG-15 pilot was literally ejected out of the cockpit (but without using the ejection seat) by the subsequent explosion of his aircraft and then he managed to open his parachute while falling to the ground. The pilot and gunner in the Il-10 were instantly killed in their exploded aircraft.

The first successful ejection from the MiG-15 in Bulgaria was reported on 12 May 1953, when Leitenant Angel Kybarsky from the 19th IAP bailed out after inadvertently entering into a spin, from which he was not able to recover.

By any criteria, the MiG-15 and its improved derivative dubbed MiG-15bis were the most capable fighters available in mass numbers in the first half of the 1950s to the Soviet allies of the Eastern Bloc. In Bulgarian service the MiG-15 fared pretty well and saw some real-world actions in the tensest Cold War times between 1953 and 1956, having been tasked to counter the frequent unsanctioned overflies of foreign aircraft.

A fine study showing Bulgarian pilots in an improvised briefing in front of a MiG-15 at a forward airfield with grass-covered surface.

In 1953 the regiments of the 10th IAD began intensely practicing attacks on low-speed aircraft, in order to be able to counter the slow-flying intruders which violated in Bulgarian airspace, mostly at night. At the same time, the regiments began to provide aircraft on an enhanced QRA duty at Graf Ignatievo, with four pilots in the daylight shift, reduced to two in the night shift. The P-20 early warning radar stationed at Trud, some 5km (2.7nm) south of Graf Ignatievo, was able to detect and track low-flying targets, at 200m (656ft) altitude, at ranges not exceeding 30km (17nm). That is why the VNOS service continued to be used as the main tool for the early detection and continuous tracking of low-flying intruders thanks to the large network of visual observation posts in southern Bulgaria, deployed alongside the borders with Turkey and Greece.

On 31 March 1953, during a day mission at 8,000 to 9,000m (26,240 to 29,520ft) a MiG-15, flown by Starshi Leitenant Georgy Boyadzhuev, a squadron CO from the 21st IAP, crashed and the pilot was killed. The most likely cause being oxygen starvation as the pilot flew without donning his oxygen mask.

Upon the relocation of the 21st IAP to the newly-built Uzundzhovo airfield near Khaskovo, some 80km (43nm) to the southeast of Graf

Ignatievo, one of its component squadrons, the 1/21 IAE, was ordered to remain at Graf Ignatievo, to be re-organised as the 3/19 IAE, a new component squadron in the 19th IAP structure. It was an urgent measure taken to further strengthen the 19th IAP, as the regiment, set to be re-equipped soon with the MiG-15bis, was heavily tasked with the day and night QRA duty.

In early April 1953, the new qualification of the aircrews included high-altitude flights to practice intercept of high-flying aircraft, at 12,000 to 14,000m (39,360 to 45,920ft).

During the intense night training operations in bad weather conditions in December 1953 at Graf Ignatievo, the 19th IAP saw its first fatal accident. Starshi Leitenant Atanas Karaganev, the 3/19 IAE CO, crashed reportedly due to a pilot mistake when flying in thick clouds, in his first solo sortie in such challenging conditions.

In total, as many as 22 single-seat MiG-15 and MiG-15bis, plus five more two-seat MiG-15UTIs were lost in flight and ground accidents in Bulgaria between 1952 and 1960, claiming the lives of no fewer than 24 pilots.

A Bulgarian Air Force MiG-15UTI two-seater seen undergoing pre-flight preparation, including refuelling.

qualification level, with pilots declared as qualified to conduct day and night combat operations in both the VMC and IMC, and having the proficiency to perform complex combat employment techniques.

In the beginning, the senior commanders in the VVS HQ and the 10th IAD underwent an accelerated training course with Soviet Air Force instructor pilots to get the newly-introduced qualifications ratings. This training at Graf Ignatievo began in September 1952, using a trio of highly experienced Soviet instructors. In the beginning of the course, the Bulgarian trainees were required to amass 14 hours of flying in IMC on the Yak-11 before transitioning to the MiG-15UTI for flying in such conditions and finally soloing on the MiG-15 and MiG-15bis.

Intensified Training

The intense training of the pilots in the newly-established jet fighter regiments included night and bad weather operations using the original Soviet Air Force training model unchanged, with the 10th IAD leading the way. The VVS adopted the Soviet combat aircrew qualification rating system, where the rating was assigned depending on the state of combat readiness in different weather conditions — and it is still in use today in Bulgaria in a little-changed form. The 3rd Class rating, implying a limited combat readiness state, was a basic qualification for performing a range of relatively simple day-only combat missions, in visual meteorological conditions (VMC) only.

The next combat training qualification level, known as the 2nd Class rating, was usually attained after three to four years of active flight training after graduating from the People's Air Force School. At this stage pilots were considered to be qualified to fly more complex combat missions, both day and night in VMC. The 2nd Class rating also allowed pilots to perform daytime combat missions in instrument meteorological conditions (IMC) and land in minimum visibility conditions.

The 1st Class rating called for the highest combat readiness/

The 1st Class training was completed in September 1953 by the first group of eight Bulgarian fighter pilots, who then began flying as instructors for the night and IMC (bad weather) training of the remaining pilots in the fighter regiments to get them to the 2nd and 1st Class rating. They were: Polkovnik Simeon Simeonov, Major Atanas Atanasov, Capitan Atanas Dimitrov and Starshi Leitenants Toma Kovachev, Todor Trifonov, Philp Tsekov and Georgi Bozhilov. Then, the best pilots in each of the VVS jet fighter regiments began accelerated training for IMC operations at night in early 1953, with their training programme comprising 30 flight hours.

To solve the issues with the reliable detection of intrudes at low altitude and the guidance of the QRA fighters, a system of radar-equipped auxiliary guidance posts was deployed across the whole of Bulgarian territory.

By early 1954, the forces on QRA duty were represented by four aircraft at each of the five main airfields — including one pair held in Readiness No 1 and another in Readiness No 2 state.

The Readiness No 1 state – with pilots sitting in the cockpit – called for a launch of the pair immediately after receiving the scramble

The first group of eight VVS pilots, trained by Soviet instructors in an accelerated course for bad weather operations at night at Graf Ignatievo, graduated in September 1953, receiving the so-called 1st Class rating. From left to right: Philp Tsekov, Toma Kovachev, Dimo Dimov, Atanas Dimitrov, Simeon Simeonov, Atanas Atanasov, Todor Trifonov, Georgy Bozhilov.

A photo dating to the early 1950s, taken at Graf Ignatievo. Bulgarian Air Force Commander-in-Chief, General Major Zakhary Zakhariev, is the second to the right, and the fourth from the right is the 10th IAD CO, then-Polkovnik Simeon Simeonov. The first on the right is the 19th IAP CO, Podpolkovnik Zhelyazko Zhelyazkov. The third and the sixth on the right are Soviet Air Force officers, posted as advisors to the Bulgarian Air Force. The photo dates to 1953 or 1954.

A Bulgarian MiG-15 and a MiG-15bis (the aircraft nearest to the camera) sitting at the flight line next to each other. In the mid-1950s, some of the VVS fighter squadrons were equipped with a mixed fleet of the straight and improved 'Fagot' versions. The improved MiG-15bis was introduced for the first time with the Bulgarian air arm in August 1953.

order, while No 2 required them to get airborne within 5 minutes from receiving the scramble order. Until 1954, the jet fighters held on the QRA duty at night were augmented by Yak-9P fighters of 14th OIAP, deployed to forward locations near the borders with Turkey and Greece, in the so-called night ambush flights and pairs. For this purpose, the Yak-9Ps used the forward airfields at Malevo and Musmishte near the border with Greece in addition to providing QRA duty well inside the country at Dobroslavtsi, Sarafovo and Gorna Oryakhovitsa airfields, on an as needed basis.

The student pilots at the People's Air Force School began training on the MiG-15 for the first time in early 1957, with their syllabus comprising around 40 hours. A total of 47 pilots were trained in the first year of operations at the 2nd UABP at Kamenets, with the syllabus including circuits, simple and complex manoeuvres, formation flying, air-to-air attacks, ground target strafing and air navigation, in daylight only. In 1958, the MiG-15 training was extended to 48 hours (comprising about 175 sorties), with 35 student pilots graduating the course and then immediately posted to the front-line units. In 1960, the 2nd UBAP at Kamenets had a fleet of 18 single-seat MiG-15s (including six equipped for blind landings) and seven two-seat MiG-15UTIs (five equipped for blind landings).

MiG-15bis enters Service

The MiG-15bis was the ultimate representative of the single-seat 'Fagot' model family, powered by an increased-thrust engine and sporting a better equipment standard. Its development became possible thanks to the availability of the more powerful VK-1 turbojet, rated at 26kN (5,951lb st. or 2,700kgf). The new engine provided maximum speed at high altitude of 1,076km/h (581kt), while at low level it reached 1,045km/h (564kt) and rate of climb increased to 50m/s (9,840fpm).

The new engine had exactly the same size and weight of its predecessor, the VK-45F, and its installation onto the MiG-15 necessitated only a few minor design alterations. The list of the other improvements included a stretched fuselage (due to the longer jet pipe of the new engine), a strengthened wing structure, a refined elevator design, and a newly designed wing fence to prevent stalls. The pilot had a better protection provided by a 64mm-thick armoured windshield, and the cockpit pressurisation was also improved. Pilots also received the PPK-1 anti-G suite for better sustaining the G-forces in turning flight, when pulling from 1.085 to 8G; this equipment was copied from a North American F-86 Sabre fighter captured in Korea. In 1952 the MiG-15bis received a rear-view periscope, mounted on the top of the canopy arc. The air brake panels were strengthened and the new

A young MiG-15 pilot from the 15th IAP stationed at Ravnets is seen here posing in the cockpit in this early-delivery single-seater in a classic propaganda photo from the early Cold War years.

'Fagot' version received powered ailerons for better controllability in the roll axis in high-speed flight.

The MiG-15bis, the first batch of which was delivered in August 1953 to equip selected squadrons in the three regiments of the 10th IAD, was also equipped with the so-called 'blind-landing' instrumentation suite, the OSP-48 incorporating an ARK-5 automatic direction finder, an RV-2 radar altimeter and a MRP-48 marker beacon receiver. The first batch comprised 20 aircraft, augmented by 32 more taken in March and April 1955 to equip initially the 10th IAD's three regiments. The new aircraft were better suited for operations in instrument meteorological conditions and also featured a slightly better flight performance and controllably characteristics than the 'plain' MiG-15s. In order to facilitate the operations of the fighters equipped with 'blind-landing' instrumentations suites for day/night IMC operations, the 10th IAD airfields at Grad Ignatievo, Uzundzhovo and Ravnets began to be equipped with the specialised lightning systems, including the AMP-90 landing searchlights, Luch-1 approach and runway lights and the PAR-BM marker radio beacons. These were also gradually installed on the airfields of the 1st and the 4th IADs, where QRA fighters were based.

By January 1954, the 19th IAP — already known as the VVS's leading all-weather day/night fighter unit — fully re-equipped with the more capable MiG-15bis and had a total of 24 pilots declared combat-ready for day operations in clear weather, and 22 of them were also cleared for clear-weather night flying. Nineteen of the regiment's pilots were also cleared for flying combat sorties in clear weather at night and only two of them were declared combat ready for combat missions in bad weather at night.

Intrusions along the Southern Border

Violations along the southern border were most often carried out by aircraft entering from Greece in the Lyubimets – Sviengrad region, a plains area alongside the Maritsa river valley. As early as 1950, the US Central Intelligence Agency established a station in Greece for active operations in the Balkans. At the time the CIA aimed to overthrow the Enver Hoxha regime in Albania, as well as discrediting the communist regimes in Bulgaria and Romania. Its covert action unit, the Office of Policy Coordination (OPC), began a range of activities to destabilise the pro-Moscow government in Sofia — it was to happen through a combination of psychological warfare and the insertion into country by air or land of agents of Bulgarian nationality, mainly recruited from Displaced Person camps across Europe. The Bulgarian plan was approved by the CIA on 19 April 1950, shortly afterwards followed by the Romanian plan for creation and/or development of indigenous anti-Moscow underground movements. Among the aims was also conducting psychological warfare operations against the communist regime in Sofia.

In 1950, the first CIA air operations were carried out over Bulgaria, reportedly in close cooperation with the Greek Air Force and the Greek secret services. In March 1950, the so-called QKSTAIR project for destabilising the regimes in Bulgaria, Albania and Romania was approved and later renamed BGCONVOY. The purpose of the CIA operations within the frame of the QKSTAIR/BGCONVOY project was to establish illegal networks of agents and nation-wide covert resistance movements. The plan also included a psychological and propaganda war to be waged domestically. The BGCONVOY project had been approved and funding had been allocated for two years of operations. A special 'black radio station', named Goryanin, was established to broadcast programs in the Bulgarian language, creating the illusion of secret broadcasts on the territory of the country and the existence of a serious local resistance movement against communist rule.

Centres were set up for the operation in the US, France, Switzerland, Germany, Italy and, of course, Turkey and Greece. It should be noted here that the Turkish government had eventually refused to allow the CIA to establish bases in their territory to be used for training and infiltration of agents into Bulgaria. This left the agency with only one real choice for use as a base for the operation. It was Greece, from where the CIA intended to operate aircraft for parachuting agents or infiltrating them through the land border. The destabilisation activity against Bulgaria was launched in December 1950, but the use of agents proved to be of low-effectiveness as the Bulgarian state security services were good enough to capture or kill almost all agents as soon as they were infiltrated into Bulgaria by land and air.

The CIA's destabilising plan, in addition to the various activities, foresaw funding for a seven-strong air crew and technical personnel needed to perform airborne parachute delivery operations and dropping agitation leaflets. US Air Force (USAF) provided the air support to the operation in the form of three Douglas C-47 transport aircraft, with up to a 2,300kg (5,000lb) payload and capable of transporting up to 27 troops. The USAF in Germany furnished the aircraft for use in project BGFIEND, aimed at conducting destabilising actives against Albania. Since Greece was the main foothold for fighting against the Enver Hoxha regime, it is believed that these aircraft were also used in operations over Bulgaria and subsequently over Romania.

Two of the three C-47 Skytrains were intended for liaison flights, transporting CIA agents and staff between different bases in Europe, as well as between different cities in Greece, with USAF crews. The third aircraft, which had been designated to perform special missions over the territory of Albania and Bulgaria, was fully staffed by a CIA-contracted crew. Its actions are said to have been highly effective in the beginning in Bulgarian airspace, where it had encountered little or no resistance. In March 1951, in one of the first missions, it got as far as the Bulgarian city of Tutrakan on the Danube river at night and dropped agitation leaflets. Soon after, it began committing regular intrusions into Bulgarian airspace. By mid-August 1951, the CIA-operated aircraft dropped over 2 million agitation leaflets over Bulgaria. One of the regular targets for the destabilising and reconnaissance activities was the newly-constructed at the time 'Friendship Bridge' across the Danube river near the big industrial city of Rousse, used for connecting Bulgaria and Romania.

Bulgaria reacted in every possible way against the CIA operation, but its reaction with military means proved to be of little or no effect in the beginning. Later on special measures were taken by both the Air Force and the Air Defence branches to counter the regular intrusions committed at night. The CIA's October 1951 report stated:

> The distribution of agitation leaflets from the air has been discontinued. The flights for dropping leaflets are currently considered unjustified because of the risk for the slow-flying C-47. And also because such flights tend to attract the attention and alert of the Bulgarian air defence, thus jeopardizing far more important future operations.

Thus, it was intended to combine psychological warfare with flights for the delivery by air of highly-trained agents and the supply of the insurgent movements.

Some of the aircraft and operations with intrusions into Bulgarian airspace were not intended solely for operations in Bulgarian territory. For example, on 18-19 October 1951, a CIA-operated aircraft launched from Greece to deliver two groups of operatives — the first was made by agents recruited by the United States and France, and the second by an American-Dutch action team — intended for operations in Romania. Both groups were successfully delivered by parachute over the territory of Bulgaria's northern neighbour — these were also the first agents transferred by air from Greece, with the aircraft crossing the entire territory of Bulgaria from the southern to the northern border. On the way back, the aircraft was reported to have encountered flak, probably engaged by the AAA batteries protecting the 'Friendship Bridge' near the city of Rousse, and then it also had a close encounter with a Bulgarian fighter in the Pleven area, but the Bulgarian pilot had reportedly failed to detect the CIA aircraft. At that time, the Karlovo-based fighter unit, 14th OIAP, was kept on the QRA duty at night. The CIA pilots are highly likely to have encountered a Yak-9P piston-engined fighter, which was scrambled for intercepting the intruder, most likely from Karlovo or Gorna Oryakhovitsa. According to recently declassified CIA documents from the daily reports to the director of the intelligence agency, the US aircraft had returned intact from this mission. Most likely it was a C-47 twin-engine transport, used at the time in regular night undercover operations in the Balkans.

The transportation of agents for reconnaissance and sabotage activities to the territory of Bulgaria took place on a monthly basis. At the same time, the first Bulgarian paramilitary unit was set up in Munich, West Germany, staffed by anti-communist emigrants ready to act to liberate the country from the communists and participate in some of the CIA-managed covert operations in Bulgaria.

In early November 1951, a CIA Special Operations Officer discussed with the Greek Air Force a plan to train two Greek pilots in Germany on the RF-51 Mustang prop-driven reconnaissance aircraft to be provided by the USAF. With these camera-equipped Mustangs donated to the Greek Air Force, Greek pilots were to participate in covert reconnaissance operations over Bulgaria and Romania, and later on eventually over the Soviet Union. It is unclear if this plan was ever initiated and implemented, but no deep intrusions of Greek aircraft in daylight had been reported at the time.

5
BULGARIAN AIR DEFENCES' DEEPENING WOES

In the early 1950s Bulgaria's fledging air defence system was divided into an air defence component for the interior of the country (Air Defence service), covering with large- and medium-calibre AAA, most if not all strategic sites in Bulgaria (urban and industrial centres), and an Army Air Defence component set for battlefield deployment. All the anti-aircraft systems were called upon to provide decisive resistance to the air intruders, flying mostly at night, and at low altitude. However, it proved ill-suited to do this rather demanding job with the required effectiveness in the early 1950s.

Veteran AAA officer Mircho Kirov recalled:

> These air intruders were coming from the northern coast of Africa or from Greece, overflying the territories of Bulgaria and Romania, and even reaching to the city of Ploesti in Romania. We fired at them during their flight over Bulgaria. In one of the intrusions, an unidentified aircraft flew towards Plovdiv and our AAA batteries opened fire. It approached from the Dimitrovgrad area where it was already engaged by the 70th ZENAP (AAA Regiment). As it approached Plovdiv, the intruder was also engaged by the batteries of the 65th ZENAP, providing the air defence of Bulgaria's second largest city. A total of 570 rounds were fired at the intruder, but without any effect.

> In another intrusion in southern Bulgaria, the intruder aircraft flew over Dimitrovgrad and Plovdiv, crossed through the entire Bulgarian territory to enter into Romania, reaching Ploești before returning on the same route. Then it flew over Plovdiv at low level, just above the base of the tank brigade. We had an AAA unit stationed there, next to the city cemetery. The aircraft dropped propaganda leaflets and the area of the AAA battery and the division's CP was obliterated with these leaflets. I called them on the phone to find out what's going on there, and the unit's commander replied, "Comrade Major, come here to pick up some leaflets".

There were almost no fighter pilots launched on QRA duty who had not been fired on at least once by their own AAA. Some of the most experienced pilots of the time, such as Major Dimitar Dimitrov – Dimitriy, at that time commander of the 1st Squadron of the 18th IAP at Dobroslavtsi, barely survived when receiving flak from the AAA batteries on positions around Sofia during a night scramble to intercept an intruder. 21st IAP pilot, Major Sava Netsov, flying a

A four-ship MiG-15 flight in engine start-up readiness, waiting for the launch signal.

A MiG-15 pilot in the cockpit in readiness for engine start-up.

Kumaritsa) near Sofia, also had a near miss with an intruder at night. In 1954, he was scrambled, together with another pilot, Peter Kolev, to visually search for a low-flying target flying towards Sofia alongside the Struma Valley. Stoyanov, flying a Yak-23, eventually managed to detect a twin-engine intruder aircraft south of Vladaya, some 10km (6nm) west of Sofia, approaching on a collision course. While manoeuvring for an attack, however, the intruder began turning and descending and eventually disappeared in the dark of the night. The other pilot from the pair, Peter Kolev was at a lower altitude and also missed the target. Escaping into the southerly direction, again low over the Struma Valley, the intruder received flak from an AAA battery near the city of Dupnitsa.

Since 1952, the CIA activity over Bulgaria was intensified thanks to the strengthened air support. The 580th Air Resupply and Communication Wing, created to support US objectives in the Cold War, was deployed specifically at Wheelus Air Force Base in Libya and one of its tasks was to support the CIA operations. Its main mission was to render air support to the agency's operations throughout the Middle East in addition to Western and Soviet-controlled Europe, and the Soviet Union.

The wing was equipped with specially modified B-29 heavy bombers able to fly low over the terrain, used for long-range night infiltration missions. The SA-16 Albatross amphibians and the C-119 Flying Boxcar transport aircraft were also included in the wing's fleet to be used for unconventional warfare missions. From Africa, the USAF aircrews performed special missions throughout the entire European theatre of operations, most likely including a proportion of the special night missions to Bulgaria and neighbouring Romania, as well as to Ukraine and the entire Black Sea basin.

In 1953 the pace of the CIA activity over Bulgaria increased notably. On the night intrusion on 22 June 1953, a total of 350,000 agitation leaflets were dropped over six selected regions of the country. Over the next month, the secret flights continued. On 22 September, on another moonlit night, a CIA aircraft flew over the major cities and regions in south-eastern Bulgaria. Packs of sewing needles and razor blades — increasingly scarce items at the time in the country — were dropped in this mission, presented as a gift from the Free World to the Bulgarians who resisted the communist regime. Propaganda leaflets were also dropped, announcing news about the Berlin Uprising against the Soviet occupation in June that year.

Yak-23 in 1951 and scrambled from Graf Ignatievo, had to apply all his flying skills first to find an intruder — which eventually proved fruitless — and then to avoid being hit by flak from the AAA batteries located in the Plovdiv area which fired at his aircraft.

Another of the emblematic names in Bulgarian aviation from the 10th IAD, Capitan Georgi Penchev, briefly mentioned in front of one of the authors:

At one time, we amassed more flying time during QRA scrambles than in regular training flights. On one occasion I had crossed paths with an aircraft coming from Greece when still in climb, just after take-off. It dropped the propaganda leaflets over the airfield and continued on its route. The leaflets were promptly collected and command authorities banned us from reading these. There was AAA protection of the airfield, but it had reportedly failed to open fire on this occasion. But the AAA batteries in Plovdiv were firing. Often, when scrambled to take-off against an intruder, we were engaged by the Plovdiv-based AAA units.

Capitan Kircho Stoyanov, an experienced pilot and Second World War veteran, serving at the time with 18th IAP at Dobroslavtsi (then

The frequent flights of enemy aircraft at night in Bulgarian airspace was the chief reason for the adoption of a new instruction on the conduct of the QRA duty, with three different levels of combat readiness. Adopted on 20 January 1954, it called for placing in Readiness No 1 and No 2 state at daytime of one fighter pair at all five main airfields housing fighter regiments, while at night the QRA duty was reduced to one or two aircraft at each airfield.

The MiG-15 was the soldier-aircraft which saw mass front-line use in Bulgaria in the 1950s, amassing hundreds of QRA launches to intercept intruders in Bulgarian airspace, but with a very low success rate.

Hunting for elusive 'Johnny' the Intruder

The situation with the air intrusions became very tense in 1953 and further worsened in 1954, but the Communist propaganda machine daily trumped how well the Bulgarian People's Army was prepared and trained to counter any provocation of world imperialism. There were huge investments in the procurement of modern armament to strengthen the country's defence capabilities but at the same time the intruder flights went deep into Bulgarian territory without encountering any serious resistance. As a rule, their routes passed over the main airfields of the fighter branch such as Dobroslavtsi, Karlovo, Graf Ignatievo and Uzundzhovo, where they dropped anti-government agitation leaflets.

In a textbook case of the lack of coordination between the flying units at Plovdiv airfield and the Air Defence service, an Il-2 attack aircraft was seriously damaged by flak near Dimitrovgrad and had to perform an emergency landing at night. This accident led to a sharp reduction in the night training activity of the 5th Attack Division in Plovdiv, equipped with the Il-2 and Il-10, and the 9th Night Light-Bomber Division in Yambol, flying the Bulgarian-made Laz-7.

Polkovnik (Ret) Georgy Razsolkov was a CO of the 3/19 IAE and he recalled how his pilots trained to counter the frequent air intruders at night:

Among pilots, these uninvited guests committing frequent intrusions at night were simply known as 'Johnny'. The radar technology had poor performance at the time due to its low technology state rendering these useless in the detection of tracking of this kind of intrusion, and vectoring fighters to intercept the intruders. On the other hand, enemy overflights were mostly conducted on moonlit nights, at low altitude, alongside the valleys of the Struma, Mesta, Maritsa and Tundzha rivers. We often gathered to discuss what and how to do in an effort to stop at last these impudent air intrusions. So, we decided to block all the approach directions by sending aircraft to loiter in pre-designated areas into all suspected approach directions.

In an effort to improve efficiency, a number of reorganisations of the country's air defence were made, while accelerating the night training of the pilots in all jet fighter regiments. In each of the three then existing jet fighter divisions — 1st, 4th and 10th — the QRA aircrews were selected among the most experienced pilots, grouped in specially designated squadrons to take on the most intense QRA periods.

Starshi Leitenant Iliya Elenski.

The psychological atmosphere in the VVS became unbearable — and it seems that whatever goals the CIA had set in its psychological warfare against the Bulgarian military, these were achieved and even overachieved. Despite the fast-track introduction of modern jet combat aircraft in mass and the constant reorganisations in a bid to improve efficiently, a single prop-driven Douglas C-47 Skytrain utility transport aircraft, crewed by experienced contract pilots, had eventually managed to keep both the Air Force and Air Defence services under serious pressure.

As a consequence, at all levels — from the Government, through the Ministry of People's Defence to every and each squadron and flight CO — strong pressure was applied in order that the air violations be stopped at last. In an effort to rise the ever-decreasing morale in the fighter aviation branch, it was announced that pilots who shot down an enemy aircraft in Bulgarian airspace would get the 'Hero of the People's Republic of Bulgaria' award — this was the highest state award in the country at the time. Furthermore, there were rumours circulating among pilots that material rewards and even cars had

Iliya Elenski as a young Leitenant seen here with his Bulgarian colleagues and a Soviet Air Force instructor during his jet conversion course in the Soviet Union in 1950 or 1951. He is the first from the right in the first row.

The scramble

The QRA duty was provided by flights and on special occasions even by entire squadrons. The best-trained pilots in each fighter regiment were compelled to literally live in the QRA aircraft. They had no permission to leave the garrison for weeks in order to keep the enhanced QRA duty, solely intended to counter 'Johnny' the intruder.

In the meantime, dozens of low-level air intrusions made it possible to identify the general pattern of the enemy operations and thus plan effective methods to counter the overflights. The 3/19 IAE, the 3rd squadron of the 19th IAP, commanded by Capitan Georgi Razsolkov, was considered to be the best trained for conducting night intercept operations at the time so it was ordered to bear the brunt in the hunt for 'Johnny' the intruder at Graf Ignatievo — from 15 March until 15 October 1954, a total of 180 days of non-stopping effort. The squadron had been assigned to the enhanced QRA duty at night at Graf Ignatievo since the beginning of March 1954 with four pilots (augmented from time to time with another two flying the Yak-11) while a MiG-15 pair was also sent from time to time for QRA duty at night at Uzundzhovo airfield situated between Khaskovo and Dimitrovgrad. The 21st IAP, home-based at this newly-constructed airfield, lacked pilots trained for night operations, especially in bad weather. Two Yak-9s also joined the QRA effort to counter the 'Johnny' in August 1954.

Todor Totev recalled the QRA duty at the forward airfield, situated only 45km (24nm) away from the border with Greece:

been foreseen for the successful 'Johnny' shooters. But the biggest motivating factor for everyone was that a successful intercept would promise to reduce at last the unbearable tension and nervousness at the QRA aprons.

General Major (Ret) Todor Trifonov, at the time a pilot from 19th IAP, recalled:

The head of the Air Force Political Affairs Department, Polkovnik Panchev, once came to visit Graf Ignatievo. He told us: "The intruder aircraft shall be taken down!" It was as if we didn't know about it. Then, in front of us, he announced that whoever takes the night intruder down, would become a recipient of 'Hero of the People's Republic of Bulgaria' award. Finally, as we parted, he shook hands with everyone with the wish to "take him down". He shook hands with all the pilots and moved on. One of the technicians said: "I'm not a pilot". But Panchev replied: "It doesn't matter – I'm not a pilot too, but I'm insisting the intruder to be taken down.

So, taking down the elusive 'Johnny' the intruder was the main task of everyone in the fighter aviation branch.

Polkovnik (Ret) Todor Totev was at that time a fighter pilot in the 3/19 IAE at Graf Ignatievo and shared his recollections:

There was a reward of 50,000 Bulgarian Leva offered in addition to the promise to get the 'Hero of the People's Republic of Bulgaria' award in case of downing the intruder. But we had never been attracted so much by these rewards. We were committed to fulfil our duty and state service as Bulgarian citizens and Air Force pilots. When dispatched for the QRA duty at Uzundzhovo airfield, even the soldiers from the guard squad there were telling us: "We consider our job to be difficult, but at least two hours we are walking around when on duty while you are sitting strapped in the cockpit all the time."

In these QRA duties we were sitting all the time in the QRA aircraft with the radio on, waiting for a green flare in the air, the signal for an immediate launch.

In Uzundzhovo, our pair — Elenski and myself — was the most [often] on the QRA duty. He was my flight commander and I was his wingman. We were partners in the air with aircraft and also on the ground with motorcycles. We flew a lot and were very well used to each other when manoeuvring in the air. He was a very good pilot, and thanks to him, so was I. A lot of people envied us for being so well coordinated in the air, because no one flew like our pair.

When we began the QRA at Uzundzhovo, *Podpolkovnik* Stoyan Velkov, the 21st IAP CO, provided us the opportunity to select soldiers from the units situated around the airfield. They were infantrymen, but very conscientious boys. They had to notify us on the presence and the direction of the flight of the intruder aircraft. At that time, all the VVS prop-driven aircraft were withdrawn into to the northern part of Bulgaria, and so mainly fighter jets remained in the southern part of the country. We instructed the soldiers, at the suggestion of the Uzundzhovo CO, as soon as they hear prop aircraft noise overhead, to launch a red flare. The direction of the flight of the enemy aircraft had to be then indicated by a green flare, launched into the same direction.

Georgi Razsolkov continued his recollection:

Let's assess the operative situation from the CO's point of view. The intruder aircraft flew at a low speed, not exceeding 300km/h while its minimum speed was 150km/h. It was an unarmed transport aircraft with a three-man crew — two pilots and a navigator or a flight engineer. It crossed the border with Greece at low altitude, at night, flying at 200m above terrain to enter deep into the Bulgarian territory. It had several typical routes. The first was Kulata – Pernik – Sofia – the sub-Balkans Valley. Another route had their entry points in Bulgarian territory at Dospat or Gotse Delchev, then flying in northerly direction to Razlog and continuing to Velingrad and Pazardzhik. Then the aircraft turned to fly at low level over the Maritsa or Stryama river valleys, reaching Karlovo, and finally turning to the right to fly over the Tundzha river valley, returning to the border with Greece.

Former 3/19 IAE pilot, Polkovnik (Ret) Todor Totev is seen in the centre of the photo, posing here the late 1970s in front of a MiG-19PM fighter-interceptor. At that time, he was working as a pilot in the Bulgarian agricultural aviation, used for domestic and international crop-dusting operations.

[Our] own forces comprised MiG-15 fighters equipped with a HF communications radio that tended often to lose the frequency tuning. The aircraft lacked radar and was equipped with an optical sight only. The armament comprised of two 23mm NR-23 cannons (160 rounds) and one 37mm NR-37 (40 rounds). So in these missions it was required first to visually detect the target and then to get into attack position. It proved, however, next to impossible to be made at night, to detect a target in moonlight, unless you are at less than 50m distance. We used at the time to place an aircraft on the runway and try to detect it visually at night, but it turned out that we had to be in a close proximity in order to be able to see it.

Even the Li-2 two-engine transport aircraft were mobilised in the action to counter the elusive night intruder. The slow-flying Li-2s, identical to the C-47 Skytrain, were used as practice targets for night intercept training of the 3/19 IAE aircrews. There were also night practice shootings at a sleeve target towed by Il-2 attack aircraft, flying at 240km/h (130kt). During these intense practices, it had been found that the only way to visually detect the target in a moonlit night was when the fighter was flying below it. Given the low altitude of the intruder — below 200m (660ft), the Bulgarian jets were forced to fly at ultra-low level for bottom to top target detection.

Georgi Razsolkov adds to the picture:

Our navigation support from the ground was almost non-existent. The P-3A early warning radar was able to provide information on targets flying at low-level at 10 to 15km range only. When an intruder was detected in our airspace, we got scramble orders. Each of us was tasked to occupy a certain area, loitering there, sitting and waiting for the intruder to appear. In this operation, we blocked the river basins of Tundzha and Maritsa. At Maritsa, this happened in Pazardzhik, and the loitering area had its centre at Stryama. We also blocked the approach direction to the north of Harmanli and

to the south over the city of Maritsa (today Lyubimets). We also had a loitering area situated next to Karlovo. We took off when the VNOS service notified us for the presence of intruders. The visual observation posts represented a phone on the border with a soldier. When hearing airplane noise, the soldier had to turn the phone and report about the noise. When this happened, we launched and occupied all the pre-designated loitering areas. The whole squadron launched, leaving only two aircraft in reserve.

Johnny's End

It was especially tense during the national holidays, in clear weather. Then almost certainly 'Johnny' the night intruder flew over Bulgaria to drop agitation leaflets. It was no exception on the night of 8 September 1954. At that time, the 1/19 and 2/19 IAEs of the 19th IAP were deployed to Dobroslavtsi and under the leadership of the 10th IAD CO, Polkovnik Simeon Simeonov, their pilots were preparing to demonstrate the MiG-15 in the forthcoming military parade in Sofia on 9 September. The 3/19 IAE, as always, was placed in its full complement on the QRA duty at Graf Ignatievo, while Starshi Leitenants Iliya Elenski and Todor Totev were dispatched to Uzundzhovo during 5 September, to act as an ambush element. As expected, 'Johnny' made a daring intrusion in the full moon night. At 22:00 of 8 September, the CP at Graf Ignatievo issued an alert order to the QRA forces as 'Johnny' the intruder was once again detected flying over the country. The QRA fighters at Graf Ignatievo launched in the air immediately, while the Uzundzhovo pair took off at 22:13.

Georgi Razsolkov recalled this memorable and a rather stressful mission:

I still remember how I took off from Graf Ignatievo in the easterly direction to get to Area No 1, watching all the villages well-lightened. I went on to loiter in an area to the east of the city of Pazardzhik, but I failed to see the intruder. It managed to pass next to me unnoticed, coming from Dospat, then turning to fly over the Maritsa river valley and so passed through Totev's loitering area. He also failed to detect the intruder and it was only near Lyubimets

Starshi Leitenant Ilyia Elenski had reportedly managed to detect and engage an intruder at low level in the Svilengrad area, next to the border with Turkey and Greece along the Maritsa river valley, on the night of 8 September 1954. Art work by Stoyan Popov.

Bulgarian technicians seen while working to pre-flight a MiG-15, a specific version produced under license in Czechoslovakia and delivered to the 11th IAP in Gabrovnitsa in November 1953.

were flying only 100 to 150m above terrain), we were not able to hear each other. After a while, the CP ordered: "Return home! Elenski exited from the attack pass."

Decades later, the prominent Bulgarian aviation researcher, journalist and writer, Tsvetan Tsakov made an interview with Iliya Elenski for his book *The 21st Century – Who's Who in Bulgarian Aviation*. This is how the main character describes his encounter with 'Johnny' the intruder on this memorable night:

While Totev flew to Parvomay, I entered into my designated search area. In the area of the Sazliyka river, I detected the intruder and reported on the radio: "Target found, entering into attack." And I unleashed the first series of shots. For the first time there was an air battle between a jet fighter and a propeller aircraft, at night, facing a very experienced enemy. He had the advantage at low altitude and used it to a full extent, all the time manoeuvring. In an effort to reduce my speed and go down close to the opponent's speed, I extended the undercarriage, activated the air brakes and placed the flaps in landing position. So I got behind the target in a little, just enough to take a good position for attack and succeeded in it. In the second series of shots — this time long and accurate — the target began turning to the

when Elenski flew in close proximity to it.

Todor Totev also recalls the sequence of events that followed the scramble of the QRA pair at Uzundzhovo:

That night I was the first to launch from Uzundzhovo. Elenski went to the area between Simeonovgrad and Lyubimets, while I was loitering in the region of Stara Zagora. There were no external aids for aircraft detection so I had to rely on my eyeballs. I saw a purple light and then a reddish one, and I almost got stuck in a thresher machine near Stara Zagora. At the last moment, I pulled out, and the CP informed me: "Elenski is working on the target." These were the only instructions. I said: "Direct me to go help him." We were on the same radio channel, but because he was flying very low (we

right while pouring smoke.

Todor Totev continued to recall, adding what his colleague shared with him post-mission:

Elenski had faced the enemy aircraft on a collision course. That night we flew at 80 to 150m above the terrain. He saw the target and initiated a tight U-turn with a very high bank angle in an effort to get behind it. The intruder was a twin-engine propeller aircraft, likely an A-26 Invader, while Elenski flew a MiG-15bis. In order to be able to stay behind the target, he first deployed the flaps but this had not been enough to hold its position. So he had to extend the undercarriage and then put the target into the sight and opened fire. It turned out that he only fired with one of the NR-23s. He succeeded to set on fire the port engine. During the attack he thought the he was shooting with the big gun (the 37mm NR-37) but in fact all the time he had been pressing on the air brake actuation button.

Georgi Razsolkov also recalls a part of these events as he also was a direct participant in the counter-air operation that night:

When the intruder was flying towards him, Elenski saw a flare in the air. One of the soldiers on the ground launched the flare. He then

1954 proved to be a rather busy year for the Bulgarian QRA fighters. The three fighter regiments of the 10th IAD alone reported as many as 130 launches of their QRA aircraft against air intruders crossing the border with Greece, mainly at night.

went on to say that he just saw the intruder to the left, flying next to him. He noticed initially the intruder's shadow, and then initiated a manoeuvre to get behind the target. He said that it was a propeller aircraft, flying at 300km/h top speed, which is the minimum speed for us. And Elenski overtook the target, so he had to lower in a prompt manner the flaps and the undercarriage in an effort to kill the excessive speed. He did everything possible not to get in front of the target and eventually managed to unleash a series of 23mm shells.

At that time, Elenski got above an alerted AAA unit in the Lyubimets area. We had no coordination with them. And the AAA opened fire on his aircraft, which had a light on. When Elenski lowered the undercarriage, a white light came on below to indicate that the landing gear had locked. Then we did not dare turn off these lights when on the QRA duty and so the AAA began delivering flak at our MiG-15. The flak was all around the Elenski's aircraft and so he was forced to exit from the attack.

Todor Totev continued with his recollection:

The intruder was set ablaze while heading towards the border with Turkey, overflying the village of Capitan Andreevo at an altitude of 30 to 50m, and then it fell into Turkish territory, some 3 to 5km from the border line. On the next day, Podpolkovnik Velkov called on the phone the commander of the AAA unit located in Lyubimets, asking him: "Which aircraft were you shooting at?" They answered him: "The one who was with a light on." So, they were shooting at the Bulgarian MiG-15bis that night. Elenski banked his aircraft sharply to the right and saw the AAA shells exploding to the left and to the right. And then, realising that he had failed to use the NR-37 cannon, he again tried to track down the enemy. If a projectile fired from the big gun had hit the intruder's aircraft, it would have fallen and remained in our territory.

Georgi Razsolkov added:

At that time, our coordination with the AAA units was almost non-existent. The coordination, in general, was made by areas of responsibility, and we were banned to enter into the areas of responsibility of the AAA units. But it this case, we were not informed about the existence of such areas reserved for AAA engagements – the command authorities could have told us at least where the AAA positions were in order to avoid what happened

with Elenski. And we were only given the signal "I'm a friendly aircraft" — for the particular day what colour of flares to launch, and in which sequence to blink with the aircraft position lights. But once the AAA started shooting at you, that's when you had to mark yourself as a friendly aircraft.

A Hero, but not exactly…

Georgi Razsolkov remembered the post-mission messy situation at Graf Ignatievo:

At that time, the 10th IAD CO, Polkovnik Simeon Simeonov, was at a parade in Sofia to celebrate on 9 September 1954 the tenth anniversary of the Socialist Revolution in Bulgarian. On 10 September, he called both myself and Elenski — he as a participant in the air combat and myself as the 3/19 IAE CO. We were standing from morning until noon straight in front of him and the question was why Elenski had failed to fire with the big gun, the NR-37. Imagine in what emotional state Elenski was then. This was an air combat, in the air at night, and he had no experience in this kind of combat.

Polkovnik Simeonov asked: "Why you had not attempted to ram the intruder"? But at two hundred meters' altitude the ramming could led to the death of the crews of both the attacker and the attacked aircraft.

The case was viewed by the high levels at the Ministry of People's Defence more as a failure, while Starshi Leitenant Elenski was considered as being a pilot who lost his chance.

Georgi Razsolkov continued his story:

So, it was not clear at the time whether the intruder had been downed or not. Then a week passed and Polkovnik Simeonov told us that the attacked enemy aircraft was set on fire but then it had fallen three kilometres into Turkish territory. There was no physical evidence, however, for the shoot down. Then there were rumours about emergence of some necrologies with death announcements in Greece. We were promised that if we took down an intruder, we would be rewarded with a car and will also get the 'Hero of the People's Republic of Bulgaria' award. But in the event, all that remained a fiction.

Todor Totev added to the story:

The Bulgarian fighter pilots used the Li-2 transports as practice targets for low-level day and night intercepts. The slow-speed twin-motor type was fully identical by silhouette and speed performance with the CIA-operated Douglas C-47 Skytrain, operating regularly over Bulgarian territory between 1951 and 1954.

Then a Starshi Leitenant from Capitan Andreevo, who then came to Uzundzhovo, told us that he was on the border that night and saw the intruder ablaze and also listened to moans from the crew of the downed aircraft. Whoever said that didn't happen, you know: it's not true. This officer confirmed the intruder had been downed.

Great promises were made for Elenski that he will become a hero. And so the commanders said whoever takes down the first intruder aircraft will get the 'Hero of the Republic of Bulgaria award'. But nothing happened! They didn't award him. They didn't even give him a medal for this achievement.

All this did not prevent, however, General Polkovnik Simeon Simeonov from describing Elenski's air combat on 8 September 1954 in a raised propaganda style in his memoir *Hardened Wings*, published in 1974. It was mentioned there, among other things:

After two days, an obituary was printed in a foreign newspaper, which reported the deaths of three pilots who had perished in the course of their official duty.

This propaganda-inspired story was then reproduced in the *Official History of the Air Force of the People's Republic of Bulgaria*, published in 1988. The book *Graf Ignatievo's People and Airfield*, published in 2003, also formalised the case. However, many open questions still remain; who, where and how was flying in the Bulgarian airspace at night, and what kind of aircraft (and what crew) was engaged by Elenski on 8 September 1954?

Today, many doubt that Elenski ever managed to take 'Johnny' the intruder down that night. The authors have heard a version, raised by veteran pilots, saying that in fact Elenski's success was considerably exaggerated by the ubiquitous Political Affairs officers at the time, in an attempt to boost morale and fighting spirit, which were in a serious decline due to the never ending failures to intercept the frequent overnight intruders. But to date, almost all the pilots, witnesses of that time, are sure of one thing: Elenski's attack was eventually successful. The best proof, they say, is the fact that for several months the violations of the Bulgarian airspace ceased. The low-altitude intruder never again bothered the duty units of the Air Force and Air Defence services. So, this is claimed to be the best evidence that 'Johnny' the intruder was shot that night.

What Bulgarian pilots did not know then or after is that in the

autumn of 1954 the program period for which the Operation BGCONVOY funding was secured by the CIA, had expired. Gradually, the need for this type of operation — waging psychological warfare and agent infiltration — diminished as the operations were considered as being ineffective and the expenses were subjected to a review. Declassified documents under Operation BGCONVOY tend to indicate that no further funding was provided for the CIA's destabilising missions in the Balkans at the time, and as a consequence BGCONVOY had gradually degenerated into specific special projects, which continue to be still hidden in top-secret archives.

To date, it is a fact that Bulgarian fighter pilot Iliya Elenski had an encounter and unleashed shells on an air intruder at night. Subsequent claims, however, of shooting down 'Johnny' the intruder still remain unconfirmed and unproven. For many years, despite the controversial attitude in socialist Bulgaria, Starshi Leitenant Elenski remained as one of the hero pilots of the Cold War.

In total, between 1950 and 1955, the CIA's BGCONVOY operation resulted in dropping over 5 million agitation leaflets — with political, satirical and religious content — on Bulgarian territory. In addition to the aircraft delivery, which was acknowledged to be a risky method, agitation leaflets were also dropped by free-floating balloons.

At the time, there were plans for sending infiltration teams made up of recently trained agents (held in Greece and Germany) in the late spring or summer of 1954. Most likely it was one of these infiltration flights encountered by Elenski during the QRA scramble on 8 September.

In mid-1954, the intensity of the operations in Bulgarian airspace was seriously reduced and the CIA eventually terminated Operation BGCONVOY on 30 June 1955, while the original targets set were to be pursued by follow-on secret projects.

More Airspace Violations

A new wave of violations in Bulgarian airspace was reported in March 1955, this time committed by high-performance jets, apparently aimed at probing the strengthened air defence capabilities in this buffer zone of the southern flank of the Eastern Bloc, otherwise far away from the Soviet Union's borders. This zone was gradually saturated at that time with modern air defence equipment, such as jet fighters, large-calibre AAA with radar guidance and long-range surveillance radars. The first intruder, a fast jet aircraft of an unidentified type, was detected on 28 March, crossing the border with Yugoslavia at 03:25 in the northwest part of the country, near the village of Martinovo, Mikhailovgrad District, and then it flew in the north-easterly direction until crossing the border with Romania near the city of Lom on the Danube river. It continued the flight over the cities of Craiova and Bucharest in Romania before entering Bulgarian territory again near Rositsa village in Tolbukhin district. The unidentified aircraft continued its flight over Balchik airfield, then passed south of Bourgas, not far away from Ravnets airfield, took a westerly heading and flew south of Yambol and north of Dimitrovgrad before turning in the north-westerly direction to pass to the north of Graf Ignatievo airfield and then to the north of Sofia, close to Dobroslavtsi airfield. The intruder exited Bulgarian airspace over the village of Kalotina, re-entering into Yugoslavia at 04:58. Two MiG-15 pairs were scrambled to intercept the night intruder but the pilots of both of these had failed to visually detect the target. The analysis of the speed/altitude/range profile of the intruder in this daring flight in Bulgarian and Romanian airspace tended to indicate that it was an English Electric Canberra twin jet — it flew at an altitude between 500 and 800m (1,640 and 2,624ft) above

The 10th IAD Command Post at Graf Ignatievo, responsible for the command and control of the QRA fighters when scrambled to intercept air intruders.

terrain, maintaining a speed of between 600 and 800km/h (324 and 432kt). In this single sortie it had managed to overfly more than the half of the six military installations considered to be of strategic importance for Bulgarian defence and over the most important industrial areas. Its route also passed nearby or directly over no fewer than six military airfields. In addition to this, the intruder overflew a good many Romanian defence installations and industrial areas in this very successful reconnaissance mission.

The Bulgarian AAA units in position near Dimitrovgrad, protecting the newly-built heavy industrial area there, engaged the low-flying target at 04:31. The AAA was only able to deliver barrage fire as the SON-9 AAA guidance radar failed to track the target, and the searchlights also proved ill-suited to detect and track the intruder. The 100mm and 57mm guns expended a total of 40 rounds without any success.

On 5 May 1955 another daring violation was committed at night, this time by an unidentified twin-engine prop-driven aircraft, which crossed the border with Greece near Krumovgrad at 23:13 and flew in a north-easterly direction over Khaskovo, Nova Zagora and Gorna Oryakhovitsa. Then it turned into the westerly direction, flew near

Mezdra, Svoge, Godech and Kalotina, crossing the border with Yugoslavia at 00:14. Two MiG-15 pairs were scrambled but both of these failed to get to the intruder.

The next violation of Bulgarian airspace, this time in broad daylight, was reported on 3 June, when the radars detected an air target crossing the border with Turkey near the village of Rezovo on the Black Sea coast, maintaining the northerly heading. Its route stretched over the coastal cities of Akhtopol, Michurin, east of Pomorie, Obzor and Goren Bliznak village, flying at between 1,000 and 1,200m (3,280 and 3,936ft) with a speed of 220km/h (119kt). Then the aircraft flew over the big coastal city of Stalin (as Varna was known for a brief period) where it was engaged by AAA which expended 24 rounds and forced it to land at 12:37 at the civilian airport at Aksakovo near Stalin. The civilian aircraft with a Turkish registration had a two-man crew, who were detained as agitation leaflets in Turkish were reported to have been found onboard. The Bulgarian air defence scrambled no fewer than four pairs of fighters — from Bezmer, Ravnets, Uzundjovo and Graf Ignatievo — in an effort to intercept the intruder. None of these fighters had, however, been able to visually detect the Turkish aircraft due to its relatively low altitude, combined with bad weather

A well-packed MiG-15 flightline — most likely at Ravnets — the home base of the 15th IAP, responsible for the air defence of the southern sector of the country's Black Sea coast and the adjacent territories alongside the border with Turkey.

conditions prevailing in the eastern part of Bulgaria.

The next violation of Bulgarian airspace was reported on the next day, 4 June, at night. At 23:00 Moscow time, an unidentified twin-engine aircraft crossed the border with Yugoslavia near Miloslavtsi village, maintaining the westerly heading. It flew over Dimitrovo (as Pernik was renamed for a brief period in the early 1950s), Vladaya, Sofia, Vrazhdebna, Chelopechene and Slivnitsa, leaving Bulgarian airspace at 23:54, entering into Yugoslavia

---

VVS Strength in 1955

By late 1955, the VVS had a fleet of no fewer than 155 MiG-15s and MiG-15bis plus 32 MiG-15UTIs, enough for equipping eight fighter regiments with a total of 24 squadrons; the fighter branch also had six MiG-17PF radar-equipped all-weather fighter interceptors and about 15 Yak-11 prop trainers. In addition, the VVS continued the operation of about 30 Yak-23s and Yak-17Us in one front-line fighter regiment with three squadrons plus one advanced training squadron with 16 jet aircraft.

The remaining Yak-23s and Yak-17Us were handed over to the attack branch, where the type equipped one regiment, the 20th ShAP, between 1957 and 1958.

---

with an easterly heading. This time the unidentified twin-engine jet aircraft flew at 6,000m (19,680ft), maintaining an average speed of 600km/h (324kt). It was detected and tracked by five early warning radar sites in the western part of Bulgaria, and was also tracked by one radar-guided searchlight and two searchlight stations. The VVS QRA assets scrambled to intercept the intruder included four fighters: one MiG-15 was launched from the 19th IAP at Graf Ignatievo; another aircraft from the 21st IAP at Uzundzhovo; and the third came from the 11th IAP at Gabrovnitsa; while a Yak-23 from the 22nd IAP had also joined the action from Bezmer. All of these fighters were ordered to loiter in designated areas next to their own airfields. That same night, the 43rd IAP at Dobroslavtsi carried out flight training operations. The CCP urgently re-tasked one of the pilots in the air, Capitan Peter Kolev, to intercept the intruder. At 23:39 he reported visual detection of the intruder's lights and pressed into attack. At 2,000m (6,560ft) distance, however, the intruder switched off its lights and began turning. The Bulgarian pilot lost visual contact with the target and was not able to regain it.

The intruder was also detected and tracked by the radars serving the AAA batteries on position around the newly-built heavy industrial area in Dimitrovo, some 30km (16nm) west of Sofia, but was not engaged as the Yak-23 had the precedence in mounting the attack against the air target flying towards Sofia.

The combat report, submitted by the Minister of People's Defence, General Polkovnik Peter Panchevski, to the deputy head of the Council of Ministers, Armeiski General Ivan Mikhailov, noted that the radar troops had operated in a fully satisfactory way during the intrusion. The intruder was detected just in time by the fighter sent to intercept it, but the pilot proved inexperienced in intercept operations at night and thus had failed to attack the target.

The next airspace violation, committed on 27 July, saw the most tragic episode of the Bulgarian air defence history, which is also among the bloodiest incidents in Cold War history, with the main player in it being the 18th IAP from Dobroslavtsi.

6

FLIGHT LY402 DOWN

The QRA pair of the 18th IAP at Dobroslavtsi airfield, placed on duty at 07:00 on 27 July 1955, comprised of the experienced pilot, Capitan Boris 'Chapo' Petrov and his wingman, young Lieutenant Kosta Sankiisky, who was on his first ever QRA duty that day. The experienced Petrov and the young Sankiisky had no idea that this Wednesday was going to be the most fateful day in their lives, as they would cause the loss of many innocent civilian lives.

This was, in fact, the first occasion when the Bulgarian air defence system operated as expected in principle against an intruder aircraft. The result was there — an intruder aircraft entered Bulgarian airspace and was shot down in a prompt manner. The aggressive purges of experienced and combat-hardened VVS personnel in the late 1940s and the accelerated training of a large number of new pilots, technicians and other aviation specialists, supplemented by the large-scale re-equipment and introduction of jet fighters, had resulted in no one capable of responding adequately to the frequent violations of Bulgarian airspace for four full years since 1950. That is why the pilots standing on QRA were put under tremendous pressure to deal with US, Greek and Yugoslavian aircraft carrying out covert reconnaissance and destabilising operations in Bulgarian airspace. The end result of all this immense pressure and nervousness was seen on 27 July 1955, with 58 innocent civilian passengers and the crew of an Israeli airliner losing their lives.

Khristo Ivanov was a pilot and deputy CO of the 18th IAP at the time of the incident and he recalled about his involvement in it:

Our regiment was placed on the QRA duty that day. I was Deputy CO at the time, responsible for the flight training. That day I was also the acting CO of the 18th IAP, as the CO, Major Vasil Draganov, was on a temporary deployment with one of the squadrons to Tolbukhin airfield, for practicing bad weather flying. In the early morning we commenced regular training flights at Dobroslavtsi — on the landing circuit and in the dedicated training areas around the airfield — in accordance with the flight operations schedule for the day. The QRA pair began its day shift, starting-up the engines for a check, then checking the operability of the radios and finally reporting that they are ready for commencing the duty shift. I was also acting as the chief air traffic controller that day and authorised the take-offs of several Yak-23s of the 43rd IAP, involved in scheduled training sorties. Not long after I received a call from the 4th IAD's CP post that a violation of the state border had been detected. The CP ordered the pilots to get into the Readiness No 1 state, when they are sitting strapped in the cockpit, ready for engine start-up. Then a red flare in the air signalled to the pilots that they shall start-up the engines and launch as soon as possible, with their vectoring to the target provided by the 4th IAD's CP. I issued orders to all pilots in the air to land as soon as possible and then went to the CP. The combat control officers informed me that there is no contact with the intruder aircraft. Our pilots had not reported that they got the target. In addition, our radars were very primitive at the time and not able to see the target at this range.

Starshi Leitenant Elenko Nedyalkov was a flight leader in one of the three squadrons of the 18th IAP at the time of the incident and a direct witness of the 27 July 1955 events. He recalled:

I was on the QRA duty in the night shift and my pair was replaced by Petrov and Sankiisky in the morning of that day. I was a flight leader at the time and Sankiisky was a young pilot serving with my flight. I instructed him how to act if necessary. This was his first QRA duty, the first combat launch and the first combat sortie. They launched and we stayed on the QRA apron to see what will happen with their mission. We then switched on the radio of one of the spare aircraft but the radio contact with them was with interruptions because they were flying at low altitude. In the next moment, I heard Petrov reporting and I understood that they had just gunned down a four-engine aircraft which refused to obey their warning signals. The fighters landed and we gathered to meet them in front of the QRA building. The MiG-15s were taxiing in with their noses sooted from the powder gases of the expended rounds. Sankiisky was very modest when he climbed down from this aircraft. I asked him to say what happened in the air and he replied: "Commander, we brought it down."

In one of the most tragic Cold War incidents, Bulgarian MiG-15s were involved in the shooting down of an El Al Airlines Lockheed L-149 Constellation passenger aircraft on 27 July 1955. This is one of the fighters, serialled 'Red 67', involved in the shoot down, with technician, then Starshi Leitenant, Iliya Penchev seen to the right who confirmed the identity of the aircraft used in the mission.

Starshi Leitenant Georgy Vukov, an armament technician in the QRA team on 27 July 1955 recalled in front of one of the authors:

I was on QRA duty that day. The fighters were launched and returned back to the base with their ammunition expended. Only Petrov had 20 rounds remaining from a total of 40 for the big gun (the 37mm NR-37), so he fired 20 rounds in the mission. All the ammunition for the two NR-23s was expended. In turn, Sankiisky expended the all the ammunition of the three guns.

Starshi Leitenant Georgy Todorov, an aircraft technician from the QRA team that day, shared his recollections of the day:

Sankiisky taxied in to the QRA apron at a very fast speed after the landing, with an open canopy as it was a hot day. He thought that he

Leitenant Kosta Sankiisky.

Capitan Boris Petrov.

Starshi Leitenant Iliya Penchev, an aircraft technician from the QRA team on 27 July 1955, is seen here performing checks in the cockpit of one of the MiG-15s serialled 'Red 67', used in that tragic mission to down the El Al Constellation.

or destabilising mission. It was, in fact, an airliner, belonging to Israeli airline El Al. In no time the Bulgarian pilots turned from heroes to victims of yet another hot episode of the ravaging Cold War. The innocent victims of their attack, mounted in yet unclear circumstances, numbered 58.

What happened near Petrich

The El Al Lockheed L-149 Constellation airliner was shot down by the QRA pair from the 18th IAP on 27 July, at 07:35 local time. The fighters opened fire, scoring numerous hits on the airliner, causing it to explode mid-air at low altitude, with its remains failing on Kozhukh hill near the city of Petrich. The

[had] gunned down a military aircraft and still was not aware about the truth. It was clear that all the ammunition had been expended as during the taxiing I noticed that his [aircraft] is with an altered balance. Both MiG-15s taxied back to the QRA apron and we all gathered there. Petrov, according to me, had some suspicions when climbing down from his aircraft that the gunned down aircraft was a civilian one. He told me: "Georgy, we had killed innocent people". We were the first ones with whom he had shared his recollections from that eventful sortie, sitting on a concrete block on the apron, excited and sweaty.

About 200 or even 300 people collected at the QRA apron. Kosta Sankiisky was also with us, with a worn jacket; he was very emotional, and much more exited after his first QRA sortie but not yet realising to a full extent what had happened. But it was all clear for Capitan Petrov.

And soon afterwards it became clear that the still burning wreckage found on the ground next to Rupite village in the south-western corner of Bulgaria was not of a CIA-operated airplane sent on a spying

Border Troops posts and patrols on the border with Greece were the first witnesses of the shoot down. The first information about the incident was received in the Border Troops Directorate in Sofia — it was a wire from the CO of the 3rd Border Troops Detachment in Petrich with the following text:

A two-engine aircraft of unidentified nationality was spotted flying over Markovi Kladentsi area, mark 1553, in a direction towards the city of Petrich. Then it turned in the eastern direction towards General Todorov railway station. Already during the aircraft appearance an explosion was heard and it crashed in the vicinity of General Todorov railway station. Three or four parachutists jumped from this aircraft. The aircraft has not been fired [at] by our line outposts. The crash area has been blocked. I started the pursuit for arresting of the parachutists.

The border troops in Petrich area undertook urgent measures to seal the border and avoid the escape of the alleged parachutists. They were the forward defence of the state and their patrols had experience

A view of the crash site from the eastern slope of Kozhukh hill, on the bank of the Struma.

Another view at the crash scene on the eastern slope of Kozhukh hill, next to the water pump station at Struma riverside, used for the irrigation of the nearby fields.

in reporting the intrusions of foreign aircraft, crossing the Bulgarian borders. But nobody was prepared for the situation at the crash site near Petrich.

Sofia asked for a detailed report upon the return of the CO of the 3rd Border Troops Detachment from the crash site. The truth was communicated to Sofia shortly afterwards, with the text of the new wire saying: 'It is an Israeli aircraft and 15 people in it have burned out. There are no parachutists detected. The aircraft has been placed under guard…'

The next wire, sent shortly afterwards, informed Sofia as follows:

An airliner route sheet has been found, for the Israel-Vienna route. About 20 burned out people have been found, including five or six children, four parachutes, one of which burned out. A few passports have also been found, including one British, one radio, one bag with letters of different origin and belongings for the fest in Warsaw. Capitan Nikolov from the Border Troops Directorate was in the Interior Ministry station in the city of Sandansky and informed us from there that the aircraft has been under fire by jet aircraft which then turned back into Sofia direction.

Post-Shootdown Shock

The initial euphoria had been followed by a sudden sobering. While Dobroslavtsi was still celebrating the first shot down air intruder of the Bulgarian borders, the Council of Ministers and the Ministry of People's Defence were facing the dilemma of what to do after receiving the first information supplied by the Border Troops.

The group of generals which gathered and worked in the Air Defence Central Command Post (CCP) during the QRA scramble went on to report to the Prime Minister, Valko Chervenkov.

There was no information yet about the downed aircraft type and the grave consequences from this act. These became known a bit later that same day, thanks to the information provided by the Border Troops.

There was little hard information in the afternoon hours on 27 July, but even this little bit was shocking. A passenger aircraft had been downed and civilians had been killed. The special government commission to investigate the events which led to the Israeli aircraft being shot down included: Mincho Neichev — Minister of Foreign Affairs, Armeyski General Peter Panchevsky — Minister of People's Defence, Yordan Chobanov — Chief Prosecutor of the Republic, Georgi Tsankov — Minister of Interior, Dr Peter Kolarov — Minister of People's Health.

Meanwhile, the Ministry of People's Defence (MoPD) established its own commission to deal with an internal investigation, which was also to assess the Air Defence and Air Force operations on 27 July. Headed by General Major Avgust Kabakchiev, a former VVS Chief Engineer, it was tasked to review all details of the actions of the Air Defence and Air Force units that morning, in order to provide an answer why the air defence units and the QRA fighters had reportedly failed to identify the intruder and why they went on to shoot it down.

Polkovnik (Retired) Vidyo Penev, at the time Major and an Inspector Pilot in the VVS HQ's Combat Training Department, was among the members of the MoPD commission and he recalled 'We went to the crash site the same day together with the Soviet military advisor, General Major Redkin and Podpolkovnik Tsvetkov, the Deputy Chief Military Prosecutor. The witnesses said that the aircraft disintegrated in the air.'

In fact, the effort to seal off the crash site proved fruitless. The border troops tried to block the access to both sides of Kozhukh Planina hill, but many locals were able to get to the crash site and started grabbing all valuable belongings from the passenger's luggage scattered around. There were cases of apparent looting at the crash site, committed by local villagers. Penev recalled:

When our group arrived at the crash site near Rupite village in the afternoon of 27 July, a Militiaman was trying, but without any success, to take a suitcase of a passenger of the downed Israeli aircraft, grabbed by the mayor of the nearly village, who was also the Communist Party Secretary in that village. This 'privileged' looter considered the suitcase he had found at the crash site to be his property and the Militiaman reportedly failed to convince him otherwise. Unfortunately, this case was not isolated one that day.

On the next day, the Border Troops summarised all the information gathered at the crash site in a new wire to Sofia. It described the sequence of the events in the air and on the ground:

100,000-43-7.35-27.7.55. An explosion, accompanied by a big bang lasting for several seconds, was heard from Ograzhden Planina direction and Markovi Kladentsi area. A four-engine aircraft had emerged from the direction of the explosion, flying at about 1,000-1,500m altitude, heading towards the city of Petrich. The aircraft initiated descent and when over the area between Martinovo and Shtarbanovo villages, it began turning to the northern direction — most likely to go down in the meadows near Karnalovo village. While still turning, another explosion was heard and the aircraft broke up into several parts, which eyewitnesses in the city of Petrich thought as being parachutists. The aircraft continued flying and losing altitude, perhaps for a few more hundred meters and then fell in the Kozhukh area. From its appearance to the moment of the crash, the aircraft was tracked. There were no other aircraft seen together with it, and belongings were also not spotted falling from the aircraft.

After the aircraft crash I have ordered strengthened duty at No 1 to 14 border outposts. I also tasked patrols to carry out surveillance of the field. Immediately with 2 people [it most probably refers to 20, and this is a technical mistake — author's note] — soldiers and officers — I arrived at the crash site, blocked the area and cleared it from local population which worked there, and then began extinguishing the fire and recovering the corpses from the fire and Struma river, collecting them in a single place, together with all belongings and papers, and placed guards, as the aircraft fell on both slopes of the Kozhukh. The rear part of the aircraft, one of the wings, two engines and most of the belongings and documents fell on the western slope of the Kozhukh, and the aircraft body and the passengers — on the eastern slope, next to the riverside of Struma. Upon arrival of the government commission, they issued an order to place all the belongings, documents, etc. in bags, and then these bags were sealed. The corpses, after medical manipulations, were lined up in coffins. All this was transported to Sofia at 23:45 on 27th this month by motor vehicles. The medical processing of the terrain was carried out immediately after despatching the corpses. Today in the morning I'm carrying out an additional search of the area to look for hidden belongings, upon finding such belongings, these will be additionally dispatched.

The information has been sent by telegram No 18. Chief of the 3rd Border Detachment, Podpolkovnik Krastev.

Shocking News spreading around the World

The first news about the incident was already spreading during the Bulgarian fighter attack runs against the ill-fated El Al L-149 Constellation 4X-AKC. The radio stations in Athens and Thessaloniki received the following SOS on a ground-to-air frequency: "SOS DE 4X-AKC" from the Israeli airliner, which had been under fire at that moment. This message was relayed immediately by Athens Air Traffic Control (ATC) to Lod ATC in Israel. Athens Flight Information Centre declared an emergency and search and rescue services were alerted. In fact, even before taking search and rescue actions, Athens ATC was informed that the aircraft had been spotted falling in flames near the Greek-Bulgarian border, next to the Bulgarian village of Shtarbanovo, and passed this information to Lod ATC.

And the news spread around the world in a few hours that communist Bulgaria had shot down an innocent passenger aircraft with 58 people onboard. Israel, Great Britain and other interested countries immediately began asking the Bulgarian Ministry of Foreign Affairs (MoFA) for details. Israel sent an official diplomatic note to Sofia, asking for details about the incident, but the Bulgarian authorities remained silent for a while. The MoFA told the Israeli Embassy that there was a government commission for the investigation and it is expected to publish its official position. It was not until 28 July, at 11:00, that the Bulgarian Telegraph Agency (BTA) issued a brief communiqué about the incident near Petrich that happened on 27 July. The Communist Party official newspaper, *Rabotnichesko Delo* (*Worker's Affairs*) published a short news story, based on the BTA information. It said that an Israeli aircraft, identified later on as such, had entered Bulgarian territory without prior notice at 07:35 in the city of Tran area. According to the information, the aircraft flew over the Bulgarian cities of Stanke Dimitrov, Blagoevgrad and Petrich. The air defence was not able to identify the aircraft and after repeated warnings shot it down. The aircraft fell on the ground and broke up in an area north of Petrich. All people in the aircraft perished.

The Victim

The L-149 Constellation was a 63-seat passenger airliner, with four examples taken by El Al in 1950 and 1951. Aircraft 4X-AKC (c/n 43-10316), originally manufactured in 1945 as a C-69 military transport and later on converted to the civilian L-149 standard, was on a scheduled passenger flight (Flight Number 402/26) from London to Tel Aviv via Paris and Vienna. It was, in fact, the spare aircraft, dispatched the previous day to serve the route from Tel Aviv to London due to a technical problem with the originally intended aircraft of the same type. 4X-AKC arrived at London Heathrow from Lod Airport at about 18:00 and departed back at 20:15 GMT. It was to fly to Lod near Tel Aviv with refuelling stops at Paris and Vienna. The crew included two pilots, a flight engineer, radio operator and three flight attendants.

The captain was Stanley Reginald Hinks, born in 1920, holder of Israeli Airline Transport Pilot License No 85. His total flying experience was 9,422 hours, including 3,199 hours on the Constellation of which 115 hours were flown during the last three months. He had flown six flights on this route as captain. Hinks was a former Royal Air Force pilot and a Second World War veteran.

The First Officer on this flight

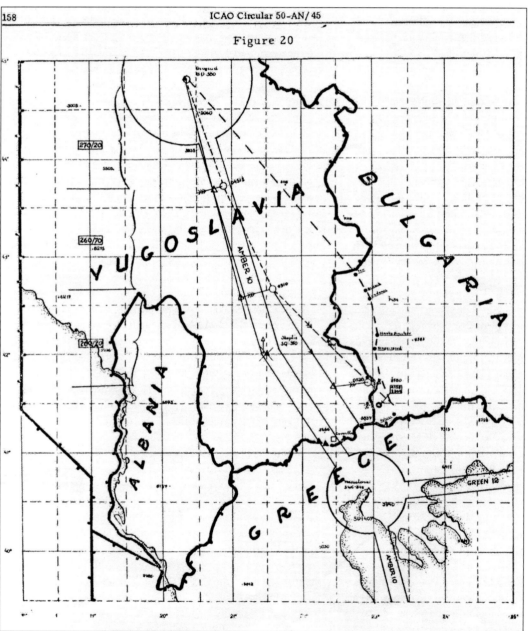

158   ICAO Circular 50-AN/45

Figure 20

Flight LY402's route in Yugoslavia and Bulgaria. The dashed line shows the actual route of the aircraft, with an entry point on Bulgarian territory at Tran, as reported by the country's Air Defence service. This represents a serious deviation from Airway Amber 10, and no reasonable explanation has been given why this had occurred in the early morning hours on 27 July 1955. The route of the aircraft, according to the Bulgarian version, is well inside Bulgaria, while the Israeli report version maintains that Flight LY402 entered Bulgarian airspace not far away from the shoot down site.

was Pinchas Ben Porat, born in 1914, and holder of Israeli Airline Transport Pilot License No 77. His total flying experience was 4,617 hours, including 1,324 hours on the Constellation of which 187 hours were flown during the last three months. During this flight he was being checked for company captaincy on the Constellation. Ben Porat was an Israeli volunteer in the first Israeli-Arab War and one of the first pilots in the newly-established Israeli Air Force. The South African Cyril Sydney Chalmers, born in 1921, was the Flight Engineer, and Israeli Raphael Goldman, also born in 1921, was the Wireless Operator.

The aircraft landed in Paris at 21:22 and then in Vienna at 01:39 GMT. It left Vienna at 02:53 hours. According to the flight plan filled at Vienna, its estimated time of arrival over Belgrade was 1 hour and 43 minutes after take-off, at 04:36.

At 04:33 GMT Flight LY402 reported overflying Belgrade and continued on its route passing over the city of Kralevo, the next reporting point (without navigation aid) and then it was set to overfly Skopje, another reporting point. At Skopje, the Airway Amber 10 international route changes its direction (magnetic heading) from 161° to 142°. The wind forecast for this part of the route, to be used in the flight plan, was 270°/20kt at an altitude of 5,488m (18,000ft). The aircraft was cleared to fly at 5,335m (17,500ft). The wind as forecast required a correction of 4° to the right, giving a heading of 165°. This was the heading provided in the flight plan.

Skopje Airport at the time was equipped with a Non-Directional Beacon (NDB) rated at 1,200W aerial output power, working normally at the time of the flight. The distance between Belgrade and Skopje is 269km (177nm) and no other radio aid was available; the time for the leg was 44 minutes and the planned arrival was at 05:17, but in fact Flight LY402 reported overflight of Skopje at 05:10.

The Constellation had to enter Greek territory at the city of Gevgelia. At that moment the crew had the option to use the Thessaloniki NDB, rated at 350W. The distance from the reporting point at the Yugoslavian-Greek border at Gevgelia to Thessaloniki is 107nm. This reporting point had no navigational facility. Later on the US airline Pan American Airways shared information that the Thessaloniki NDB was not reliable, and reliable reception was possible only in a small area over the beacon.

The Constellation was fitted with two Bendix radio compasses and two Bendix-made VOR units. The navigation system was complemented by a magnetic compass and one Flux-gate compass, swing and adjusted on 18 March 1955. Both pilot positions were fitted with full instrument panels, including three directional gyros. There were also two marker receivers, a radar altimeter and Loran installed at the navigator's unused position. Later on, the Israeli investigators found out that the VOR could work reliably at 70 to 80nm, while the NDB signals could not be received in a reliable manner in case of thunderstorms and static electricity in the air.

The range of the NDB, owing to thunderstorms, could not have

Bulgarian Official Position

On 3 August, when the internal MoPD commission, appointed on 31 July completed its work, the Government Commission for Investigation issued its report and on its base the Bulgarian Telegraph Agency (BTA) released a detailed communiqué on the official Bulgarian position. It contradicted the Israeli position that the aircraft entered Bulgarian airspace in proximity to the Greek-Yugoslavian border, insisting that Flight LY402 flew more than 200km (110nm) in Bulgarian airspace. The Israeli commission claimed that the aircraft (based on testimonies of eyewitnesses, Yugoslavian citizens on the border line) had violated the Bulgarian border in proximity to the Greek border, after overflying Skopje, and Flight 402 was in Bulgarian territory for 40km (22nm) only. Had this been true, however, the case tends to indicate that the Bulgarian air defence had responded almost instantaneously, sending the MiG-15s to patrol well in advance into the area of the attack in the proximity of Petrich, but this was far from a real-world situation.

been considered reliable for steady course indication. This also applied, and even to a greater extent, to the Skopje beacon which was surrounded by static.

The Thessaloniki NDB was considered as being of low reliability by definition due to its low output and the possibility of coastal refraction of the nearby sea surface. The report issued by the Israeli Commission of Enquiry into the Flight LY402 accident also noted that the effectiveness of the NDBs may have been reduced by sunrise conditions.

Crossing the Bulgarian Border

The Bulgarian MoPD Commission, headed by General Major Avgust Kabakchiev, included four members — Polkovnnik Atanas Semerdzhiev from the Bulgarian Armed Forces General Staff and Polkovnik Alexander Dechev — VVS Chief of Staff, complemented by Polkovnik Vasil Velichkov and Major Vidyu Penev from the VVS HQ. The commission was appointed by an aural order by the Minister of People's Defence, Armeyski General Peter Panchevsky and was tasked to carry out a detailed review of all the documents and proofs in the CCP and the 4th IAD CP, created and used during the airspace violation on 27 July. It also got the tapes from the gun cameras of both MiG-15s and the documents governing the QRA organisation in the 18th IAP.

The pilots and all officers and soldiers on duty that day were interrogated, together with the eyewitnesses who observed the crash at Kozhukh hill. The authors have analysed the content of all these documents, which had stayed classified for five decades, in an effort to reconstruct the sequence of the events that unfolded in the early morning hours of 27 July 1955. The report of the commission uses Bulgarian local time (GMT+2), but in some of the documents Moscow time (GMT+3) had also been used. In particular, the Moscow time was used by the CCP, to meet a Soviet requirement for a standardised time of all air defence systems in the Eastern Bloc countries.

By 1955, the 1st Polk VNOS, responsible for the visual and radar air warning in the western part of Bulgaria, alongside the borders with Yugoslavia (on the western border) and Greece (on the southern border), had its CP co-located with the CP of the 4th IAD at Dobroslavtsi airfield. The regiment controlled six radar sites served by five radar companies — at Medkovets (also used to support the intercept operations of the 11th IAP at Gabrovnitsa), Dobri Dol (near Kyustendil), Igralishte (near Sandanski), Bozhurishte (near Sofia) and Lomski Fort (near Sofia, also used to support the intercept operations of the 18th and the 43rd IAPs). The equipment at the sites comprised a total of nine radars — three P-3As, two P-8s and four P-20s.

The network of visual observation posts was organised in five component companies of the 1st Polk VNOS, deploying a total of 60 posts. The companies were headquartered at Vidin (12 posts), Mikhailovgrad (12 posts), Kyustendil (13 posts), Blagoevgrad (15 posts) and Gotse Delchev (8 posts).

According to the MoPD Commission report, Flight LY402, straying off course into Bulgarian territory from Yugoslavia was initially detected by the visual observation posts (VOPs) and the radar surveillance posts. Two radars detected and tracked the aircraft even before its border crossing, at their maximum range. RTS-712 and RTS-701 were the radar sites placed on the alert duty that day. According to the initial data, when crossing the border, the altitude of the target was between 2,000 and 2,500m (6,560 and 8,200ft), and then it climbed to 4,500m (14,760ft) upon reaching Blagoevgrad, flying in the southerly direction. The visual observation posts were ordered to go into full combat readiness. During its flight in Bulgarian airspace, Flight LY402 was tracked by a total of five Bulgarian radars and it also crossed the area of responsibility of no fewer than 14 individual VOPs which issued a total of 17 reports. Some of the VOPs also provided information on the actions of the Bulgarian fighters which gunned down the Constellation.

The VOPs, however, failed to provide a reliable identification of the target type. The NP-VNOS 141 post, for example, identified the target at 08:12 (Moscow time) as a four-engine aircraft while the NP-VNOS 140 reported it as a C-47 cargo aircraft. Four other VOPs identified it as the Li-2 (the Soviet-built licensed C-47 version). The other VOPs reported engine noise from an unidentified aircraft, while another registered the flight of the Bulgarian QRA fighters scrambled from Dobroslavtsi.

As a result, at 08:13 (Moscow time) the Main Command Post (MCP) of the VNOS Service reported the air intrusion detected by the network of visual observation posts deployed alongside the border with Yugoslavia to the Air Defence CCP.

Major Khristo Ivanov, 18th IAP Deputy CO, provided the following information during his interrogation by the MoPD commission:

On 26.07.1955 I was appointed as the responsible duty officer at the CP of Military Unit 25900 (4th IAD) and assumed the duty on 26.07.55, at 8:00. On 27.06.1955, I was the air traffic controller and at 6:20 I went on to the flight line for a pre-flight briefing.

Due to the lack of a substitute at the CP, I ordered the duty combat control officer, Leitenant Kulev, they [were] to look for me at the Start Command Post (airfield tower) in case of a scramble or if somebody is asking for me.

The flight operations launched at 7:00 and at 7:07 the duty combat control officer informed me that there is data from the radar on an aircraft flying to the west of Tran, over Yugoslavian territory. I instructed him to order the QRA fighter pair to go into a higher alert state, as the aircraft was flying with a 140° heading, in proximity to the Bulgarian border. After the launch of the QRA pair I was not able to return immediately to the CP because there were aircraft in the airfield landing circuit and in the training areas around. That is why I ordered the Chief of Staff, Capitan Petkanov, to go to the CP and manage the intercept of the intruder until my arrival there.

Capitan Khristo Petkanov provided the following information to the commission during his interrogation:

On 27.07.1955 the military unit carried out flight operations and I was at the flight line to organise the operations. The pre-flight briefing was held from 6:20 to 6:40. The flights opened at 7:00. Then the CP of Military Unit 25900 launched a green flare, signalling a higher alert state (of combat readiness) for the QRA fighters. Not long after, a red flare was launched (ordering their launch) and I got into the duty *Gazka* (motor vehicle) at the flight line to get

to the CP. I knew that the acting 18th IAP CO, Major Ivanov, is the responsible duty officer at the CP. Upon my arrival at the CP, the QRA fighters had already launched and their vectoring was undertaken by using radar data.

The CCP in Sofia was also activated upon detection of the airspace intrusion in Tran area. Major Angel Karchev was the responsible duty officer there and he provided the following testimony:

At 8:10 (Moscow time) we got information supplied by the VNOS Service on the Bulgarian-Yugoslavian border, in Tran area. In the same minute I issued a command to the 4th IAD CP, placing them into a higher alert state, and then began clarifying the situation unfolding in the air.

After receiving the report for the state border violation at 8:13, the 4th IAD CP reported for the launch of the QRA pair. I approved the decision and tasked them to intercept the intruder in Breznik area, if possible, taking into consideration the bad weather prevailing in the area.

The state border violation was confirmed by NP-VNOS 139, 140 and others, informing that it is a four-engine aircraft of an unidentified type.

At 8:21 I ordered the CP in Dobroslavtsi to intercept the target (which was reliably tracked by the radar at Dobroslavtsi) and find out its nationality. In case it is wearing the Yugoslavian insignia, it shall not be fired [at], and instead shall be forced to land at Dobroslavtsi or assisted to return to own territory.

At 8:15 I declared the combat alert state.

After issuing the above instructions, at 8:16 I reported on the phone to Polkovnik Zikulov about the intrusion and the instructions issued by me. He approved my decision. At 8:17 I reported to General Georgiev, who also approved my decision. In the following minutes I rang generals Zakhariev and Bachvarov and the Minister of People's Defence, General Panchevsky, but I was not able to find them on the phone line.

From today's point of view, the most interesting is the information from the interrogation of the pilots, Capitan Petrov and Leitenant Sankiisky, undertaken the same day by the head of the 18th IAP Special Service (Military Counterintelligence).

The information provided by Capitan Boris Petrov says:

On 27 July 1955, at 7:12 we got the scramble signal from the CP. After taking off and retracting the undercarriage, the CP ordered to reload the guns and take a compass course (CC) towards the city of Breznik, at 5,000m altitude.

About four minutes later I reported that I'm over Site 15 (Breznik), at 1,500m, as due to the bad weather condition it proved impossible to climb out to 5,000m. We got an order that the intruder is over the city of Stanke Dimitrov and we shall climb to 4,000m, flying to a point five to ten kilometres to the south of Stanke Dimitrov, on a 180° heading.

I tried to jettison the external tanks, but these failed to separate immediately. There were a few more attempts made, and eventually the port one separated first, followed by the starboard tank.

At this moment, the 4th IAD CP lost radio contact with the QRA pair. The CCP, situated in Sofia's neighbourhood of Lozenets, however, had connection with the VOPs and the radar sites in the western part of the country. The main cause for the communication loss was related to the poor performance of the HF radios installed on the first MiG-

15 versions, provided with only four pre-set frequency channels and their maximum range was 60 to 80km (32 to 43nm). As a result, the QRA pilots Petrov and Sankiisky were left without control from the ground and had to deal alone with the air intruder to be intercepted soon in the southwestern corner of the country.

Capitan Khristo Petkanov said in his testimony in front of the MoD's investigation commission:

Leitenant Petkov was the officer on the radio, issuing vectoring commands to the pilots. We maintained the communication with them until reaching [the] Blagoevgrad area and then lost contact. We kept calling the aircraft on the radio but [got] no reply from them. In order to regain the contact, I ordered take-off of the leader of the second QRA pair, Capitan Peev, to be used as an airborne relay station — i.e. relaying the commands issued by the CP in Dobroslavtsi to the QRA pair.

Captain Peev was ordered to loiter in a zone north of the airfield. We maintained a good contact with Capitan Peev, but he was not able to establish contact with the QRA pair, which was flying south of Blagoevgrad. At that time, the next responsible duty officer, Major Atanasov was in the CP, and shortly afterwards Major Ivanov arrived as well.

According to our calculations of the flight time, the fighters were about to violate the state border so we issued a command [that] they [were] to return to the base. It turned [out] that the QRA pilots, Capitan Petrov and Leitenant Sankiisky, had listened [to] the command issued by the relay aircraft (Capitan Peev) and the CP, but we were not able to listen [to] them. We lacked radar data on the position of our aircraft south of Blagoevgrad.

Major Khristo Ivanov confirmed in his testimony that the situation with controlling the QRA fighters during the intercept proved to be difficult due to the communication loss:

I was at the CP at 7:30, when Capitan Petrov's QRA pair lost radio contact and we had to order the launch of Capitan Peev (also from the QRA flight), to relay the commands issued by the CP to the QRA pair. He was dispatched to loiter north of the airfield, but due to the low clouds (cloud base was up to 2,000m) he was not able to climb out to the ordered level of 4,000m.

It proved impossible to regain the radio contact with the QRA pair until their return to Blagoevgrad area. When, according to our calculations, they were to reach the border line, I ordered the officer carrying out their guidance, to order a U-turn to the pilots.

At that moment the picture at the CCP was augmented by data provided by radars able to cover the intercept area in south-western Bulgaria. Major Karchev said in his testimony:

At 8:31 (Moscow time), the 4th IAD CP reported that due to the loss of radio communication with the fighters, it is going to launch an aircraft to relay the issued commands. This way, the 4th IAD CP issued orders by radio, and the CCP was not interfering in the control of the QRA pair.

From 8:28 to 8:40, Polkovnik Zikulov, the Chief of Staff, arrived at the CCP and assumed the command duties. At 8:40, generals Georgiev and Zakhariev arrived at the CCP. We got information that the intruder is nearing the southern borders, that there is a lack of information about the position of [our] own fighters and by report from the 10th IAD CP — Graf Ignatievo and the report of the redirected QRA pair in the Sandansky area, that the intruder

is in the Greek territory. I reported to General Georgiev that the intruder had exited our airspace without being intercepted by the QRA pair.

At 8:36 I ordered the QRA pair to return home. The order was relayed by the 4th IAD CP at 8:37.

At 8:55 I ordered the fighters to land as soon as possible due to the approaching storm and the rapidly deteriorating weather.

Air attack

After losing the ground control, QRA pilots Petrov and Sankiisky had to deal alone and unafraid with the intercept and stopping the intruder. Their testimony however, had raised some questions and the information given by them is deemed insufficient to reconstruct the complete picture of the encounter with the Israeli airliner and its subsequent shooting down.

Capitan Petrov's testimony says:

I closed to the intruder aircraft from the port side and saw it was a four-engine transport. I was not able to identify its nationality. I got in front of it and issued a signal to obey to my commands and turn to the left. The aircraft, however, instead of turning to the left began turning to the right. I did a second approach, to the starboard and fired warning shots. Then I mounted two more attacks with warning shots, to the starboard, in order [for] it to follow me with a left-hand turn, or in total one warning attack without firing and three more attacks with warning shots to the starboard.

The intruder aircraft continued not to obey the commands and instead turned to a 220° heading. In this situation, I had to open fire, in order to destroy it. After a few real attacks by me and my wingman, the aircraft lowered its undercarriage, but retained the 220° heading.

In this situation, I mounted another attack with exit to the starboard, followed by a left-hand turn. The attacked aircraft changed its heading to the south — 180°, and retracted the undercarriage, flying perpendicular to the Belasitsa mountain ridge, in an effort to cross it.

At that moment its port engine caught fire, but the aircraft retained its heading to the south. We followed with new attacks, in order to avoid crossing the Belasitsa mountain ridge. The aircraft began turning to the left and did a U-turn, flying into the northern direction, then began descending more steeply and at a 200 to 300m altitude exploded and hit the ground in Petrich area.

Then we gathered together in pair and returned to the base.

Sankiisky's testimony was much shorter and also leaves many unanswered questions:

On 27 July 1955, we, the QRA pair pilots, were scrambled in a combat alert. At 7:13, just after take-off, at 100m altitude, we got an order to reload the armament.

The CP ordered us to fly to Site 15, then climbing to 4,000m and fly to Site 61. We detected the intruder aircraft at 4,500m altitude. We began issuing warning signals to it in the Simitly area. The aircraft maintained a heading of 220° to 230° and did not respond to our warnings, continuing to the Malashevska Planina mountain with lowered undercarriage. Assuming that it was applying a tactical manoeuvre, we opened real fire against the intruder in order to destroy it, because it was approaching the border with Yugoslavia. Under fire it turned to 180° and began increasing its speed, flying to Belasitsa mountain and retracting the undercarriage.

The intruder aircraft was set ablaze and destroyed by our fire, at

Fragments of the downed aircraft with multiple holes, most likely caused by shell fragments, shown in the report of the Israeli Commission of Enquiry.

in Sofia, Nansen-Nir Baruch (Charge d'Affairs at Sofia) joined them from Sofia. The group was also supplemented by the British Military Attaché in Sofia, Stevenson.

Border troops securing the crash site had been given explicit directives both to provide assistance to the Israeli commission and also prevent the presence of VVS representatives who had been working on the scene for three days. Subsequently, important parts and instruments from the aircraft were found to be missing — apparently dismantled. The VVS technical specialists appeared to be interested in certain parts and instruments of the aircraft — it is unclear whether this had been done for any intelligence purpose, to look for compromising equipment on board, or simply to try concealing some of the parts badly damaged by the projectiles fired by the MiG-15s.

400m altitude it exploded and increased the dive angle. It collided with the ground and broke up in pieces. Upon order by the leader I closed to him and safely returned back home.

Major Khristo Ivanov mentioned the following in the closing part of his testimony:

When the radio contact was restored, I ordered them to maintain the 360° heading to the airfield, looking for signals from the direction finder. I asked on the radio if they have encountered the intruder aircraft and they reported that it had been intercepted and destroyed in the city of Petrich area.

Israeli Investigation Board at Work on Bulgarian Soil

On 28 July, the acting head of the Israeli Legation in Sofia (Charge d'Affairs), Nansen-Nir Baruch, obtained permission to visit the crash site. He was attended by Mack Gark, Secretary of the British Embassy and Paul Gardner, Attaché in the British Embassy. Locals confirmed during conversations with them, albeit in a restrained manner, that the aircraft was under fire and had exploded in mid-air.

Amid the horrific sight, the Israeli representative noted the lack of victims' bodies and their luggage. No one had explained why the state commission had decided as early as the evening of 27 July to remove the corpses together with the collected luggage and belongings from the crash site. This reinforced Israeli suspicions that the Bulgarian authorities had something to hide at the crash site.

The Bulgarian authorities imposed a set of strict restrictions on the Israeli Commission of Enquiry which had eventually been allowed to conduct a crash site survey. It was restricted to three members only, and the duration of the crash site survey was set from sunrise to sunset, in a single day. The commission was forbidden to conduct surveys and interrogations of witnesses on Bulgarian territory. After three days of waiting, visas were eventually issued for the commission members who crossed the Bulgarian-Greek frontier at the Kulata border checkpoint, not far away from Petrich. Representatives of the Israeli Legation

VVS officers were expected at the crash site as of 28 July, but they had not appeared. It remained unclear exactly when they had eventually managed to recover parts and instruments from the crash site. The presence of VVS officers there was confirmed by a wire, sent by the Border Troops Commander-in-Chief to the 3rd Border Troops Detachment CO in the early morning of 30 July. It proved that between 28 and 30 July in the morning, VVS officers worked at the crash site to examine parts of the aircraft and collect some of the parts of interest.

The conduct of the Israeli commission itself was described in a top-secret memo to the Commander-in-Chief of the Border Troops Directorate of the Ministry of Interior, General Major Chakarov. In it, Podpolkovnik Stefan Krastev, CO of the 3rd Border Troops Detachment in Petrich, reported:

On 30 July, 1955, at 12:45 minutes Bulgarian time, on the railway bridge near the village of Kulata, Petrich area, based on Telegram No 4379, dated 29 July 1955, of the Chief of Staff of the Border Troops, I met the Israeli representatives. I met them on the bridge in the presence of Comrade Molerov from the Ministry of Foreign Affairs and I told the Israeli representatives that out of the five people they have indicated, only three could cross the border, to which they agreed. Mordechai Laufer, Zivi Tohar and Joel Palgi went to our territory. When crossing the border, they handed over their personal passports. Israeli representatives coming from Greece were accommodated into pre-prepared motor vehicles and transported to the crash scene. There, they took pictures of where the aircraft crashed, searching for bullet holes and taking pictures when they found such holes. Particularly impressive was the activity of the British Military Attaché, who came from Sofia. He crawled the most at the place, paying attention to small pieces of paper. During the inspection, Israeli officials kept making notes on pocketbooks and periodically looking at an air navigation map. After surveying the area on the east side of the Kozhukh hill, the representatives

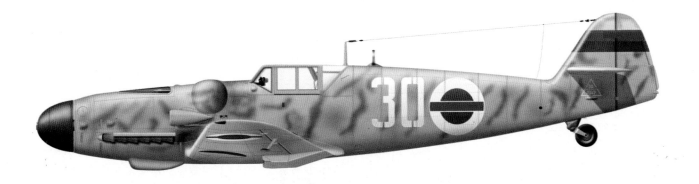

The Messerschmitt Bf 109G-2/6 remained in active use with the Bulgarian air arm until the second half of 1950, and during the last years of service it assumed the role of a training fighter. A significant proportion of the survivors at the time were aircraft inherited as war trophies in May 1945, taken brand-new from Zeltweg airfield in Austria. As many as 22 newly built aircraft were taken and ferried back to Karlovo while two more were lost during the ferry flight between Austria and Bulgaria. By 1946, the active Bf 109G fleet in Bulgarian service accounted for 62 aircraft, including 59 maintained in airworthy condition and by 1950 the numerical strength reduced to below 40 examples in the G-6/10/12/14 versions.

A total of 120 Ilyushin Il-2m3 attack aircraft were delivered to the Bulgarian air arm in 1945. The last of these remained in active use until 1953. In the 1950s, the depleted Il-2m3 fleet was used to equip one attack fighter regiment, the 20rd ShAP, based at Krumovo airfield, a component unit of the 5th ShAD, an attack aircraft division headquartered in Plovdiv. In addition, it was used by one artillery fire corrections squadron based at Karlovo – Marino Pole between 1954 and 1958. By 1952, the Il-2m3 fleet numbered 41 combat aircraft in addition to eight trainers with dual controls.

The Ilyushin Il-10 attack aircraft was taken into service with the Bulgarian Air Force in 1951. Seventy-four combat aircraft and six trainers with dual controls were used to equip the headquarters flight and two attack regiments of the 5th ShAD, an attack division based at Plovdiv airfield. Its 17th ShAP, a component regiment, was based at Plovdiv, the 23rd ShAP at Krumovo and the 17th ShAP at Gorna Oryakhovitsa. In 1953, the VVS took delivery of 30 more Il-10s, this time made in Czechoslovakia, which replaced the last Il-2m3s serving with the three squadrons of the 20th ShAP at Krumovo. The last Il-10s remained in active service with the Bulgarian air arm until 1958.

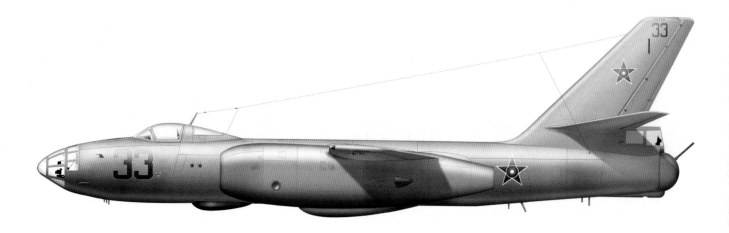

The Ilyushin Il-28 twin-jet bomber was inducted into service with the Bulgarian Air Force in 1954. Three aircraft were taken on strength in the autumn of 1954 — including two bombers and one trainer with dual controls — assigned to a squadron with the 28th BAP, a bomber regiment stationed at Balchik, moving in 1955 to nearby Tolbukhin. There the jet bomber aircraft were transferred to the inventory of 26th RAP, a reconnaissance regiment, where the type continued to serve in both bomber and reconnaissance roles together with a fleet of 17 Tu-2Ts, ten Fw 58s, three Laz-7Ms and one Fi 156.

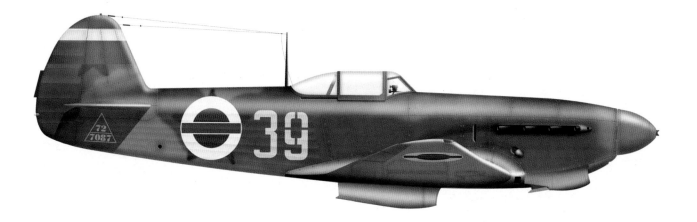

A number of Yakovlev Yak-9Ds were included in the batch of 120 Yak-9 fighters taken on strength by the Bulgarian air arm in mid-1945. This is a long-range derivative of the well-known Yak-9 family, equipped with additional fuel tanks. The type remained in front-line service with the VVS until 1954, when the last survivors, serving with the 14th OIAP at Karlovo – Marino Pole, specialised in night operations, were retired. This aircraft wears the so-called OF-insignia, introduced by the Bulgarian air arm in 1945.

The Yakovlev Yak-9M prop fighter saw intense service with the VVS in both the front-line and training role. In the former, it was augmented by the more modern Yak-9P, delivered second-hand in 1950, mainly used as night-fighters to counter the sharply increased violations of Bulgarian airspace from Greece and Turkey. The Bulgarian air arm reported no fewer than seven fatal accidents with the Yak-9M/D/P while two more pilots managed to bail out safely with parachutes during the type's nine years of service. In addition, at least ten more aircraft were damaged beyond repair in hard landings. This aircraft wears the Soviet-style national insignia, adopted in late 1949.

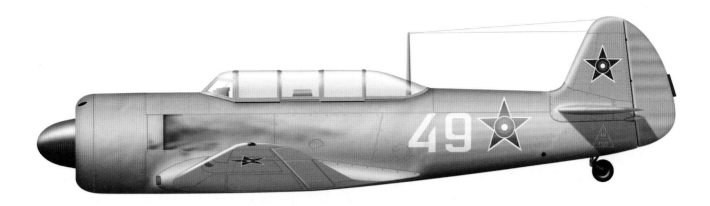

The Yakovlev Yak-11 entered service with the Bulgarian air arm in 1950. A total of 45 aircraft were delivered, initially set to be used for the advanced and night training of the pilots in the newly-established jet fighter regiments, and later on the type was handed over to the People's Air Force School in Dolna Mitropolya, where it remained in use until 1965.

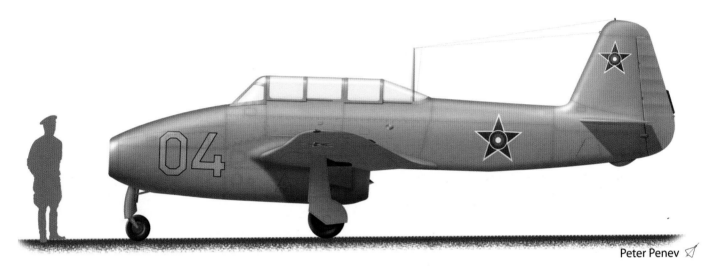

Peter Penev

The Yakovlev Yak-17UTI two-seat jet trainer was a follow-on development of the first Soviet jet fighter, the Yak-15. It lacked armament and featured a tricycle undercarriage, introduced in order to level the nose and provide better visibility for the student pilot in the front cockpit. The Bulgarian air arm took on strength 16 Yak-17UTIs, all of these being second-hand examples, with the first batch of five delivered in crated form in May 1951. The last aircraft were taken in 1955 and remained in active use until 1958. Despite its primitive design and the intense use for jet conversion and continuation training, the Yak-17UTI proved reliable enough in Bulgarian service, with only one aircraft lost, due to pilot error.

Yakovlev's designers used the fuselage of the war-proven Yak-3 piston-engine fighter as a base for designing their first jet-powered model, the Yak-15, which was further developed into the Yak-17, while the Yak-23 was the last representative of the family line, retaining the keel airframe layout, but with a much more powerful engine for a sharply increased performance. It, in fact, developed to perfection Yakovlev's 'trademark' concept of a lightweight, fast, reasonably-armed and highly-agile fighter, but there were no further reserves for future performance enhancements. In the early 1950s, the Yak-23 was considered to be an obsolete yet simple fighter in terms of systems and demonstrated pretty good reliability in Bulgarian service, able to be flown effectively and safely by relatively young and inexperienced pilots.

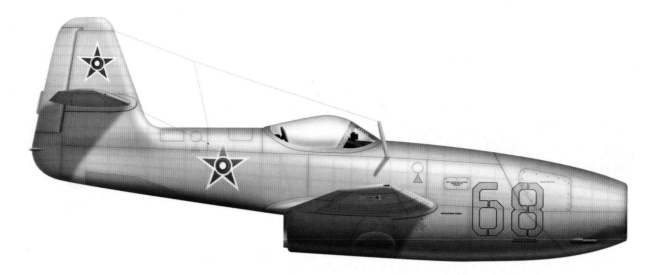

At the height of its service in Bulgaria, 120 Yak-23s, together with 16 Yak-17UTIs, were used to equip as many as six fighter regiments with about 15 squadrons, each flying eight single-seaters. The attrition was relatively light and the last aircraft continued service in the fighter role with the 43rd IAP at Dobroslavtsi (as the aircraft shown here) until 1958. The short-legged, lightweight fighter for front-line use also equipped one attack regiment, the 20th ShAP at Krumovo airfield near Plovdiv, but its service there proved short-lived, lasting for only two years between 1956 and 1958.

Peter Penev

The Bulgarian-made Laz-7 was used as a light night bomber and trainer. A total of 163, including the prototypes, were produced at the DFS Lovech (renamed as the Zavod-14) factory, with the first production-standard exampled rolled out in 1949. The type entered regular VVS service in 1950 with the People's Air Force School in Dolna Mitropolya, where the Laz-7 was used in the initial and basic training role until 1954. The type was mainly used to equip the two light night bomber divisions with a total of six regiments. In addition, it was used for liaison and training in the attack and bomber regiments.

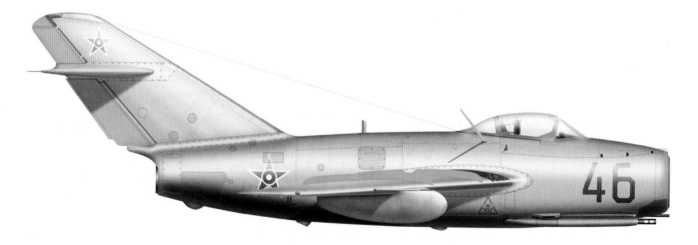

The Mikoyan and Gurevich MiG-15 jet fighter featured swept wings and vastly improved performance compared to its predecessor Yak-23, and was rushed in significant numbers to Bulgaria in 1952-54, initially to equip the three fighter regiments of the 10th IAD at Graf Ignatievo, and then two of the regiments of the 4th IAD at Dobroslavtsi, followed by the three regiments of the 1st IAD at Tolbukhin in 1955. The MiG-15 bore the brunt of countering the increased number of intrusions of unidentified aircraft into Bulgarian airspace coming from Turkey and Greece.

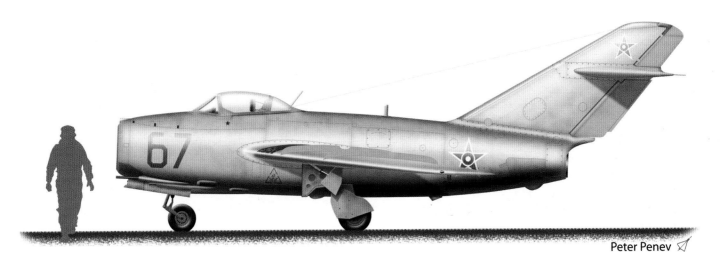

Peter Penev

According to former QRA team technician, Illya Velev, this MiG-15 serialled 'Red 67' from the fleet of the 18th IAP at Dobroslavtsi, was involved in the Flight LY402 shoot down. The MiG-15 pilots from the QRA pair at the 18th IAP had mistakenly identified an El Al Lockhhed L-149 Constellation as a four-engined military transport or bomber and opened fire, according to the pilot testimony, after it ignored their initial warning signals and warning shots. The ill-fated airliner was eventually shot down near the border with Greece, with all fifty-eight people onboard killed in the crash, making it one of the worst incidents of the Cold War era.

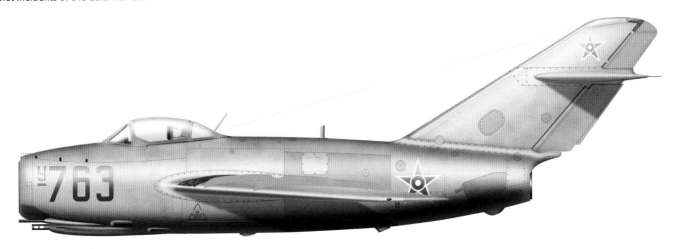

The MiG-15bis is the ultimate representative of the MiG-15 model family, with better performance and equipment standard. The VVS took delivery of 67 such jets, the first of which arrived at Graf Ignatievo in crated form in August 1953, while the last batch followed two years later. Some of the VVS fighter squadrons in the mid-1950s operated in mixed fleets of 'plain' and improved MiG-15s. In the early 1960s, the MiG-15bis fleet was handed over to the fighter-bomber regiments and it was also operated for a while by one of the training squadrons of the 2nd UBAP at Kamenets.

The MiG-17F had the distinction to become the most successful and widely used first-generation jet fighter in Bulgarian service, with the last examples continuing their faithful service in the fighter role until 1983 with the 21st IAP at Uzundzhovo and the 18th IAP at Dobroslavtsi. This is a Soviet-made MiG-17F from the first batch of 12 aircraft delivered in February 1957 to equip one squadron at the 11th IAP at Gabrovnitsa. On 20 January 1962, Leitenant Milush Solakov escaped from Bulgaria with this aircraft, flying from Gabrovnitsa to Acquaviva delle Fonti, near the large city of Bari in the southern part of Italy. The aircraft sustained serious damage in the emergency landing and following return to Bulgaria it was declared a write off.

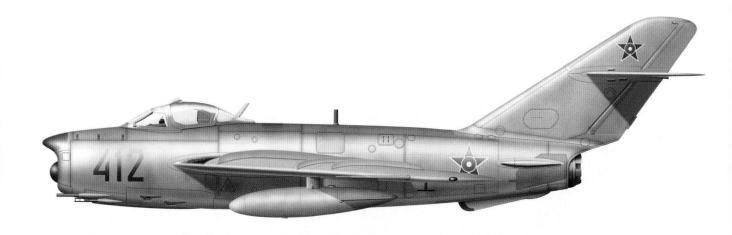

The 12 MiG-17PFs originally delivered in 1955 saw a long service in Bulgaria, having been retired only in 1983. The MiG-17PF is an all-weather interceptor, equipped with the RP-5 Izumrud-5 radar with a maximum detection range against a four-engine bomber of 9.5km (5.1nm), while small twin-engine bombers, such as the Il-28, could be detected from 7.5km (4nm). The radar, however, proved ill-suited for the interception of targets flying below 3,000m (9,900 feet) due to ground clutter, and the minimum altitude of the fighter during intercepts was limited to 2,500m (8,200 feet).

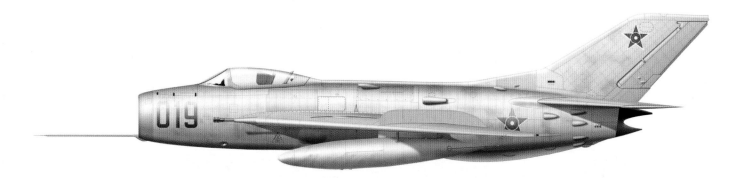

As many as 60 MiG-19S supersonic fighters were taken on strength by the Bulgarian air arm in 1957. The type remained in service until 1977, flying with two principal regiments, the 19th IAP at Graf Ignatievo and the 21st IAP at Uzundzhovo, fielding a total of five squadrons. Later on, a handful of these were also provided to the 1/11 IAE at Gabrovnitsa, together with a dozen MiG-19Ps. This particular version suffered from an unusually high accident rate in Bulgarian service, amounting to about 45 losses per 100,000 flight hours or one loss per 2,200 flight hours.

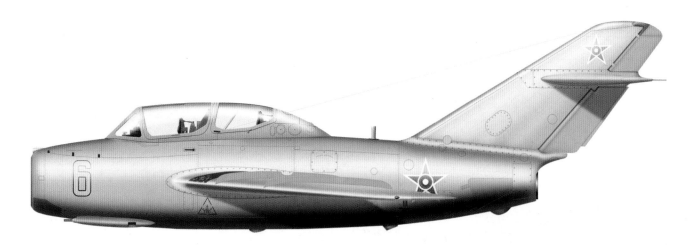

The MiG-15UTI two-seat trainers were the most intensely operated aircraft in every Bulgarian fighter regiment in the 1950s and 1960s, used for the continuation training and proficiency checks of all pilots flying the MiG-15, MiG-17 and MiG-19. The two-seat MiG-15UTI 'Midget', used the basic airframe and powerplant of the single-seater, and had its second cockpit (occupied by the instructor) inserted in the place of the fuel tanks, thus reducing the internal fuel tankage. This aircraft wears a rare four-digit serial which tends to indicate that it was among the first delivered aircraft, taken on strength in 1951 or 1952. The VVS took delivery of no fewer than 61 two-seaters between 1951 and 1960, representing a mixture of Soviet- and Czechoslovak-built examples.

As many as 310 Yak-23s were rolled out at the GAZ-31 aircraft plant in Tbilisi in the Soviet Socialist Republic of Georgia, and after a short service stint with the Soviet air arm most of the aircraft were transferred to Soviet satellite countries in Eastern Europe such as Bulgaria, Poland, Czechoslovakia and Romania. The Yak-23 proved to be a faithful type in Bulgarian service, reasonably reliable and easy to handle and maintain. The type was also briefly used in the attack role, but this was a short-lived initiative due to a combination of organisational and technical issues which eventually saw the end of the use in 1958.

The MiG-17F, seen here, is among the longest-lived fighter types in Bulgarian service — until 1983, while the MiG-17 powered by a non-afterburning engine continued its active use in the fighter-bomber role until 1987. In turn, the use of the MiG-17 in the advanced training role in Bulgaria continued until 1986.

The force-wide MiG-17 introduction in the second half of the 1950s coincided with sharp growth of the Bulgarian military capabilities following the formation of the Warsaw Pact, with the VVS achieving at last its desired status of an air arm with a potent fleet and trained crews.

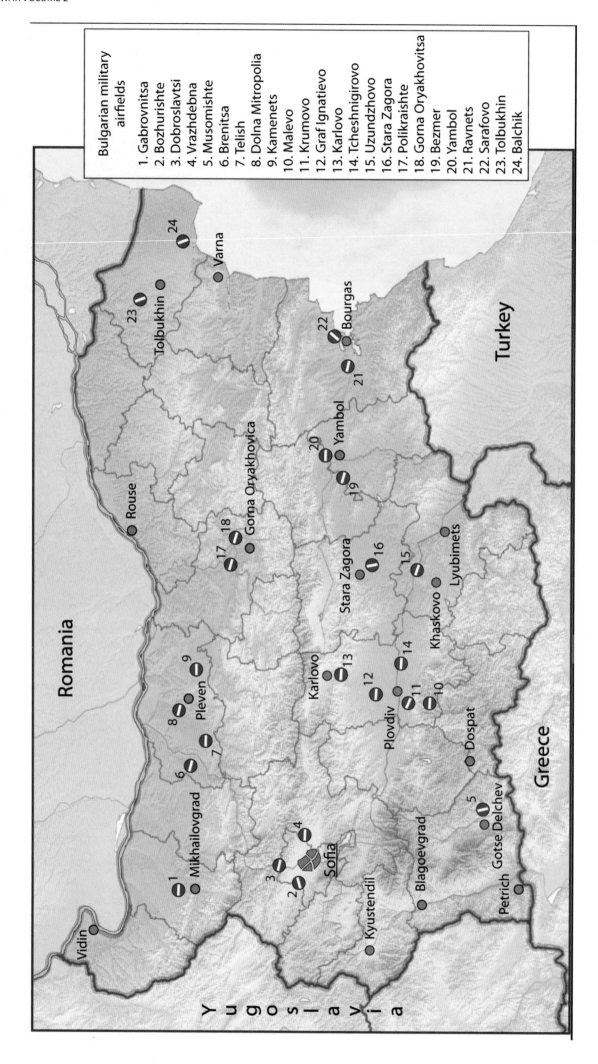

Bulgarian military airfields

1. Gabrovnitsa
2. Bozhurishte
3. Dobroslavtsi
4. Vrazhdebna
5. Musomishte
6. Brenitsa
7. Telish
8. Dolna Mitropolia
9. Kamenets
10. Malevo
11. Krumovo
12. Graf Ignatievo
13. Karlovo
14. Tcheshnigirovo
15. Uzundzhovo
16. Stara Zagora
17. Polikraishte
18. Gorna Oryakhovitsa
19. Bezmer
20. Yambol
21. Ravnets
22. Sarafovo
23. Tolbukhin
24. Balchik

gathered together and probably clarified their findings for the cause of the aircraft crash, then they went on to the west side of the Kozhukh, where the aircraft tail and part of its wings fell. Here, in the same way, they inspected the area, took pictures of the parts and searched for bullet holes. Looking at the tail of the plane, the Israeli representative who had come from Sofia told me in Russian language: "This is a barbaric job, what is that pilot as he had never seen the tail and opened fire on a passenger plane?"

I replied that the Bulgarian government had told its word on this issue. Upon completion of the crash scene survey, the representatives came together again to clarify some issues. During the inspection, the Israeli representatives spoke Hebrew and I could not figure out what. Only Comrade Malin Molerov may have only understood what their conversation was. Upon completion of the crash scene survey, the commission left and at 19:20 it crossed back the border, and those from Sofia left to Sofia.

On 3 and 4 August, the Israeli commission worked on Yugoslavian territory by interviewing officers and soldiers from border posts across the Bulgarian-Yugoslavian border. Eyewitness accounts from the Greek border post in the Promachontas area also proved valuable. In Bulgaria, the search for answers went in parallel but the process was well-hidden from the curious eyes of foreigners.

Israeli Commission of Enquiry Report

The Commission of Enquiry confirmed that the Flight LY402 report on overflying Belgrade was accurate and it was confirmed by the local air traffic control authorities. The noise of the aircraft was heard by the air traffic controllers as the overfly report had been issued. And here the big unknown appears — at which point Flight LY402 had deviated from the Airway Amber 10? At 05:10 GMT the aircraft reported overfly of Skopje, but this happened seven minutes earlier than planned. The expected time of crossing the Greek border was also reported — at 05:28. And right at this moment Belgrade ATC received a report from Flight LY402 that it was crossing the border at 5,488m (18,000ft), and changing transmission to Athens ATC. Nine minutes later Flight LY402 radioed a distress call: "SOS". This message had been issued repeatedly for two minutes and then the aircraft went silent. Different witnesses on Bulgarian, Yugoslavian and Greek territory were observing what happened in the air. Very soon it became clear that 4K-AKC was attacked mid-air and its wreckage fell on Bulgarian territory.

The Israeli Commission of Enquiry noted in its report that the premature report over Skopje beacon was probably due to an erroneous indication of the radio compass influenced by the thunderstorms which were well-developed near the actual flight path, and also mentioned that the easterly trend of the flight path could not have been checked by air to ground observations owing to the fact that the aircraft was passing over clouds.

The report also noted that Flight LY402 encountered stronger than forecasted winds, at 260°/70kt on its route between Belgrade and Skopje, but the pilots could not have been aware of the wind speed increase and would not, therefore, have made any correction to the course. The aircraft must, therefore, have continued on the same bearing as before (165°) until reporting over Skopje at 05:10. At this time, as the report says, the aircraft would, in fact, have left the airway.

Assuming they were at Skopje beacon, the pilots at 05:10 changed course to the new heading of Airway Amber 10, at 142°, corrected for the forecasted winds to 146°, and maintained this course for 18 minutes, reporting crossing the Greek-Yugoslavian border.

The Israeli report maintained that at this moment, in fact, Flight LY402 was close to the Yugoslavian-Bulgarian border at a point approximately 48km (26nm) north of the Greek border. Continuing for a further few minutes on this course, the aircraft would cross into Bulgarian territory, and Yugoslavian eyewitnesses reported to have observed the aircraft crossing the border.

The Commission of Enquiry report also referred at this point to the findings of the Bulgarian Investigation Commission, which said that Flight LY402 entered Bulgaria near the town of Tran (Trn) and after penetrating Bulgarian airspace for 40km (22nm), flying in south-easterly direction, eventually turned to the south and overflew several Bulgarian towns. To the south of the town of Stanke Dimitrov it was intercepted by two fighters which warned it to land. Taking into consideration that Tran is on a bearing of 135° (magnetic) from Belgrade and at a distance of 272km (147nm), such a course could be regarded as quite unrelated to the pilot's flight plan or the direction in which they were making.

The report claims that the winds in this region were as predicted and pilots were assisted for 130km (70nm) out of Belgrade by reliable track indicating navigational aids (VOR); furthermore, they were experienced pilots, familiar with the route. So, it was not acceptable for the Israeli Commission of Enquiry that they could have flown for some 41 minutes on an entirely arbitrary course, then turning sharply south on an entirely new course without apparent reason, and therefore reporting without comment over the Greek border.

The report also challenged the conclusion in the report of the Bulgarian Government Commission for Investigation that the fighters warned Flight LY402 to land "in conformity with established international regulations. In spite of this it would not obey and continued on its flight towards the south in trying to escape." The Israeli report's authors noted that it is unconceivable that an unarmed civil aircraft with an experienced crew and 51 passengers aboard would not obey orders adequately given by two armed fighters. Further, the subsequent behaviour of the fighters, as claimed in the report, was inconsistent with any previous warning having been given. The fighters attacked the aircraft a second time when is had lost considerable height and was evidently seeking for a place to land. A last attack was carried out at a time when the course of the aircraft was to the north, further into Bulgarian territory. The aircraft had already been hit and was obviously making an approach for a forced landing either in the Struma valley or on an abandoned airfield further north.

Finally, the Israeli report noted that no radio warnings on the frequency fixed by the International Civil Aviation Organisation for aircraft communication in this region were intercepted by either Greek or Yugoslavian aeronautical stations keeping watch.

The Israeli investigation team inspection of the crash site listed its finding in the report:

1. That many parts of the aircraft had been removed from the places where they original fell.

2. That a most thorough search had been made of the wreckage. Lining had been ripped off and all closed structures had been opened for examination.

3. That there were holes of various calibres too numerous to detail in the short time available.

4. That all traces of bodies, luggage and personal belongings had been removed.

5. That nearly all cockpit equipment, such as radios, instruments,

electrical panels, had been removed and were not available for examination. Only one radio compass indicator and some completely smashed radio sets were found.

Before leaving, Israeli officials requested interviews with eyewitnesses of the aircraft crash who could give further information. They requested particularly to see the fighter pilots who shot down the aircraft and were obviously the only witnesses to give a full and detailed information of what had happened. The commission also requested to interview the commanding officer who directed their mission and in addition, eyewitnesses along the flight path. A request was also made for the return of aircraft parts that had been recovered from the crash site. MoFA's Malin Molerov responded that this request would be referred to the authorities in Sofia. In fact, no answer had been received during the Israeli commission's work and in the event it was obliged to prepare its report without this vital evidence being available from Bulgaria. The only Bulgarian evidence at the time was the official communiqué of the findings of the Bulgarian Government Investigation Commission, which established beyond any doubt that the aircraft was attacked and shot down by Bulgarian fighters.

The commission proceeded forward with work on Yugoslavian territory where the local authorities proved cooperative. On 2 August four members of the commission interviewed witnesses, assisted in their work by Yugoslavian civilian and military representatives. The witnesses were all military personnel from points along the border with Bulgaria. Three of them made their observations from a post 48km (26nm) north of the Greek border and two were from a post situated 20km (11nm) north of the Greek border. One further witness was at the time of the accident at a point situated at 18km (10nm) from the Greek border. The commission also collected information from the Yugoslavian Civil Aviation authorities

As a result of the work of the Israeli commission in Yugoslavia, it stated in the report that, after careful consideration it could not accept the findings on this point as set out in the official Bulgarian Communique. Its report said that a Yugoslavian witness, stationed at a point 48km (26nm) from the Greek border, saw a large aircraft flying in an easterly direction over Bulgaria and two fighters approaching it from the east. One of the fighters took up a position between the large aircraft and the border line, while the other manoeuvred around the large aircraft. All three witnesses at this point heard bursts of machinegun fire but none of them saw signs of a hit. Then the two witnesses at the point 20km (11nm) north of the Greek border heard an aircraft to the north-east of their position and heard bursts of machinegun fire. They then observed the aircraft moving in a south-easterly direction towards the Greek border. After this they heard more machinegun fire. The aircraft was flying in a south-easterly direction and was about 7km distant from the observation post when it disappeared from view.

A witness at a point 18km (10km) from the Greek border also spotted the aircraft to the north-east of his position and observed it flying to the south east and losing height. He heard machinegun fire but did not notice smoke from the aircraft when its disappeared over the mountain.

Witnesses of the accident from Greece also provided information to the Israeli commission. The first group from a border post in the mountain told the investigators that they saw the aircraft approaching over a mountain from the north-west. When it appeared, smoke was trailing from its right-hand side. Before the aircraft came into view, one witness heard what he took to be heavy gun fire and another he thought was thunder. The aircraft was observed flying in a south-easterly direction, losing height but under control. When south of

Petrich, it started to turn towards the north-east, heading for the plain north of hills 224 and 281. A little beyond this to the north there was an abandoned military airfield. All three witnesses interviewed said that when the aircraft was over hills 224 and 281, it broke up and fell in pieces. Part of the debris fell on the northern-western slopes of the hills and burned for a short time. The other part fell on the south-eastern slopes and continued burning for more than an hour.

When the aircraft broke-up in mid-air, it was at an altitude of approximately 610m (2,000ft).

Other witnesses from a point further west along the same border heard machinegun fire before the aircraft appeared and then saw it coming low over the mountain with fire and smoke at the root of the right wing. They also confirmed in a general way the previous witness reporting on the flight path. However, they saw in addition, two jet fighters above the aircraft. One of the jets disappeared immediately after the aircraft turned north but the other escorted it right to the time when it broke up. After this it circled and flew to the north. These witnesses also heard a loud explosion at the time the aircraft broke up.

Another group of three witnesses, civilians, in the village of Promachontas reported shots immediately before the aircraft broke up. Of this group, three saw the fighter.

Efforts were made to obtain exact information from the witnesses regarding times. However, as all estimates appeared completely unreliable on cross-examination, it has not been possible to place reliance on this type of information, the report says.

Then the report continues with reconstruction of the flight path from a point presumed to be in Yugoslavia at 05:28 to the mountain over which it first appeared to the Greek eyewitnesses. This distance is 17nm, and the mountain (Ograzhden Planina) is about 6,000ft in height, with the aircraft described as coming low over it, with the commission assuming the altitude of some 8,000ft. As the aircraft had reported being at 18,000ft over the point at 05:28, the report noted that it must have reduced speed to the minimum in order to make a rapid descent. In must have averaged about 150kt over this distance which it would then have covered in seven minutes, bringing it over the mountain at 05:36. In this situation, the report considers that loss of pressurisation may have been a likely cause of this steep descent, as a result of damage to the fuselage caused by one of the earlier bursts of gunfire. As Yugoslavian witnesses heard fire when the aircraft disappeared from view and Greek witnesses said they heard fire just before the aircraft appeared smoking into their view, it seems that when the aircraft was hit for a second time a fire started as the aircraft came over the mountain.

The SOS message was received at 05:37 which would be immediately after the fire started. Here the report asks why no SOS message was received earlier, assuming that this was a matter for conjecture. The cause of the sudden loss of pressurisation may not have been immediately apparent to the aircraft captain. It may be that it was only at the second attack that he realised that the aircraft was under fire. The aircraft continued flying towards Petrich accompanied by the fighters, losing altitude steadily. After crossing the Strumitsa river, it turned left between Petrich and the Greek border, then headed in a northerly direction towards the Struma (Strimon) valley until its reached the hills 224 and 281.

The report notes that right up to this point the aircraft appeared to have been still under control and the pilot was making for a landing on the Strimon plain and possibly on the abandoned military airfield north of the hills. One of the fighters accompanied the aircraft to the end.

From the report of the wreckage and technical investigation, as the report noted, it can be seen that certain damage was inflicted in the air, immediately before the break up. Explosions of large-calibre projectiles in the rear part of the fuselage — damaging the control mechanism of the elevators and rudders — would not have permitted the aircraft to maintain controlled flight.

The report also says that projectiles had penetrated the tanks of the right wing and it is clear from the scatter of the pieces that the wing had exploded in mid-air. The left wing tanks had also been hit by bullets which must have started a fire followed by an explosion.

The technical investigation pointed to the aircraft having exploded and broken up over the hills as the result of a final attack. This had been supported by eyewitnesses' evidence. Nearly all of them told the commission that they saw the aircraft breaking up in mid-air and some of them also saw a fighter flying next to it. Those a little further to the east along the border line heard the explosion and some of them also heard gunfire.

The report also noted that from the condition of the wreckage and the eyewitness accounts of the break-up in mid-air, together with the statement of the Bulgarian Government, it may be conclusively presumed that there were no survivors.

The conclusions of the report, made by the Israeli Commission of Enquiry were as follows (the original orography is retained unchanged):

On the 27th of July, 1955, at approximately 05:50 GMT, a Constellation aircraft of Israel civil registration (4X-AKC) en route from Vienna to Lod, was fired upon in three phases by two Bulgarian jet fighters and in last attack was destroyed over Bulgarian territory.

The first firing took place in the area of the Yugoslav-Bulgarian border at an altitude of approximately 18,000 feet. The Commission is satisfied that the aircraft did not receive any warning prior to this firing.

Several minutes later the second firing took place over Bulgarian territory at an altitude of approximately 8,000 feet. The aircraft was then evidently in process of descent seeking a place to land and was showing signs of fire. Nevertheless, it continued its controlled flight. At the time of this attack it had covered some 17 nautical miles within Bulgarian air space.

After approximately five minutes the third attack took place at an altitude of about 2,000 feet. The aircraft was still under control, heading northward deeper into Bulgaria and making for a forced landing. As result of this last attack, the aircraft broke up in mid-air.

The aircraft entered Bulgarian air space being approximately 35 nautical miles off track on a course which would have brought it to the Bulgarian-Greek border after traversing approximately 26 nautical miles (6 to 7 minutes flying) of the south-western corner of Bulgaria. The Bulgarian statement as to the course with the track of the aircraft is inconsistent with the facts as proved.

In the circumstances of wind and weather on this flight, the crew could not have been aware of the aircraft's drift from track. In any event, the cause of the disaster was not this deviation but the action of the Bulgarian fighters in shooting down the aircraft. There were no survivors.

Eventually, each of the investigation commissions in Bulgaria and Israel sorted out what it knew and what it assumed, but without coming to a common cause of what happened in the air in the south-western corner of Bulgaria. As a consequence, the case had gradually and entirely crept into the realm of diplomacy and international law.

The unwillingness of the Bulgarian authorities to share, even partially, the results of their investigation with the Israeli Commission of Enquiry, and allow access for undertaking investigation in

Bulgaria, could be seen as one of the main contributing factors for the appearance of the Israeli version of the flight path of Flight LY402. This flight path reconstruction made in the report, particularly for its part in Bulgarian airspace, was undertaken solely based on the testimony of Yugoslavian eyewitnesses on the frontier, at points situated between 10 and 20km north of the Greek border, who were all military servicemen. Taking into consideration the rather tense political relations between Bulgaria and Yugoslavia at that time, and the serious hostility still existing between the countries (each of them has been actively involved in covert military and intelligence operations against the other since 1948), such testimonies could be hardly accepted as fully reliable and impartial.

Looking at the map, it can be also concluded that there was no practical possibility to have the QRA pair from Dobroslavtsi launched at 07:10 to 07:15 to perform the successful intercept and engage Flight LY402 in the Petrich area in case it crossed the Yugoslavian-Bulgarian border at a point which is about 20km (11nm) north of the Greek border at between 07:28 and 07:30. In such an unlikely event (as maintained by the Israeli Commission of Enquiry), at the time of the QRA pair launch from Dobroslavtsi, the Israeli aircraft would have been at a point about 30km (16nm) north of Skopje (as indicated on the map released by the Israeli Commission of Enquiry in its report) and at 30 to 40km (16 to 22nm) from the Bulgarian border, flying in south-easterly direction. No doubt, at this position it would have been invisible for the Bulgarian visual observation posts deployed next to the border, and could be only detected by the Bulgarian radars situated in the south-western part of the country, still near Airway Amber 10, and with a course hardly to be predicted as leading to an immediate violation of Bulgarian airspace.

Criticism from above

On 27 July 1955, later in the day, after hearing the reports of all the generals in his cabinet, the Minister of People's Defence, Armeyski General Peter Panchevsky, sent a note to the Prime Minister of the People's Republic of Bulgaria, Valko Chervenkov, with the initial and unverified information. It briefly described the path of the intruder aircraft into Bulgarian territory and what happened according to the combat report of the Air Defence Commander-in-Chief:

In the Blagoevgrad area, the fighters have detected a four-engine propeller aircraft without national insignia and markings (according to the report of the pilots). They signalled the intruder to follow them and fired warning shots in front of the cockpit but the transport aircraft had failed to obey the order. When it entered the forbidden border area in the vicinity to General Todorovo village, 10km south of the city of Sandanski, our fighters opened fire and at 08:34 [Moscow time – author's note] it was shot down. The actions of the fighter pilots and the intruder have been documented on gun camera tapes.

By noon and the later part of the day, after getting information from the crash site, as well as from reports published by international news agencies, the truth of what happened in the air near Petrich became clear to the whole world. In a nutshell: Bulgaria shot down a properly-marked Israeli passenger aircraft. This became number one news story and the world news agencies rushed to tell how Communist Bulgaria shot down a regular passenger aircraft and killed innocent passengers. Valko Chervenkov was extremely annoyed with the brief and incomplete report submitted by his Defence Minister. On 28 July, he provided his angry response to the Minister of People's Defence, with the following text:

Aerial gunnery results

One of the first jobs of the MoPD Commission was to interrogate the pilots and check their actions in the air during the intercept and attacks. The tapes of the gun cameras gun, which recorded the shooting, were analysed in detail. There were a total of 133 frames analysed from the tape of Capitan Petrov's aircraft gun camera and 97 more from that of Sankiisky. The records of the MoPD Commission comprised these analyses:

A)   Data from the tape of Capitan Boris Vasilev Petrov

Series No 1: Frames from 133 to 130 – fire opened to check the armament operability – time 7:28:46.

Series No 2: Frames from 129 to 107 – fire opened against an aircraft in the 0/4 aspect [tail-on], from 800m distance. Average drop of 35 mils. No probability of hits. The projectiles passed below and to the port – time 7:29:36.

Series No 3: Frames from 106 to 104 – the aircraft is not visible into the frame – time 7:33:10.

Series No 4: Frames from 103 to 102 – the aircraft is not visible into the frame – time 7:33:10.

Series No 5: Frames from 101 to 81 – fire opened against an aircraft in the 0/4 aspect, from 800 to 620m distance. Drop – up to 15 mils. Time 7:35:58. The aircraft is with lowered undercarriage. No probability of hit, the projectiles passed below the aircraft.

Series No 6: Frames from 80 to 40 – time from 7:35:02. Fire opened in the 0/4 aspect, from 700 to 500m distance, with a drop from 10 to 80 mils. There is probability of hit into the aircraft. The target is crossing the crosshairs, passing from left to the right.

Series No 7: Frames from 39 to 35 – the aircraft is not visible into the frame – time 7:31:05.

Series No 8: Frames from 34 to 27 – time 7:31:54. Fire opened in the 0/4 aspect, from 800 to 700m distance, with a drop of 10 mils. There is probability of hit into the aircraft.

Series No 9: Frames from 26 to 11 – no time is recognisable on the frames. Fire opened in the 0/4 aspect, from 750 to 650m distance, with a drop of 10 mils. There is probability of hit into the aircraft. Frames No 21 and No 20 show smoke.

Series No 10: Frames from 10 to 1 – no time recognisable on the frames. Fire opened in the 0/4 aspect, from 700 to 600m distance, with a drop from 0 to 50 mils. There is probability of hit into the aircraft.

B)   Data from the tape of Leitenant Kosta Krumov Sankiisky

Series No 1: Frames from 1 to 3 – time 7:28:07.

Series No 2: Frames from 4 to 12 – time 7:29:22. Fire opened in the 2/4 aspect, from 700 to 650m distance, with a lead of 20 mils and drop of 0 mils. There is probability of hit into the aircraft.

Series No 3: Frames from 13 to 20 – time 7:29:25. Fire opened in the 2/4 to 1/4 aspect, from 700 to 600m distance. Lead – 10 to 0 mils. There is probability of hit into the aircraft.

Series No 4: Frames from 21 to 26 – time 7:29:25. The aircraft is not recognisable into the frames.

Series No 5: Frames from 27 to 36 – time 7:29:35. Fire opened in the 2/4 to 1/4 aspect, from 650 to 500m distance. Lead – 15 mils. There is probability of hit.

Series No 6: Frames from 37 to 49 – time 7:29:32. Fire opened in the 1/4 aspect, from 550 to 400m distance. Lead – up to 15 mils. There is probability of hit.

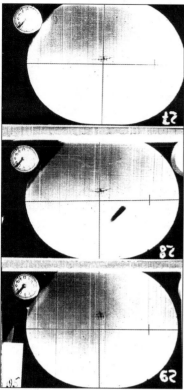

Gun camera frames from No 27 to No 29 from Petrov's aircraft show how fire was opened from 800 to 700m distance tail-on.

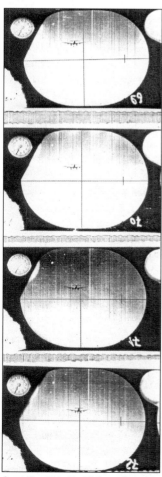

Gun camera frames from No 69 to No 72 from Petrov's aircraft, with fire opened by him from 700 to 500m distance, in a tail-on attack.

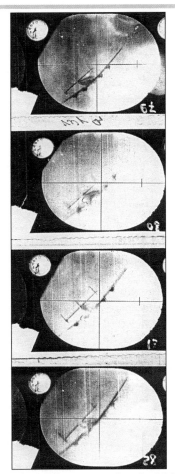

Gun camera frames from No 79 to No 82 from Sankiisky's aircraft, where he attacks side-on from 300 to 100m distance.

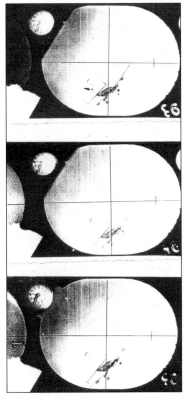

The gun camera frames from No 93 to No 95 from Sankiisky's aircraft. This is the last attack, with firing from a very close distance — the last rounds were unleashed from 150m distance — and the Constellation was turning with its undercarriage in lowered position near the city of Petrich, before exploding and braking up mid-air over the Kozhikh hill.

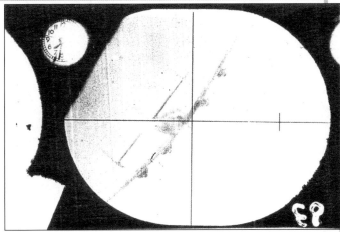

Gun camera frame No 83 from Sankiisky's aircraft, showing rounds being unleashed from a point-blank range.

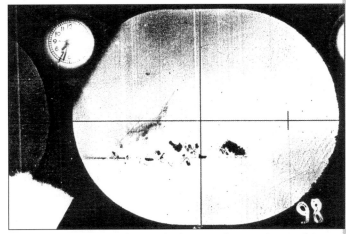

Gun camera frame No 86 from Sankiisky's aircraft, again showing firing from a point-blank range.

Series No 7: Frames from 50 to 54 – time 7:30:25. Fire opened in the 2/4 aspect, from 500 to 400m distance. Lead – 0 mils. Projectiles passed behind the target.

Series No 8: Frames from 55 to 68 – time 7:30:32. Fire opened in the 1/4 to 0/4 aspect, from 300 to 150m distance. There is probability of hit.

Series No 9: Frames from 69 to 84 – time 7:31:45. Fire opened in the 2/4 to 1/4 aspect, from 300 to 100m distance. There is probability of hit.

Series No 10: Frames from 85 to 97 – time 07:33:15. Fire opened in the 2/4 to 1/4 aspect, from 400 to 150m distance. Lead – 50 to 20 mils. The aircraft is with undercarriage down. There is probability of hit.

Author's note: There is no data about an accurate synchronisation of the gun camera clocks, but nevertheless analysis of the frames provides good information on the number of rounds unleashed in the series, and the sequence of the attacks performed by both pilots.

Comrade Panchevsky
Before submitting a report to the Prime Minister, the facts should be well checked. The conclusions of the authorities that directed and shot down the aircraft must not be taken faithfully.

1.   Are there or are no distinctive markings on the aircraft? How did it fly over Yugoslavia without identification markings?

2.   Pilots from the downed aircraft have reported to Vienna that they have been attacked by Bulgarian fighters. Why do you not know what and when exactly the pilots from the downed aircraft have reported? The company knows this. The Israeli Embassy knows this.

3.   There is no conclusion in your report, your opinion is missing. What are the conclusions?'

As a result of the sharp criticism, Armeyski General Panchevsky had requested servicemen from Simitli and Petrich to send him further testimony from ground witnesses. Moreover, there was an anti-aircraft battery stationed in Simitli. The testimony of Polkovnik Grozdan Stoilov Petrov, CO of Military Unit 40550 in Simitli, is of particular interest. Using this information and the testimony of other eyewitnesses on the ground, allowed for the reconstruction of this stage of the flight and intercept:

On 27 July 1955, at 07:05, I was alerted by the visual observation posts that there is a violation in the northwest. I alerted the AAA artillery units. At 07:20 an aircraft was spotted above Simitli, at an altitude of about 3,000-3,500m, in parallel to which two jet fighters were moving — one above it and slightly forward and the other to the right in retreat.

The right-hand fighter clearly gave signalling by rocking its wings. The big aircraft I personally thought was a B-29 did not respond. It attempted to turn to the west over Krupnik. In the meantime, the fighter, moving to the right in retreat, overtook the target and crossed its path. Then the big aircraft speeded up to the south. At this time, the right-hand fighter opened fire and the first one did not respond. Afterwards, all three aircraft disappeared in the Kresna Gorge. Immediately I went to the village of Pirin by car, and at 08:25 I arrived at the accident scene. I don't know any further.

Obviously, Polkovnik Petrov's clock had not been exactly set, but his testimony can provide enough information about the time intervals and what happened in the sky above Simitli. Shortly thereafter, Panchevsky corrected himself by sending to the Prime Minister an extremely detailed report on what happened, but the truth had not pleased anyone.

Investigation goes to Dobroslavtsi
In the early afternoon of July 27, Polkovnik Vasil Zikulov (Air Defence Deputy Chief of Staff) was the first to arrive in Dobroslavtsi. He was also the first one to inform the command personnel of the 4th IAD about the tragic news — that the QRA pair shot down an Israeli passenger aircraft instead of a spy aircraft. An immediate interrogation of the pilots began, with questions where and how they did it. Particularly important were the gun camera tapes and the analysis of the frames. Former weapons technician Georgy Vukov recalled that moment:

The photographers checked [the tapes – note by the authors] and I went on to check these personally, including the time of the shooting

recorded, and how many shots were unleashed. In the afternoon it was all clear. By that time the photo tapes were developed and the prints printed. The attacks on the target were made at 07:30 as both clocks on the MiG-15s were working in a proper manner. The command authorities wanted to get the photos immediately, and both cartridges with the tapes were forwarded by a motor vehicle to the VVS HQ.

Khristo Ivanov recalls the tough moments after the initial celebration in the morning hours at the CP in Dobroslavtsi:

We met them as heroes. They came to the division's CP. The division CO was also there. Minutes later, a call from the VVS HQ informed us that a passenger aircraft had been shot down. And this same Constellation was a former military aircraft, bomber. So, its silhouette was misleading.
The next day it was announced that a government commission had been set up to investigate what happened and punish the guilty.
The division commander told us: "You, Petrov and Sankiisky, and the responsible duty officer at the main command post, Major Karchev, shall report to the Minister of People's Defence, Armeyski General Peter Panchevsky". The next day, by noon, we went to the Minister. In addition to Panchevsky, one Soviet general, his adviser, was also in the cabinet. Before the minister could say anything, the Soviet general said to us, "Well done!" Panchevsky laughed, we sat down and told him what happened. He said there was nothing wrong and reassured us. The next day we had to report to the government commission.
The next day (29 June 1955), already in the Communist Party House, the Government Commission for Investigation had a meeting. The Minister of People's Defence, the Minister of Foreign Affairs Mincho Neichev, the Chairman of the Commission, the Prosecutor General and General Zakhary Zahariev were still at a round table full of people. One by one we were introduced and talked about.
As far as I know, there was a dispute in the commission. The rules called when fighter jets intercept an intruder, they should fly in formation with the intruder and rock the wings — this is the 'follow me' signal. The second thing is to instruct the intruder where to turn and direct it to land. If not following the instruction, then pilots shall fire warning shots with tracer projectiles. If the aircraft rejects to follow the fighters after their warning shots, then pilots are instructed to shoot at it. There was a dispute as to whether the pilots had issued warning signals during the mission. The gun camera tapes were used to prove the fact that the pilots issued the warning shots as required. They were firing and the tracer projectiles passed in front of the aircraft.

The VVS Commander-in-Chief, General Major Kiril Kirilov, defended his pilots:

That is, we will not blame them. And if I was there, I would command and shoot. How can you fail to follow an order; then you would have to shoot the pilots because of they had failed to follow a command! What if it was a four-engine bomber?
So, the QRA pilots were misled. They didn't realise until the very last moment that they were shooting at a passenger aircraft. How will they know this? Do you imagine how many violations of the Bulgarian airspace were recorded at that time and what would be the consequences if you missed the target. Well, you're going straight to Court Martial. It was a very hot situation then.

Radio Chatter[1]

08:13 – CP: Damba [the CP code name] gives adjustment [of the radio frequency].

08:14 – CP: 487 Line [heading] 270, Kupol [altitude] 20, Reload [a command to reload the guns].

08:15 – QRA pair: I'm 487 [the call sign of the leader Capitan Petrov], Kupol 20.

08:15 – CP: 487, the Vorona [Crow – the code name of the target] is 20km to the west of you.

08:15 – CP: The Vorona at 10km.

08:16 – CP: 487, go to Site 72.

08:16 – QRA pair: Understood, go to the area.

08:17 – CP: 487, switch on IFF.

08:17 – QRA pair: IFF on.

P: 487, for you Kupol 50.

QRA pair: Say again, not understood.

CP: Kupol 50.

QRA pair: Got it.

CP: 487, report position.

QRA pair: Say again, not understood.

08:18 – CP: 487, are the clouds dense?

08:20 – CP: 487, immediately take Line 70. Increase speed.

08:20 – CP: 487, what is the cloud base?

CP: 487, where are you now?

CP: 487, what is the cloud base?

QRA pair: I'm at Site 91.

CP: Go to Point 7261.

08:22 – CP: 487, take a Kupol above the clouds.

CP: 487, what is the visibility?

08:23 – CP: 487, at which site you are now?

08:23 – CP: 487, what is your Kupol now?

08:24 – QRA Pair: Now Kupol 40.

08:24 – CP: Maintain this Kupol.

08:24 – CP: 487, Line 180, increase speed.

QRA pair: Understood.

CP: Be careful with the Fence [the border line with Yugoslavia].

CP: 487, descend to Kupol 25.

08:25 – QRA pair: Say again.

CP: Descend to Kupol 25.

QRA pair: Not understood.

CP: Descend to 25. The target is to the south of you.

CP: 487, hold the Line.

08:26 – CP: 487, where you are now?

08:27 – CP: 487, give adjustment. Damba-3.

08:32 – CP: 487, give adjustment.

08:33 – CP: 487, take care for the Fence.

[At 08:31 an aircraft with the call sign 470 took-off from Dobroslavtsi to be used as a relay of the radio communications between the CP and the QRA pair]

08:32 – CP: 470, over the point, Kupol 40 above the clouds.

08:33 – CP: 487, take care to avoid the Fence.

08:34 – CP: 487, I'm Damba-3. Go to 15km to the east of Point 72.

08:34 – CP: 470, relay to 487 to go to the east, 15km from 7267.

08:37 – CP: 470, do you hear 487?

Relay aircraft: I do not hear 487.

487, for you Horizont and More [code words for immediate return to the airfield and landing].

08:37 – CP: 470 to take Kupol 40.

08:38 – CP: 487, I'm 470, take Kupol 40.

CP: 470, do you hear 487?

Relay aircraft: Not hearing?

08:39 – CP: 487, take Kupol 40.

08:40 – CP: 470, give adjustment and enter into contract with 470.

CP: 470, giving adjustment.

CP: 470, do you hear 487?

Relay aircraft: 487, request Strela [guidance, indicating the direction to the airfield].

Relay aircraft: 487, I'm 470, request Strela.

Relay aircraft: 487, request Strela, they do not hear you.

Relay aircraft: 487, south of Point 2 there are another two of the neighbours [most likely these were MiG-15s from the 10th IAD at Graf Ignatievo].

Relay aircraft: 487, how do you hear me?

Relay aircraft: 487, I'm 470, give adjustment.

CP: 470, relay that they shall take Kupol 40 under the cloud base and request Strela.

Relay aircraft: 487, I'm 470, take Kupol 40 under the cloud base.

Relay aircraft: 487, to the southeast of Site 37 the other two are situated.

CP: 487, for you Line 360.

CP: 487, I'm Damba-3. Give adjustment.

CP: 487, how do you hear me?

CP: 487, give adjustment, I do not hear you.

QRA pair: I'm 487. Position to the south of Site 91.

CP: Have you seen the Vorona?

CP: 487, repeat what you have seen?

QRA pair: The Vorona was being burned out.

CP: How many engines, did you see it?

CP: 487, in which area the Vorona fell?

QRA pair: In Petrich area. I'm 487.

CP: 487, your position?

QRA pair: I'm to the west of you.

CP: Do you see the point [the airfield]?

CP: 487, what is your altitude?

QRA pair: The Vorona was at 35.

CP: 470, for you Horizont [return to the airfield] and More [landing].

CP: 487, report on normal.

QRA pair: All normal.

QRA pair: Request clearance for landing.

CP: 470, what is your position?

Relay aircraft: Approaching to land.

The aircraft landed at 8:56.

Author's note

1   The time in the transcription of the radio conversations is given in the Moscow time. This had been used as a common time in order to coordinate the operations of the air defence systems of the Eastern Bloc countries. The copy of the radio conversations in the QRA mission has been taken from the radio conversations logbook of the 4th IAD Command Post.

The pilots were under huge pressure and at a crossroad. Everyone — from the last VVS pilot to the Communist Party leadership — was looking forward to the moment when the secret air operations in Bulgarian airspace would come to an end. But no one expected this to happen in such a bloody way.

MoPD Commission Conclusions

In the meantime, within three days, the MoPD Commission completed its internal investigation, and its report summarised the results:

On 27 July, 1955, at 07:08, the visual observation post (VOP) system detected an air target in the Yugoslav territory, west of the city of Tran, heading at 90° into the direction of the city of Tran.

At 07:11 the target crossed the Bulgarian-Yugoslavian border in the region of Tran, which entered the territory of the People's Republic of Bulgaria with a course in the Tran – Breznik direction.

To intercept the intruder, at 07:13 the QRA fighter pair was launched from DOBROSLAVTSI airfield, with Capitan Boris Vasilev PETROV as the pair leader and Leitenant Kosta Krumov SANKIISKI as his wingman.

As a result of the information of the VOP system and the guidance of the fighters, they were able to detect the intruder aircraft at 07:26 in the Blagoevgrad region, heading to the south (180°), at an altitude of 4,000m. The meteorological conditions at that moment in the area of Blagoevgrad, Petrich and Sandanski were: cloudy 1–3/10 at altitude above 3,000 meters. The visibility was 20km.

After detecting the intruder aircraft, the fighters checked their weapons and took an initial position for attacking it.

The leader of the fighter pair, Capitan Petrov (according to his testimony) fired warning shots, and Leitenant Sankiisky opened fire aiming at the intruder at the 29th minute (at 07:29) in the Simitli area.

The fighter pair conducted several attacks by firing on the intruder. After the first attacks, it sharply changed the course to the southwest, towards the Bulgarian-Yugoslavian border while descending.

As a result of the attacks being carried out by fighters from the direction of the western border, the intruder once again changed its heading to the south while decreasing the altitude.

The fighters continued to attack.

The intruder lowered its landing gear in the area northwest of PETRICH, at the 33rd minute, continuing to lose altitude. Reaching the Petrich area at an altitude of about 2,000m, the intruder entered a sharp left-hand turn, rapidly losing altitude and disintegrating mid-air at about 1,000m, falling in the Kozhukh hill area – at 8km northeast of the city of PETRICH. The plane was completely destroyed, the crew and passengers perished.

From the moment of its launch to the moment of getting in the area of STANKE DIMITROV the fighter pair had a regular communication until the 25th minute. From this moment on, the communication had been lost, from where the pilots operated independently without being controlled by the 4th IAD's CP.

In order to restore the control of the fighters, the 4th IAD's CP launched a fighter from the next QRA pair, to loiter in a designated area over SVOGE in the 33rd minute. The radio communication, however, was not restored.

The responsible duty officer in the 4th IAD CP, and the acting CO of the 18th IAP, Major Khristo Stoyanov IVANOV, was at the start command post at 07:08, when the signal of a higher alert state was issued. He sent the Chief of Staff of the regiment, Capitan Khristo

Vassilev Petkanov, to the 4th IAD CP, and then he continued to control the air traffic until the landing of all airborne aircraft, and he arrived at the CP at 07:30.

The radio communication was restored only when the pilots were back to [the] Blagoevgrad area at 07:39.

Analysing the materials at its disposal and the testimony of country's Air Defence and the Air Force, and eyewitnesses on the ground, the Commission arrived at the following conclusions:

1. On July 27, 1955 an Israeli Lockheed C-69 Constellation passenger aircraft, following on the BELGRADE-SKOPJE-THESSALONIKI route, deviated off course due to unknown reasons, crossing the state border at 07:11 at Miloslavtsi village, Tran area, and violated the airspace of the People's Republic of Bulgaria by flying on the route: MILOSLAVTSI, RADOMIR, BLAGOEVGRAD, PETRICH.

2. Considering the fact that both the air route and the aircraft are equipped with modern radio navigation aids, capable of providing reliable air navigation in all weather conditions, and also that at the time of the border violation the weather was good, especially in the territory of Yugoslavia, allowing for visual orientation, the commission considers that in the case when the onboard equipment and the ground aids were in good working order, as well as the good conditions for visual orientation of the air crew, there is no reason to the aircraft's deviation nearly 130km to the left (to the east) from its route and violating our air border.

3. The deviation of the intruder aircraft (at approximately 30°) from the established route is a gross failure of the aircrew to follow the flight path of the aircraft, since even in the event of failure of the radio navigation equipment, the crew could have been able to fly the aircraft using the time/range calculations and a magnetic compass and, in the current good weather conditions, to control the position of the flight by visual orientation over the terrain.

4. The aircrew of the intruder has been completely irresponsible in controlling the flight along the route, neglecting the fact that the route passes parallel to the state border of a foreign country and, if deviated, this could lead to a violation of the foreign country's airspace.

5. By turning the intruder aircraft at the 30th minute into the southwest direction and decreasing the altitude after the fighters had issued warning shots and mounted attacks, the commission believes that the crew had realised that it was in foreign territory but did not follow the instructions of the fighters and made an attempt to exit the country.

6. The lowering of the undercarriage at the 33rd minute, which the commission assumes was a signal that it agrees to follow the fighter instructions, was undertaken by the aircraft crew after it had taken hits from the fighter's targeted fire.

7. The country's air defence forces, without any requests for foreign aircraft crossing at the state border in the area, assumed that the incoming aircraft is an intruder.

8. The VNOS Main Command Post had not been able to determine the type of aircraft due to the insufficient and contradictory data supplied by the VOPs. They reported that the aircraft is a four-engine but of unknown type.

9. The Air Defence Command Post of the country, acting upon the information supplied by the VNOS Main Post, issued an order at 07:08 for placing the 4th IAD CP into a higher state of alert and approved at 07:17 its decision to launch the fighter pair to intercept the intruder, although that the VNOS Main Post had information that the aircraft is a transport model.

10. The scrambled fighter pair from DOBROSLAVTSI airfield for intercepting the intruder aircraft, after determining that the intruder aircraft is a transport model of unknown nationality, did not show the necessary precaution, proceeding that the aircraft was a transport model, to make every effort to force its crew to land on our territory, and instead the pilots had acted strictly in accordance with the "Instructions for the actions of fighters against aircraft-intruders of the air borders and the airspace of the People's Republic of Bulgaria", item 15a, which reads: "Upon detection of an intruder aircraft, fighters shall identify its nationality by the silhouette and insignia, and then, according to the situation, shall act, by meeting the following conditions:

a) If the detected aircraft belongs to foreign countries – Turkey, Greece, Yugoslavia or the United States and England — and it had entered within 40km of our state border, it shall be destroyed without warning, and if it had entered at more than 40km from our state border, the fighters shall use all means (warning shots, signals, etc.) in order the intruder to be forced to land at one of the nearby airfields or at an auxiliary landing site. In the event that it refuses to obey to the warning signals, with a clear willingness to cross into its own territory, destructive fire shall be opened, pursuing and attacking it most vigorously to our state border line."

11. The radio communication between the 4th IAD CP and the fighters in the air had been interrupted due to the considerable distance from the airfield and the strong atmospheric interference. The Chief of Staff of the 18th IAP, Captain Petkanov, should have ordered the launch of the relay aircraft to relay the radio communications between the 4th IAD CP and the fighters earlier, and also to consider sending it not to the loitering zone in the SVOGE area, but to the south in the RADOMIR – STANKE DIMITROV area.

12. The responsible duty officer in the 4th IAD, Major IVANOV, upon receiving the report on the higher alert state from the CP, instead of handing over the air traffic control duties to another officer in command and immediately arriving at the 4th IAD CP to take over the fighter control, he decided to send the Chief of Staff, Captain PETKANOV, issued an order for all aircraft to land and remained to control their flights until the last aircraft had landed.

13. The Auxiliary Guidance Post at Dobri Dol, Kyustendil area, had the ability and was obliged to establish radio communication with the fighters and take over the guidance but it had failed to do this.

14. The Air Defence CP of the country – the responsible duty officer, Major Karchev, acted in accordance with the instructions. He has not shown the urge to establish radio communication with the fighters, to restore the 4th IAD CP's radio communication and to activate the Auxiliary Guidance Post at Dobri Dol. Instead of clarifying the situation and directing the fighter actions against the intruder, he lost time to inform and search for the commanders of the Air Defence and the MoPD.

15. The cause for the accident with the intruder aircraft and the death of its passengers and crew was the result of the fire in its port inner engine and its rear section, as well as the separation of its fin and the disintegration of the aircraft mid-air as a consequence from the hits scored by the pair of fighters.

CONCLUSION

1. The responsibility for the accident with the intruder aircraft shall be borne by the crew of the aircraft, which has deviated from the route, violated the airspace of the People's Republic of Bulgaria and signalled to obey to the fighters (instructions) in a delayed manner.

2. The officials of both the VNOS Service and the VVS, with the exception of the responsible duty officer in the 4th IAD CP, Major Khristo Stoyanov IVANOV and the officers of the Auxiliary Guidance Post at Dobri Dol, have acted in a correct manner, in accordance with the current instructions and there is no reason to claim them liable, however:

a) The fighter pilots, finding out that the aircraft was a transport model, not showing any armed resistance, should do their utmost by the means of warning attacks with warning fire, to force it to land on our territory and, as a last resort, to open destructive fire.

b) The responsible duty officers in the Central CP of the Air Defence and the 4th IAD CP should have undertaken everything possible to restore the radio communication with the fighters.

Thus, on 31 July the MoPD's Commission for Investigation submitted the first overall conclusions about the cause and the consequences that led to the downing of the Israeli passenger aircraft in the Petrich area. But that had not ended the story. The conclusions and the cause were to be then confirmed by the Government Commission and the pilots were still under threat at that time of being submitted to Court Martial. And if for them and their colleagues this was a permanent threat in case of a failure to deal with the numerous violations of various aircraft entering from neighbouring countries in recent years to carry out reconnaissance or delivery of operatives and agitation leaflets, this time the pancake had been reversed. A foreign passenger aircraft was shot down and this had created a serious diplomatic problem at the inter-state level with Israel, the United Kingdom and the United States. Traditionally, a scape goat had to be found and everyone along the chain that had triggered the actions of the country's air defence system was at risk.

On 4 August 1955, a meeting of the MoPD leadership and Air Defence representatives for the country and the VVS was held. It discussed the report of the Minister of People's Defence, Armeyski General Panchevsky, named *On the State of the Country's Air Defence* in connection with the incident of the shooting down of the Israeli passenger aircraft by air defence fighters. The report was to be approved and submitted to the Political Bureau of the Communist Party's Central Committee.

The first part of the report was presented by General Leitenant Zakhary Zakhariev while the second one, more critical of the Air Defence and the Air Force, was presented by Armeyski General Peter Panchevsky.

After reading the report, a discussion began and it had been recorded. It would be of great interest from today's point of view, because it was crucial for the attitude of the senior military command of the Bulgarian People's Army to the pilots and the fault of the individual participants in the tragic sequence of events.

Following the BTA's second communiqué on the shooting down of the Israeli passenger aircraft, published in Bulgaria and around the world on 3 August, the MoPD was ready with the detailed report of the Minister, Armeyski General Peter Panchevsky. The report contained information about the state of the Air Defence and the Air Force, as well as on the specific causes and all the known facts about the downing of the Israeli passenger aircraft. The document was first filed under No. 001064 on 4 August, when it was reported to the MoPD Council. Some of the highlights of the report will be provided below. According to the authors, the detailed reading of the documents allows the understanding of the fine nuances of the complex foreign and domestic political environment in the Cold War and the explanation and understanding of the complex mechanisms that eventually led to the death of 58 Israeli passengers and crew of El Al Flight LY402.

The MoPD Report

In his detailed report of 4 August, the Minister of People's Defence mentioned that in 1955 alone, the Air Defence Troops (VPVO) branch's numerical strength increased by 2,500, reaching 13,500 servicemen, without including the fighter aviation which is in the VVS structure. The fighter divisions at that time were equipped with the modern MiG-15bis aircraft and some of the pilots were already converting to the even more modern MiG-17. The AAA units began to be equipped with the modern 57mm and 100mm guns in addition to 360° search radars, guidance radars and anti-aircraft fire control systems for the guns.

Both the PVO and the VVS fighter aviation branch, according to the report, were equipped with a large number of radars, enabling the enemy aircraft to be detected on the territory of the neighbouring countries, well before their entry into Bulgarian airspace. At that time, the command posts of two 4th and 10th Fighter Divisions were combined with the command posts of the VNOS regiments (the visual observation posts for air surveillance, alerting and communication duties) in Plovdiv and Sofia. The Minister also reported on the newly introduced position of Deputy Commander of the Air Defence — Fighter Aviation, which was required to centralise the employment of the aviation in the event of airspace violations. The AAA was set to be consolidated into AAA brigades and divisions. The staffing of the Air Defence and Air Force services with officers was also noted — the figure was of over 90%.

The first part of the report concluded that sound foundations had been laid for the establishment of a modern air defence system in the country, and there were the necessary minimum conditions already provided for the successful countering of the persistent airspace violations.

In the second part of the report, there were seven critical points reviewed, typical at that time. Some common weaknesses were highlighted, affecting the combat readiness state, in particular: 'The VVS Commander-in-Chief is not sufficiently and persistently working on training fighter pilots for day and night operations in bad weather.' In the report, the Minister of People's Defence blamed Polkovnik Ivan Demirev, 4th IAD CO, that despite his order, Demirev was not residing in the garrison — and this had hindered his timely arrival at the CP of the division in Dobroslavtsi. Separately, the practices in the control of fighter jets involved in intercepts of intruder aircraft were insufficient. Generally, Armeyski General Panchevsky saw the reason for commanding the Air Defence and the Air Force as a lack of rigor for his subordinates:

As a result, the combat capability of the personnel when facing the enemy in the air is still weak. At the same time, it should be noted that when serious exercises are conducted with the troops, when discipline is increased, in a relatively complex environment, PVO commanders and staffs are working satisfactorily...

Conversely, during actual violations, when the situation is relatively simple, our enemy caught us unprepared and performed his mission, returning back with impunity. In an airspace violation on 8 September 1954, due to the improved combat readiness and the good work of commanders and command posts, the enemy was detected in time, intercepted and took hits, after which it did not show up in our airspace for more than 6 months.

The above referred to the reportedly successful night intercept of Capitan Ilya Elenski, who was able to detect and open fire against an intruder aircraft at night.

In his report, Panchevsky also pointed out as a weakness that, due to the lack of training, radar operators could track only three targets at a time. On the side of the report, General Zakhariev placed his hand-written note that the capabilities of the radars, in fact, do not allow more than 3-4 targets to be tracked at a time, and these were large aircraft only. He also wrote:

As a rule, pilots do not provide information on their position in the air and do not maintain a strong connection with their CP. Most of the pilots and the crews of the visual observation posts do not know the silhouettes of foreign aircraft, which is their main duty. For example, in the most recent violation, almost all the visual observation posts had reported that the offending aircraft was a Li-2 type.

This part of the report ended with the conclusion that the political work in the air defence units was not sufficiently targeted, whatever that means. Confirming his criticisms of the air defence command and the VVS, and also indirectly against his deputy, General Leitenant Zakhariev (a former VVS Commander-in-Chief), Panchevsky highlighted what happened on 27 July 1955. Then the final version of the sequence of events in the skies above Petrich followed, including the well-known facts about tracking and reconstructing the path of the intruder aircraft from its entry into Bulgarian airspace over the village of Miloslavtsi, Tran area, to the encounter with the QRA fighter pair. Analysing all the data, Panchevsky made four conclusions regarding the flight of the Israeli Constellation passenger aircraft. Conclusion 2 states:

Based on the fact that the air route and the aircraft are equipped with modern radio navigation aids, providing reliable air navigation in all weather conditions, and also that at the time of the border violation the weather conditions were good for visual orientation, there is no reason for the aircraft's deviation at nearly 130km to the left (to the east) from the route and violating our air border.

3. The crew of the intruder aircraft has been completely irresponsible in controlling the flight along the route, neglecting the fact that the route runs parallel to the border of a foreign country and that the deviation will lead to a violation of that country's airspace.

4. The Air Defence Forces of the country, without any request for the flight of a foreign aircraft at our state border, correctly assumed that the incoming aircraft was an intruder aircraft.

Regarding the actions of the 4th IAD CP at Dobroslavtsi airfield, the launch of the radio relay aircraft was judged by the Minister of People's Defence as a delayed action:

In this case, the relay aircraft has been used in a tactically illiterate manner, and instead of directing it to the south, he (Capitan Petkanov) dispatched it to the northeast, at 4,000m altitude instead of 7,000m. As a result of this tactical mistake, the aircraft launched in the air to relay commands had reportedly failed to perform its function and the fighters were left without control.

CONCLUSION: The 4th IAD CP actually did not control the actions of the fighter pair dispatched to intercept the intruder.

Regarding the fighter pilots, Capitan Petrov and Leitenant Sankiiysky, the report mentioned:

Upon detecting the target (the intruder), Capitan Petrov properly decided to close with the intruder aircraft. The instruction obliges the fighter pilot as follows: "upon detection of the intruder aircraft, the fighter aircraft are obliged to find its nationality by its silhouette and insignia."

Petrov failed to do this. He reported to the commander after the mission that the intruder was unmarked and told the Government Commission that he did not see the insignia, explaining that the instruction allowed him to attack the intruder within 40km of the border without warning.

According to my instructions and a letter from General Leitenant Zakhariev dated 9 July, 1955 the pilots are not allowed to open fire against Yugoslavian aircraft anywhere inside our territory.

The intruder aircraft was coming from Yugoslavian territory, so Capitan Petrov was not allowed to fire on the aircraft, although it had been in the 40-kilometre border zone. In both cases, Capitan Petrov had to establish the nationality of the intruder aircraft — but he had failed in doing this.

Capitan Petrov reported that with the evolution of his aircraft and with fire, he had warned the intruder aircraft that it is flying over foreign territory and instructed to follow him.

The interviewed residents of the villages of Simitli and Krupnik, where the warning was being issued at the time, could not validate Petrov's statement regarding the wing-rocking warning signals because the aircraft were at high altitude (about 4,000meters). They said that a small aircraft was spotted circling around the big one, and they also saw smoke from the small aircraft, and later on heard the sound of firing. The analysis of the photos taken by the gun camera showed that the first salvo was fired by Capitan Petrov in front of the aircraft, which can be considered a warning signal.

The analysis of the first photo from the gun camera of second aircraft, half a minute later, shows that the fire was opened against the aircraft, i.e. targeted to score hits in it.

CONCLUSION:
1. The fighter pilots generally have acted in accordance with the "Instruction for the actions of fighters against aircraft violating the air border and airspace of People's Republic of Bulgaria", but with serious deviations and violations of the instructions and directives regarding Yugoslavian aircraft that require the intruder to be identified before firing against it, and in the second case, not firing at all.

2. The fighter pilots have acted in a hasty manner. Daytime and good visibility conditions would have enabled the fighters to fulfil a common command request, namely: "If possible, the offender

should be taken alive." The reason for such an instruction is the command authorities' willingness to find out what kind of equipment is installed on the aircraft which for several years violated our airspace, always escaping intact. The pilots, involved in the pursuit, could have, in this particular setting, taken a few more minutes in order to take the intruder alive.

3. The pursuing pilots have failed to comply with the instructions for maintaining contact with the senior commander. Capitan Petrov told the Government Commission: "I didn't try to keep in touch as I didn't have time to tune in to the radio."

The investigation showed that the 4th IAD HQ performed in an incompetent manner, and in the case of 27 July 1955, also in an irresponsible manner, the schedule for the duty officers in the 4th IAD CP. Thus, Major Ivanov on the schedule was appointed on 26-27 July as the responsible duty officer in the CP and was simultaneously appointed as the chief of the air traffic control of the 18th IAP in the morning of 27 July. This gross mistake was also missed by the division CO, Polkovnik Demirev.

Polkovnik Demirev, 4th IAD CO, has reportedly failed to fight hard to improve the flight crew qualification, to promote a strictly established order in his assigned division, thanks to which many mistakes were made in the intercept and shooting down of the Israeli aircraft ...

In the sub-point of the report named "Actions of the CCP-PVO and the VNOS Service", it is said:

The responsible operations officer at the CCP-PVO, Major Karchev, correctly assessed the situation as having a violation of our airspace. He has properly commanded AAA and the QRA fighters to go into a higher combat readiness/alert state. As for the fighters on QRA duty at Dobroslavtsi airfield, the closest one to the target, the command should have been they to launch, and not being placed into a higher alert state.

In the latter case, perhaps the fighter's encounter with the target would have taken place earlier and within the effective radio range, so the fighters would have been controlled (from the ground) and hence the results could have been different.

After issuing the initial commands, Major Karchev, instead of focusing his attention on gathering target information and plotting the position of the fighters, and analysing the information received from the VNOS service, necessary for conducting the operation, he had spent too much time for searching and reporting to different commanders. Major Karchev did not take any measures to restore the communication with the fighters, nor did he assist the 4th IAD CP in this regard.

VNOS Service

a. The visual observation posts provided regular information, but it was very controversial and implausible in terms of identifying the type of aircraft. Most of the information supplied by the visual posts referred to the intruder aircraft as a Li-2 and C-47. And only one post – No 140 (Vrabcha village, Tran area), reported that the aircraft type is the C-69, at least as originally recorded by the KP VNOS recorder, Private Iliev. I personally asked Private Iliev and he reported that he had not heard the information and instead of the number 13-11 – code-number for an unspecified aircraft, he recorded 13-14, the

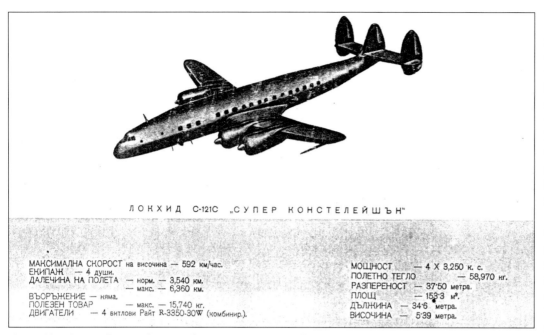

ЛОКХИД С-121С „СУПЕР КОНСТЕЛЕЙШЪН"

МАКСИМАЛНА СКОРОСТ на височина — 592 км/час.
ЕКИПАЖ — 4 души.
ДАЛЕЧИНА НА ПОЛЕТА — норм. — 3,540 км.
— макс. — 6,360 км.
ВЪОРЪЖЕНИЕ — няма.
ПОЛЕЗЕН ТОВАР — макс. — 15,740 кг.
ДВИГАТЕЛИ — 4 витлови Райт R-3350-30W (комбинир.).

МОЩНОСТ — 4 X 3,250 к. с.
ПОЛЕТНО ТЕГЛО — 58,970 кг.
РАЗПЕРЕНОСТ — 37·50 метра.
ПЛОЩ — 153·3 м².
ДЪЛЖИНА — 34·6 метра.
ВИСОЧИНА — 5·39 метра.

The Lockheed Constellation reference information, comprising of a basic picture and data, provided to the Bulgarian pilots on the QRA duty, intended to be used for the quick identification of aircraft intruding in the country's airspace. The aircraft depicted here, in fact, is the C-121C Super Constellation military transport version.

ДЪГЛАС С—47 „СКАЙТРЕН"

ОСНОВНИ ДАННИ

Максимална скорост на височина 2600 метра
370 км/час.
Далечина на полета (нормално) — 2400 км
Практически таван — 3,700 метра.
Разпереност — 28·9 метра
Дължина — 19·6 метра
Нормален товар 2700 кг или 28 души

The Douglas C-47 Skytrain reference information used at the time by the Bulgarian QRA pilots and the ground-based visual observation posts.

code-number for the C-69. As it was badly heard, he asked for the second time the visual post No 140 and he confirmed the number 13-11, after which Private Iliev corrected the number

14 to 11 and thus passed on the information to the operators (obviously these data should be verified by the investigation).

b. The radar sites tasked with detecting and tracking the intruder aircraft have done a satisfactory job but these have failed to monitor and provide accurate positional information in regard to our fighters.

The work of the Air Defence Command: the command and staff of the Air Defence did not organise well the information and call of the command officers. As a result, almost all the responsible commanders from the Air Defence Headquarters showed up at the MCP-VNOS from 07:34 to 07:50. Due to the above mistakes and disorganization, the Air Defence Command reportedly failed to actually direct the air defence operations on 27 July 1955.

The leadership of the Ministry of People's Defence is well aware that the downing of the Israeli aircraft has enabled the reactionary forces in the world to blaspheme our nation and government, and even the Soviet Union's Government, which now has no greater interest but to reduce tensions and promoting peace in the world.

The conclusion is clear that the accident was undesirable and, at the moment, harmful. On the other hand, the leadership of the Ministry of People's Defence is aware that hard work is needed to enhance the combat ability combat readiness of the Air Defence, to further improve the ideological and political education of the entire personnel of our People's Army and, above all, of the Air Defence and the Air Force.

I would like propose that the following officials should be held responsible for the downed passenger aircraft:

[here are two blank points where the Government must decide who to punish, probably in the Ministry of People's Defence – author's note].

3. The Air Defence Commander-in-Chief, General Major Georgiev, for failing to arrange the reliable notification of the officers in the Air Defence Command and HQ during the combat alert, as a result of which, on 27 July 1955, the Air Defence Command proved unable to manage the operation of the air defence assets.

- Because he had neglected to study and know the existing instructions and laws, he did not study them, he did not require his subordinates to know them and to apply them properly in their practical activity.

Given that he is a relatively young Air Defence Commander-in-Chief and he does not have the necessary special preparation for this position — he shall be punished with the rights and authority of the Minister of People's Defence.

4. The Air Force Commander-in-Chief, General Major Kirilov, for his weak leadership in the work of the staffs of the air divisions in the air and on the ground:

- For the insufficiently persistent fight against accidents in the Air Force.
- For the low discipline among some of the Air Force responsible commanders and pilots — he shall be punished by the Government.

5. The 4th IAD CO, Polkovnik Demirev, for his weak personal discipline, low demand on himself and his subordinates, for not fighting against accidents, anarchy and crashes in the division.

- That, despite his assistance from the Air Force Command, the repeated comments made to him by the leadership of the Ministry of People's Defence and the MoPD's Council, he had failed to take steps for improving the control of aviation units in the air and on the ground.
- For not being able to organise in a proper manner the work in the division's CP, and for being absent from the unit without permission on 27 July, as a result of which the airborne fighters were left uncontrolled — he shall be removed from his position and dismissed from the military service.

6. Major Ivanov, for leaving his post as a responsible duty officer in the CP, for his failure to immediately respond to a green flare signal to arrive at the CP and his failure to take over the operation after launching the fighters.

- Because, even after arriving at the CP, he failed to actively engage in the control of the fighters, he failed to direct the relay aircraft to the south in order to restore communication with the fighters — he shall be removed from his position and used with decrease of his rank.

7. Fighter pilots, Capitan Petrov and Leitenant Sankiisky, are deemed to be the ones directly responsible for the downing of the Israeli aircraft — in their actions they have made almost no attempt to identify the aircraft as being a passenger one. They did not properly issue the warning, and after the warning shots (fired by Petrov at 30m in front of the aircraft) they did not give the time and chance for the intruder aircraft to take any action to fulfil their order, but started their attacks against it, which continued until its explosion. The fatal hit was delivered in the last moment, when the aircraft lacked the necessary altitude to overfly Belasitsa, and obviously had to land. The instruction prohibits fighters from pursuing the intruder within a 15-kilometer zone from the border. Here, too, they had violated the instruction. They have not tried to communicate with the CCP, reporting what they see and how they act.

For their actions, Capitan Petrov and Leitenant Sankiisky should be brought to Court Martial and prosecuted, but given that they are good pilots, they have not had any serious violations so far and that their mistakes were the result of a number of omissions by the Air Force and the Air Defence, and that in their actions, which developed very quickly, they were driven by patriotic motives, I hereby would like to ask that the Politbureau of the Central Committee of the Bulgarian Communist Party not to prosecute Captain Petrov and Leitenant Sankiiysky, who were disciplined.

8. Disciplinary penalties should be imposed by the Minister of People's Defence onto the other officials of the Air Defence and the Air Force who have committed mistakes and violations in the case of the downing of the Israeli passenger aircraft.

Questions remaining

From today's point of view, several serious questions still remain unanswered and continue to be of interest to researchers over the years. The first is why the Israeli aircraft, having an experienced crew and flying in relatively predictable weather conditions, had deviated so far from its pre-planned route and eventually entered deep into the Bulgarian airspace? The second is related to the possibility of the Bulgarian pilots to identify the Israeli passenger aircraft as such, enter into contact with its crew and not come to opening fire?

In theory, even today, the visual identification of the Israeli passenger aircraft should be fast and easy. It was painted in white on top, with a blue line running the entire length of the fuselage, wearing an Israeli flag on the fins in addition to a five-pointed star and an "El Al" inscription on the fuselage. What Western researchers and their Israeli counterparts may not know is that in those years, the People's Republic of Bulgaria placed itself in a deep self-isolation, following the Soviet model of development.

Fighter pilots were young, with only a few years of active service and with little idea of how civil aviation worked. At the time, the TABSO civilian airline in Bulgaria maintained only a few international routes, from Sofia to the capitals of socialist countries such as Prague and Berlin. Only the Soviet air carrier Aeroflot provided a regular service from Moscow to Sofia. At the same time, there were only a handful of handbooks in the VVS for the identification of aircraft silhouettes and containing aircraft data for the 'capitalist countries'. Most likely, what the QRA pilots at Dobroslavtsi used at the time was a 1952 edition of the handbook, containing brief technical information, a photo and a silhouette in three views. In fact, the Bulgarian fighter pilots had a very basic idea of only a few types of aircraft of the likely enemy, as well as the civilian designations of the aircraft of the neighbouring countries and the big countries in Western Europe and America, which were expected to be the enemies in the event of an armed conflict.

In these handbooks, the C-121C Super Constellation was portrayed as a US-made military transport aircraft, and the Israeli identification markings and insignia — both civilian and military — were missing. At that time, no one had expected an encounter between Bulgarian military aircraft in their own aerospace with aircraft of the newly established state of Israel. This tends to explain to some extent why ground-based visual observation posts had also failed to identify the passenger aircraft as the Lockheed Constellation.

On the other hand, only ten years had passed since the end of the Second World War, and the memory of the US air raids and bombing of Sofia and other Bulgarian cities was still alive. The 4th IAD CO in Dobroslavtsi himself, Polkovnik Ivan Demirev, was one of the few remaining pilots who took part in the fighting against the USAAF B-17 and B-24 bombers in their raids on Sofia in 1944. A former non-commissioned officer in the wartime years and an experienced fighter pilot, he managed to survive the brutal purges of royal officers and airmen. Among pilots, the stories of four-engine Flying Fortresses bombing Sofia in massed raids during the Second World War had almost mythical dimensions. Poor knowledge of the current Western aircraft types — likely enemies — made every average pilot describe almost every large-size four-engine transport aircraft as an enemy bomber. A small improvement was only achieved with publishing in 1955 of the *Directory of Aircraft Weapons in Capitalist Countries*. The large-size album contained the same scanty information acquired from the publicly available aviation directories in the West in just a few lines.

One of the members of the MoPD commission, Polkovnik Vidyo Penev, before his death, told Evgeni Andonov, one of the authors of this book, the following:

And they committed a mistake that it was a 'Flying Fortress' (a four engine bomber), because the Constellation had a dark line running on the entire fuselage length over the window line, which made the windows not clearly visible, so it was not appearing to be a passenger aircraft cabin. And the pilots decided it was a Flying Fortress.

Radio communication with the Israeli aircraft cannot be considered at all at the time. None of the pilot[s] had studied English, while the aircraft radio transmitters had very limited technical capabilities, with four frequency channels only. It should be remembered that during the attack, Petrov and Sankiiyski had no communication even with their own command post at Dobroslavtsi.

Stoil Stoilov, a colleague and close friend of Kosta Sankiisky in the 1960s recalled:

The pilots were posted to Gabrovnitsa for a long time after the accident, until things cleared up. Then Sankiisky left the Air Force and came to work with me in the Agricultural Aviation branch, flying the Antonov An-2 biplane used for crop dusting. And then he told me what happened that day. When 'Bore' Petrov attacked the intruder, he unleashed a warning burst to the side and then pulled up, climbing sharply while in a turn. And Sankiisky told me: "I thought they were shooting at him (with defensive machineguns), scoring hits and setting his aircraft ablaze." So, Sankiisky opened fire directly at the intruder and shot it down. And he told me this when we were flying the An-2 as a crew. He said: "I thought that 'Bore' Petrov was gunned down, and

that that the intruder was a combat aircraft, armed with defensive machineguns. But it was misleading — in fact, when Petrov sharply pulled up at the maximum power rating after his first attack pass on the Constellation with warning shots, flames and smoke came out from the jet nozzle of his aircraft. And so Sankiisky had mistakenly taken this as being combat damage incurred by defensive fire and immediately began unleashing shells at the intruder to riddle it.

Today, when there are declassified photos from the gun cameras of both fighters, it could be seen that only 30 seconds lapsed between the warning shots given by Boris Petrov and Kosta Sankyiisky opening fire. Here, of course, the question still remains as to how accurately the clocks of the gun camera were synchronised to show the same time. The memories recalled by veteran pilots were now evidenced by the gun camera photos at the time but may largely explain why the experienced pilot Boris Petrov had no time to identify the intercepted aircraft from the side while Sankiisky was providing cover from behind. Now the gun camera photos also show that Sankiisky was the main shooter in the attacks on the Constellation.

The Smuggling Trail

It took months and as Bulgarian diplomats scratched their heads on how to get out of the diplomatic crisis, suddenly another trace had emerged from the Kozhukh area, which may shed some light on what was described as a strange behaviour of the Israeli aircraft crew. In his memoirs written in the 1970s, General Zakhary Zakhariev had provided an interesting detail:

On the other hand, the facts confirm the great insistence of the Israeli crew to go to the Yugoslavian and Greek territories. In addition to the two attempts for right-hand turns in an effort to cross back into Yugoslavian territory, the crew had hoped to pass over the Belasitsa mountain to enter Greek territory until the very last moment. Even when under fire, the aircraft continued to fly into [a] southern direction. This was confirmed by Yugoslavian and Greek eyewitnesses. Only when the crew became convinced that they would not be able to cross Belasitsa, they began turning to the left and started looking for a spot for an emergency landing. It was only right after the first warning that the aircraft would follow

Remains of the tail fin of the Constellation, photographed on the western slope of Kozhukh hill and attached to the report of the Israeli Commission of Enquiry.

our fighters, which would bring it to Sofia Airport, and this way the incident would only end with an apology on their part. The actions of the Israeli crew clearly speak of the desire to prevent our country [from] forcing the aircraft to land or by removing it from the facts to confirm the violation. This can only be done in case of intentional misconduct with a clear purpose for intelligence, smuggling or other unknown motives.

One of the reasons for the crew's great reluctance to land at our airport was revealed thanks to the local gypsy population in the accident area. After the removal of all the debris from the destroyed aircraft, they began to collect moles of molten tin, scattered on the ground, for tinning of household utensils. To their surprise, the tin they found did not want to tinplate vessels. This surprised them, and they resorted to the advice of goldsmiths to determine the metal. Specialists immediately determined that it was not tin, but pure silver. This necessitated another investigation, which showed that the crew transported around four hundred kilograms of silver hidden in the engine nacelles. I believe further comments would be superfluous.

The book *Flight 4X-AKC* published in 2003 by Dragoljub Gadzhev and the former acting head of the Israeli Legation in Sofia (Charge d'Affaires), Nansen-Nir Baruch, also contains information on the documented presence of silver onboard the Israeli aircraft. After some time had passed, through the Ministry of People's Defence channels, Minister Peter Panchevsky was informed about the newly-discovered facts. He immediately reported to Deputy Prime Minister, Armeyski General Ivan Mikhailov:

I hereby report that after all the debris of the crashed plane were collected, the local population, mostly gypsies, swarming around the ground, found a large amount of silver grains scattered on the surface and in [the] Struma river.

Collectors initially thought it was remnants of molten tin alloy, but after unsuccessful attempts to tinplate vessels with this metal, a study was conducted and found the metal to be pure silver with a sample of 800-900 carats in the form of grains-commercial stock.

A thorough study found that the silver was only found in the place where the engine nacelles hit the ground and was scattered in the direction of the separated engines, with a large amount falling into the riverbed of the Struma river.

By the end of August, [the] Narmag-Petrich commercial organisation (purchasing scrap metals) had purchased about 90kg (198lb) of silver, mostly from gypsies. They claimed that a large amount of silver, no less than 70-80kg (154-176lb), was also collected from ethnic Bulgarians but they had not offered it to Narmag until that moment.

The fact that the silver was found in the area where the engines hit the ground suggests that the silver was smuggled into the engine nacelles and some other places in the forward part of the aircraft, where only the crew had access to.

It follows from the foregoing that the smuggling of silver and other certain values by the crew of the aircraft had a direct bearing on the conduct of the aircraft in its attempt to escape when intercepted by the Bulgarian fighters, exposing the passengers and the aircraft at an excessively high risk.

The presence of contraband silver was completely ignored by the Israeli side and also seen by them as an attempt by the Bulgarian authorities to steer the tracks in the wrong direction; therefore, it was completely ignored. Nor was it ever mentioned in the numerous Israeli publications dedicated to what happened in the sky over Petrich on 27 July 1955.

Taking Action

Shortly after the downing of the Israeli aircraft, it was decided that Polkovnik Ivan Demirev should be removed from his position as the 4th IAD CO and eventually fired from the military service. The responsible operative officer on duty that day in the 4th IAD CP, Major Khristo Ivanov was disciplined with a garrison arrest sanction. From the higher command levels, only General Major Velichko Georgiev suffered — in connection with the ongoing unification of the Air Defence and the Air Force and the establishment of a common command post, he was removed from the position of Air Defence Commander-in-Chief. To a large extent, he personally took the responsibility for the incident by admitting that he had ordered the pilots to open fire. Everyone, both in the Political Bureau of the Central Committee of the Communist Party and the Council of Ministers, headed by the Prime Minister Valko Chervenkov, knew that the order given by General Major Georgiev had nothing to do with the direct actions of the QRA pilots in the air, but someone had to be proclaimed guilty.

It was decided at the highest government level that fighter pilots Boris Petrov and Kosta Sankiiysky would not be punished. All those involved in the scrambling of the QRA pair and fulfilling their responsibilities were rewarded with small prizes and rewards.

Fighter pilot Elenko Nedyalkov from the 18th IAP recalled these times:

Then the instruction changed. We had the QRA fighters with guns turned off so we couldn't open fire in the air when scrambled. The cannons were loaded with ammunition, but the hoses (for the supply of pressurised air needed for the reloading) of the QRA fighters were disconnected and I was not able to reload the guns in the air. It was a temporary measure for two to three months. After the Israeli aircraft had been shot down, the intruders began to avoid entering into Bulgarian airspace. They saw that it was a guarded territory here.

In practice, the measures were extended over time. Hoses were connected, but the instruction was made so restricting that without an explicit order no one was allowed to open fire. The psychological burden and refusal to accept responsibility remained in place until the 1980s. This feature had become known in the West and in some cases was used. On the other hand, the gradual strengthening of the air defence and air forces of the Warsaw Pact countries made the missions of Western reconnaissance aircraft even more difficult and dangerous.

In 1956-1957, along with RAF British Electric Canberra high-altitude reconnaissance aircraft, the USA began reconnaissance missions over Eastern Europe with the Lockheed U-2 flying at an altitude otherwise unreachable for the air defence fighters. But this was all about to become clear only in 1960. Until then, unsuccessfully, the air arms of all Eastern Bloc countries tried to counter another wave of intruders in their airspace. And if when encountering the high-altitude air balloons they had some success, the U-2 problem was not resolved before the deployment of surface-to-air missile systems.

The Bulgarian fighter pilots continued to encounter intruders in their own airspace, albeit less frequently until the end of the 1950s.

On 11 September 1956, for instance, an unidentified aircraft entered from the north direction at 21:11. It was a four-engine transport that entered Bulgarian airspace near the village of Bregovo on the border with Yugoslavia in the north-western part of the country. It flew in a north-easterly direction to the city of Vidin, then proceeded into Romanian territory to the city of Krayova before re-entering Bulgarian airspace near the city of Nikopol. It flew in a southerly direction, passing over Plovdiv and crossing the border with Greece north of the city of Gymurdjina (now Alexandropulis).

A MiG-17PF fighter from Graf Ignatievo was scrambled to intercept the intruder. Capitan Ilya Elenski, an experienced pilot from the 1/19 IAE of the 19th IAP, was in the cockpit. The guidance during the intercept was undertaken using information supplied by a radar site in the Gabrovnitsa airfield area. The Bulgarian pilot detected the intruder and reported: "I see the target, request clearance

Capitan Boris Petrov, seen here in the early 1960s as the CO of the 3/18 IAE at Dobroslavtsi, providing instructions to his pilots before flying operations from a grass-covered forward airfield in the western part of Bulgaria. It is most likely Kondofrei near the city of Radomir, not far away from the border with Yugoslavia.

to fire!" From the ground General Zakhary Zakhariev personally prohibited opening fire on the intruder. The pilot was instructed to give only warning shots in order to force the intruder aircraft to land at Graf Ignatievo. The warning shots, however, did not particularly affect the intruder. For a fighter pilot who had a direct encounter with an enemy aircraft intruder in the past and had possibly shot it down, accomplishing this mission was a matter of personal honour. However, the intruder aircraft continued flying, escorted, over the Plovdiv-Asenovgrad area, with numerous series of shells passing next to it. From the ground, the command authorities never cleared Elenski to open fire against the target. In the event, the intruder left Bulgarian airspace intact and continued its flight over Greece.

Tsvetan Tsekov, a fighter pilot from 18th IAP in Dobroslavtsi, recalled another intercept with the same disappointing results:

In 1955 we shot down the Israeli aircraft. There was an instruction issued soon after, stating that we could shoot at our aircraft if they went somewhere to escape, but could not shoot at foreign aircraft. Well, no secrets, they knew that.

On 6 June 1957 I flew a training sortie in pair with Zvezdomir Todorov — it was an air navigation mission on the Sofia-Velingrad-Karlovo-Sofia route. We flew MiG-15s, with the leader and the wingman required to change their position mid-sortie. Todorov flew a MiG-15bis while I flew a regular MiG-15. At one time, my call sign was called by Peter Domuschiev, the combat control officer on the ground. "For you heading ... altitude ...", these were the commands issued by the regimental CP, which redirected us for intercepting an intruder. These commands were issued at the second minute after the intrusion of a foreign aircraft — it was a Greek military transport. And a few minutes after its entry from Yugoslavia, then Yugoslavia was broken up country, we performed the intercept. "You shall force it to land in Sofia", we got a new command. We started some attacks, firing warning shots in order to scare the crew. The transport, however, went down, descending to low altitude to fly over the Struma valley in southerly direction, with the crew apparently well aware that we do not want to shoot down it.

While the intruder flew at a low altitude over the Struma valley, however, I realised that the border was not drawn in red like on the map. All mountains around us and we continued the pursuit. Zvezdomir Todorov flew a MiG-15bis and ran out of fuel earlier than me. Its aircraft had enough fuel left to return home so he turned back. I was still hanging around for some two or three more minutes. Worst of all you can't measure this time when airborne. Then, when I landed back home, the command authorities told me that I had entered together with the intruder aircraft into Greece. 20 seconds after I broke from the Greek transport, two fighters came into the area. They would shoot me down for being an intruder of the Greek airspace.

The Fate of Flight LY402's Executioners

At that time Boris Petrov continued to fly with the 18th IAP as a flight leader. Despite the pilots knowing all of the details of the downing of the Israeli aircraft, they had never tended to comment on the event openly. The case affected much more severely the young Kosta Sankiiysky. Lalyu Varbanov, a prominent Bulgarian fighter pilot, shared about his fate: 'Sankiisky was transferred to Gabrovnitsa after this case, to continue the service with the 11th IAP so he should not be in the regiment in Dobroslavtsi.'

The emotional soul of Kosta Sankiiysky proved unable to cope with the post-shoot-down psychological stress. From that time he began the heavy drinking of alcohol. So, he was moved first to the 11th IAP in Gabrovnitsa and then to the 19th IAP in Graf Ignatievo. In the event, he was banned from flying due to the drinking problem and shortly afterwards left the military service for good. A young pilot with a family, Sankiisky stayed unemployed for a while. His former colleagues, however, soon lent a hand, but managed to appoint him only as a loader at Sofia Airport. From here, yesterday's promising fighter pilot watched his pilot colleagues in the civil aviation and dreamed of flying again. He got a chance in 1960, given to him by the famous former military aviation commander Assen Dragnev, at the time appointed as the head of the TABSO Special-Purpose Aviation branch. Dragnev employed in his enterprise dozens of military pilots made redundant from service during the large-scale VVS downsizing under the Geneva Accords in 1955, or those simply fired for disagreeing with their commanders.

Thus, Sankiiysky was employed as a pilot in the Bulgarian Agricultural Aviation branch and flew an An-2 biplane used for crop dusting. However, the trauma of the downing of the Israeli passenger aircraft continued to haunt him over the years. In the late 1960s, he moved to the Transport Aviation branch of the Bulgarian Civil Aviation and converted to the An-24 turboprop-powered passenger aircraft, and later on continued service as the co-pilot of a four-engine An-12 cargo aircraft. He remained well-respected and valued by his colleagues. Many sympathised with him, realising that, although alive, he was also among the victims of what happened on 27 July 1955. Over the years, the problem of alcohol and mental trauma deepened. In 1972, he suffered a heart attack at his home and fell into a glass door. Cruelly cut, Sankiisky died of a blood loss. Such was his destiny!

The QRA technician Iliya Penchev, who did pre-flight of the MiG-15s that day recalled:

Both pilots continued flying after the accident. Sankiisky, however, began indiscriminate drinking and he was banned from flying for a while. Then they moved him somewhere in the command posts. Later on, he moved to the Agricultural Aviation because he was a violent head. Once he got drunk, wobbled and died... This thing — shooting down a passenger aircraft — cannot be forgotten and weighs on the conscience. Boris Petrov was one or two years older than me and reached the position of a squadron commander in Dobroslavtsi. They didn't talk about the case anymore and we didn't even want to remember it. And all Bulgaria knew that the Israeli aircraft was shot down by pilots from Dobroslavtsi.

Boris Petrov continued flying as a fighter pilot and ended his military career in 1965 as a CO of the 3/18 IAE of the 18th IAP at Dobroslavtsi airfield, equipped with the MiG-17F. He stopped flying due to a serious kidney disease. Like many pilots, after retiring from flying military aircraft, he found employment in the Bulgarian Civil Aviation. At the Special-Purpose Aviation branch he was appointed an aerodynamics teacher with the Agricultural Aviation branch training centre. Aerodynamics was his professional fate for decades. He retired in 1982 and passed away in Sofia in 1989. VVS veterans still remember his words decades after what happened near Petrich: 'If they scramble me today, I will shoot it down again.' Until his death, he remained convinced that on 27 July 1955 he was acting properly as the leader of the QRA pair.

On 27 July 1955, at 07:00, Kosta Sankiiysky began his first QRA duty shift, while at 07:15 he was scrambled to intercept an intruder aircraft and at 07:30 he opened fire to destroy the aircraft caught in his sight.

Today it would be easy to look at the incident from a modern perspective, but it should not be forgotten that for the servicemen of the Bulgarian Air Force in the 1950s the great Cold War was a daily, hot and dangerous routine.

The end of the story is that Bulgaria issued an apology for the shoot down of Flight LY402 and eventually paid compensation for the loss of life of the crew and the passengers. This payment was sent eight years after the tragedy, in 1963, to the families of 22 Israeli citizens on board. They got the maximum amount allowed by the Warsaw Convention, accounting for US $8,236 per passenger. In fact, Israel had applied to World Court to make a resolution of the issue of compensation, but the court ruled that it did not have jurisdiction over the case.

7

MiG-17 ERA BEGINS

The 19th IAP, the leading VVS air defence unit, home-based at Graf Ignatievo in the central part of the country, got a significant boost in its all-weather capacity in 1955, with the introduction of 12 MiG-17PF radar-equipped fighters-interceptors with afterburning engines, equipping the 1/19 IAE. These were followed by 32 more MiG-17Fs without radar, taken by 1/18 IAE of the 18th IAP at Dobroslavtsi, the 1/11 IAE of the 11th IAP at Gabrovnitsa and the 1/27 IAE at Balchik between 1957 and 1959. Later on, the MiG-17F deliveries continued, with 30 more examples taken on strength in 1960, allowing the type to be also introduced into service with the other VVS fighter regiments — such as the 15th IAP and the 22nd IAP, and more squadrons with the 18th, 11th and 27th IAPs. In 1961, 138 more MiG-17 sourced second-hand, powered by non-afterburning VK-1 engines, were taken on strength to equip the newly-reorganised fighter-bomber regiments — the 22nd and the 25th IBAPs, in addition to the 2nd UBAP and later on the 21st IAP.

The MiG-17 (NATO reporting name 'Fresco') had the distinction of being the most successful and widely-used first-generation Soviet-built jet fighter. Developed on the base of the proven MiG-15, it retained the general layout and armament of its predecessor but introduced some minor aerodynamic performance improvements and also had a better equipment standard.

Compared to the MiG-15bis, the MiG-17 featured a longer fuselage mated to new, thinner wings with a 45° sweptback angle with increased area featuring three aerodynamic fences on the upper surface on each panel (while the original MiG-15bis had only two fences); it also had increased-area air brakes. The MiG-17 retained the MiG-15's armament unaltered — one NR-37 with 40 rounds and two NR-23 cannons, each with 100 rounds, aimed by using the ASP-3N sight.

The MiG-17F, which flew for the first time in September 1951, was the second 'Fresco' variant produced in numbers, powered by the VK-1F afterburning turbojet. This new derivative of the VK-1A boasted a 25 per cent increase in thrust compared to that of the VK-1A, while at military power it was rated at 2.548kN (5,730lb st. or 2,600kgf). The afterburning engine provided the MiG-17F with a much-improved performance, especially in terms of level speed, acceleration and rate of climb. At 3,000m (9,848ft) altitude its maximum level speed hit 1,145km/h (618kt), while the rate of climb was 75.8m/s (14,917fpm). The maximum Mach number was lifted up to 0.994 at 11,000m (36,000ft) altitude and the practical ceiling reached 16,6000m (54,448ft).

The MiG-17PF was the most advanced 'Fresco' derivative, fitted with the RP-1 radar set, capable of tracking targets at up to 4km (2.1nm) to be engaged with guns in tail-on attack without direct visibility (i.e. at night and in bad weather). Integrated with the ASP-3NM gun-sight, the two-antenna radar set had a search antenna installed in the upper part of the intake lip and a tracking antenna in the centre-body. During the intercept, when the distance between

The MiG-17F was a further-refined MiG-15 derivative with better speed performance and controllability characteristics, which was used to equip about half of the VVS fighter squadrons between 1955 and 1960, with the Bulgarian air arm taking on strength a mixture of Soviet- and Polish-built examples. The Polish-built MiG-17F, shown here, can be easily recognised by the black antenna of the SRD-1M radar range-finder in front of the windshield.

A Soviet-made MiG-17 in flight. As many as 138 second-hand fighters, powered by non-afterburning VK-1 engines, were delivered to the Bulgarian air arm in 1961.

the fighter and target reduced to below 2km (1.1nm), the tracking antenna switched on automatically, enabling accurate sighting. In clear-weather conditions the pilot used the ASP-3NM gun-sight only.

Maximum radar detection range against a four-engine bomber was up to 9.5km (5.1nm), while small twin-engine bombers could be detected from 7.5km (4nm). The RP-1, however, was ill-suited for the interception of targets flying below 3,000m (9,900ft) due to ground clutter, and the minimum altitude of the fighter during intercepts was limited to 2,500m (8,200ft). This derivative was armed with three NR-23 cannons, each provided with 100 rounds. It was also equipped with the Sirena-2 radar-warning receiver (RWR) and the NI-50B navigation indicator.

A MiG-17F during a detailed technical inspection with its armament platform, containing the two 23mm and a single 37mm gun, seen here in a lowered position.

At the time it entered service in Bulgaria, the MiG-17PF had much better performance than the MiG-15 and MiG-15bis thanks to its afterburning engine and better aerodynamics, translating into a faster rate of climb and a higher practical ceiling.

The conversion training of the first group of Bulgarian pilots was carried out in Savastleika in the Soviet Union, where the Soviet IA PVO's dedicated combat training and aircrew conversion unit, the 148th TsBPiPLS was located. The group from the 19th IAP, commanded by Capitan Todor

The MiG-17 was an easy to maintain and fly aircraft, and it continued to serve in significant numbers with the VVS fighter branch until the second half of the 1970s, with the last three fighter squadrons phasing out the type in 1982-1983, while in the fighter-bomber branch the faithful type remained in use until the second half of the 1980s.

Trifonov, and consisting of eight pilots and four ground-controlled intercept (GCI) officers, arrived in Savastleika in January 1955 to practice bad weather intercepts with GCI guidance flying the MiG-17PF until June that year. The conversion course concluded with two to three intercepts in clouds and flown at night.

The first batch of half a dozen brand-new MiG-17PFs was delivered to Graf Ignatievo in the spring of 1955 to equip the 1/19 IAE, replacing the MiG-15. Six MiG-17PFs were delivered in April and assembled in May, followed by six more in November 1955. After a short period of refresher training, the first two pilots who completed the conversion course at Savastleika — Capitan Trifonov and Starshi Leitenant Krivchev — were placed on the QRA duty, with the remaining six

joining in September. The second group of eight pilots sent for MiG-17PF conversion training when to Savastleika in July 1956 and they returned home in June 1956. By December 1956, the 1/19 IAE had a fleet of 12 aircraft and 17 pilots trained for bad weather operations at night. The squadron was declared ready for large-formation counter-air operations at up to 12,000m (39,360ft) altitude.

Then the MiG-17F began gradually entering service with some of the fighter regiments between 1957 and 1959, with each of the 11th, 18th, 22nd and 27th IAPs receiving aircraft for equipping one squadron. The first batch of 12 Soviet-built MiG-17Fs was delivered to Bulgaria in February 1957, followed by 20 more examples built in Poland in March 1959 while 30 more were taken in February and

Between January and September 1956, Capitan Todor Trifonov from the 19th IAP, flying the radar-equipped MiG-17PF, managed to gun down as many as four US reconnaissance balloons. Three more were downed by other pilots from the same fighter regiment, home-based at Graf Ignatievo airfield near Plovdiv. The 12 MiG-17PFs, taken on strength in 1955, remained in active service in the all-weather fighter interceptor role until the early 1980s.

The Polish-made MiG-17Fs were the backbone of the VVS fighter-fleet in the second half of the 1950s and proved hard to fully replace with the more modern MiG-19S, outliving its supersonic successor in the front-line by five to six years.

in 1950 by the United States Strategic Air Command (SAC) and other agencies, with the first balloon launches to overfly the Eastern Bloc countries made in 1956. The official cover for this large-scale and rather expensive reconnaissance effort was that it was a meteorological and scientific undertaking. The chief objective of the effort was to gather much-needed photographic reconnaissance of the Soviet Union and its allies by employing high-flying balloons fitted with high-resolution photo cameras. The original plan called for launching up to 2,500 balloons fitted with camera gondolas, cruising at stratospheric heights to cross Soviet airspace thanks to the winter jet stream, and in this way carrying out autonomous reconnaissance missions. It would be possible to cover most of Eastern Europe and the Soviet Union's territory in these low-risk and unmanned missions, otherwise unreachable for manned reconnaissance aircraft. After exiting Soviet territory, the gondolas with the camera equipment would separate from the balloons by radio command and while descending on parachute they would be recovered mid-air or lifted from the water surface. This job was to be undertaken by specially-equipped C-119L cargo aircraft of the US Air Force, belonging to the 456th Troop Carrier Wing, operating out of bases in Alaska, the Philippine Islands, Midway and Japan.

The first wave of the operational phase of Genertix saw nine spy balloons being launched on missions on 10 January 1956 – eight from Adana in Turkey and one from Giebelstadt in West Germany. Initially, it was decided to make multiple balloon launches each day in order to saturate the Soviet air defences, but later on the launch rate was restricted to ten per day in a bid to see how things would unfold. During the next few days, balloons were launched from the other sites — on 11 January the site at Oberpfaffenhohen in West Germany was used and the next day launches were made from NAS Evanton in Scotland, while 12 January saw the first use of the site at Gardermoen in Norway. The first balloons, which crossed the airspace of the East European countries and the Soviet Union, were recovered on 13 January. Then the daily launches increased to between 10 and 20.

The Bulgarian air defence system encountered the first Genertix

March 1960. The total number of 62 MiG-17Fs proved to be just enough for equipping five 12-aircraft squadrons, and from December 1961 the fighter squadrons also began receiving non-afterburner MiG-17s, 138 of which were delivered second hand from the Soviet Union.

Meanwhile, the MiG-17PFs, superseded in service with the 1/19 IAE by the radar-equipped MiG-19P, were transferred to the 1/11 IAE at Gabrovnitsa in 1958, and the following year went to the 1/27 IAE at Balchik.

Countering the SAC Spy Balloons

In fact, the MiG-17PF gained much combat fame in Bulgaria pitted against another enemy reconnaissance system, used en masse in the mid-1950s. Operation Genetrix was a secret programme initiated

These MiG-17Fs, undergoing pre-flight maintenance, belong to the fleet of the 27th IAP based at Balchik airfield on the Black Sea coast.

These MiG-17Fs are seen lined up at Dobroslavtsi, where the type served on with the 18th IAP between 1957 and 1983.

balloons on 14 January. Capitan Todor Trifoinov was the leader of QRA pair that that day at Graf Ignatievo and he recalled:

During a QRA alert duty on 14 January 1956, I was ordered to get to the so-called Readiness State No 1, sitting strapped in the cockpit and ready to launch upon receiving a further command. I was told that there is an unidentified balloon floating in the air in northern Bulgaria, between the cities of Rouse and Varna, near Shoumen. The balloon made three passes in the same area. Four fighters were scrambled from Balchik, where the 27th IAP was based, but all of them failed to climb to the target's altitude. I asked insistently for launch permission, because my MiG-17PF had a practical ceiling 1,500m (4,920ft) higher than that of the MiG-15 but the 10th IAD CP was reluctant to issue a scramble order. They simply thought that this was a weather balloon and it [was] not worth the effort to intercept it and waste precious jet fuel and engine service life.

The next reconnaissance balloon of Operation Genertix was detected two days later, on 16 January, when Capitan Trifonov was again on the QRA duty. He recalled:

I got the scramble order at around 11:00. Having been placed in Readiness No 1, the duty officer in the CP informed me that there is a balloon in [the] Stryama area, near General Nikolaevo village,

which is not far away from Graf Ignatievo, floating at 4,500m (14,760ft) altitude. I was ordered to launch but at that time the balloon suddenly began climbing. Guided by the GCI officer, Starshi Leitenant Dinyo Radkov, I performed the intercept of the target situated at around 40km (22nm) east of Graf Ignatievo, floating at 15,000m (49,200ft) altitude. During the first attack pass I decided to fire at the target with two of the three 23mm guns, keeping the third one in reserve. When at 15,700 to 15,800m (51,500 to 51,800ft) altitude, I entered in a shallow dive and put the central mark of the ASP-3NM sight in the centre of the pear-shaped balloon. I decided not to enter the base size (the target wingspan) into the computing sight since I had no idea about its real dimensions. The tracer shells of the first short burst passed below the target. Taking into consideration the fast closing speed, I unleashed the second burst. It also passed below the target but much closer to it compared to the first bust. I began thinking to ram the target with the wing should my third burst fail to nail it. Luckily, the shells of the third burst hit the target and it disappeared, leaving only a small cloud. I sharply pulled on the stick and pushed it to the left. After ten seconds I stopped the climb out and transited into a steady descent while turning to the left. Now it was the time to report to the CP: "121st, target destroyed at 14,800m (48,544ft)".

The GCI officer, however, told Capitan Trifinov, that the target was

69

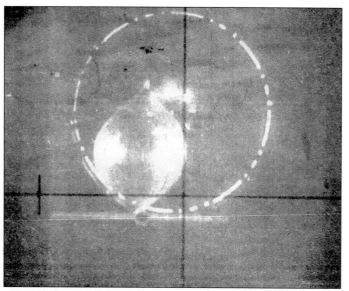

A CIA-launched reconnaissance balloon, targeted by the MiG-17PF flown by Capitan Todor Trifonov, 1/19 IAE CO, on 23 September 1956.

Capitan Todor Trifonov was the most successful balloon-downing pilot in the VVS, with four victories under his belt, all scored in 1956.

still visible on the radar screen, to the disappointment of the excited pilot. In the event, after landing, Capitan Trifonov was told by the 10th IAD CO, Polkovnik Zhelyazko Zhelyazkov, that that balloon had really been downed and its remains found on the ground. The investigation of these revealed that the payload included high-tech spy camera equipment housed in a big pod. It was also easy to explain the fact that the balloon continued to be visible on the radar screen long after it had been shot down. The pod, slowly descending on a parachute, represented a big target, reflecting radar energy for a while, misleading the GCI officer that the balloon was still there and intact after the attacks mounted by Capitan Trifonov.

According to Capitan Trifonov, he was told at the time by General Major Kiril Kirilov, the VVS Commander-in-Chief, that it was, in fact, the first US-made spy balloon shot down in the Eastern Bloc airspace. To destroy it in his first mission, flown on 16 January 1956, Capitan Trifinov expended only 39 23mm rounds.

Capitan Elenko Nedyalkov, a flight leader from the 18th IAP at

Dobroslavtsi near Sofia, was also scrambled in a MiG-15bis to intercept a spy balloon, detected over the city of Slivnitsa to the west of Sofia and not far away from the border with Yugoslavia. He, however, was not able to inflict damage in two attacks and the balloon continued on its free-floating mission in the easterly direction. He recalled the unsuccessful mission:

I climbed over 10,000m and discovered the target, a big balloon, which was still much higher than me. I continued the climb, while looking at the balloon all the time. At 12,500m I tried to get into a good attack position, but when closing to the target it increased its altitude. I passed below it and had another look at it. At this moment my altitude reached 13,000m, the speed decayed to 350km/h (indicated air speed), while by rate of climb was zero. I was convinced that my MiG-15bis with underwing drop tanks cannot climb out any more. I reported to the CP, asking for a permission to jettison the drop tanks (in an effort to get an improved climb capability) but the ground control banned this. So I did another attempt to get into attack position — this time I entered into a shallow dive with the engine at the maximum power setting to accelerate to the maximum possible speed and then entered a climb. As a result, I climbed out to 13,000m altitude, with distance to the target of 600m, firing a burst but the projectiles passed under the balloon. I had hard feelings after the failure to gun it down but what could I do? The balloon floated with the wind, slowly following in the easterly direction. I landed hoping that another of our pilots will gun it down with an aircraft specially prepared for this purpose.

After this sortie the bitter experience was taken into account and the QRA flight at Dobroslavtsi also included one MiG-15 without drop tanks (for better climb performance), ready to be used against high-altitude balloons.

The next counter-balloon mission, flown by Capitan Trifonov, occurred on 31 January, during the preparation for a day/night flying training operation. After the alarm bell rang to signal the scrambling of the pilots from the 1/19 IAE, Capitan Trifinov was the first to climb into the cockpit of his radar-equipped jet and immediately got a take-off clearance.

His MiG-17PF was directed against the balloon floating at 13,000m (42,640ft) altitude north of Pazardzhiik and to the west from the airfield, at a distance of about 30km (17nm). He climbed out and initiated the first attack run from altitude 2,500m (8,200ft) higher than that of the target. This time, having experience from the previous successful engagement, the pilot was not in a hurry so he waited to get to an effective firing distance. He pressed the trigger only when the balloon entered in full into the ASP-3NM's ring. The first burst of projectiles unleashed hit the target which immediately exploded, leaving a small smoke cloud. Capitan Trifonov recalled:

So, I detected the balloon and climbed out to 15,500m. It was noticeably below me. The combat control officers gave me distance of 20km. I waited to 15 to 20 seconds and began aiming. This time I had the experience needed, and was in a rush to open fire. The balloon entered into my sight's targeting ring in full, with the centre mesh point placed into its centre. I pressed the trigger and the projectiles hit the balloon. I saw only a small white cloud and reported that the target is destroyed. Then I heard that Capitan Angelov is entering into attack and mentally wished him god luck. The time for his attack expired, but no report of success. It's time to enter into [the] clouds and began the recover to the airfield.

After exiting from the successful attack, the happy pilot took a course back to Graf Ignatievo, entering the clouds at 9,000m (29,520ft) but then a new command was issued by the CP, which ordered Trifonov to retract the undercarriage and turn into the south-easterly direction. Another balloon was detected south of Plovdiv and it was the second target engaged by Capitan Trifonov in the same sortie — in fact, it was the same target engaged without success by Capitan Angelov minutes ago. This time he climbed out to 15,200m (49,860ft) and shot down the next balloon in the first attack pass, mounted with the sun on his back.

The same day another two pilots from the 1/19 IAE scored victories. Capitan Georgy Antov downed a balloon in his second attack pass, while Capitan Milcho Stoyanov had scored his victory but not before the third attack pass. Another pilot, Capitan Stoyan Angelov, had no luck at all, expending all his ammunition of 300 23mm rounds without managing to bring the engaged target down. In addition to his double victory, Capitan Trifonov made a weighty contribution to Capitan Georgi Antov's success, as he provided his aircraft to Antov, whose aircraft had a burst tire when taking off in from the previous sortie.

Capitan Milcho Stoyanov was directed to engage a balloon north of Sofia and he recalled the sortie for the *Bulgarska Armya* (Bulgarian Army) newspaper in 1966:

The group of the four 19th IAP pilots who scored a total of seven US-made balloons shot down in Bulgarian airspace — from left to right: Major Sava Netsov, Capitan Todor Trifonov, Capitan Milcho Stoyanov and Capitan Anto Georgiev.

Todor Trifonov, shown here as a Retired General Major in the mid-1990s together with his family. His son, Orlin Trifonov, was a VVS pilot too, serving between 1992 and 2008. He graduated from a staff academy in the UK and flying the MiG-21 participated in many NATO exercises in Bulgaria and abroad.

After taking-off I was ordered to climb out to the maximum altitude, and follow with a 290° heading. I reloaded two of the three cannons, with the third one being held in reserve. I noticed the target – a sunlit sphere, high above me. I closed, according to me, into a good distance for the attack and opened fire. I noticed however, that the projectiles dropped far before the target. I closed further and unleashed a burst again, but no hits. The distance was still too big. Meanwhile I performed another attack manoeuvre and decided that in case of missed shots I will hit the balloon with the port wing. I did not want to leave it drifting away with impunity. In the event, the third attack was successful, with the balloon bursting and collapsing. What was hanging as a beam began falling to the ground and in the next moment a parachute dome appeared, then

second and third. The equipment fell on the ground somewhere northwest of the city of Pazardzhik. Meanwhile, my airfield began to be covered by fog, so I had to recover as soon as possible.

On 1 February, the 19th IAP CO, Major Sava Netsov, was scrambled to intercept another balloon detected in the vicinity of Sofia. He fired from a point-bank range, scoring good hits and after the balloon explosion his aircraft passed through the big red ball of hot gases, with the pilot barely avoiding entering into a spin. This was the sixth balloon downed by the Bulgarian fighter force.

Capitan Trifonov had no luck, however, in another difficult mission to intercept balloons in January 1956 and experienced serious difficulties during his recovery to an alternate airfield. That day Graf Ignatievo airfield was covered with thick clouds and saw a heavy snowfall, with horizontal visibility of only 300m (984 ft). The 3rd IAD CO, Polkovnik Zhelyazko Zhelyazkov, told Capitan Trifinov that

A mission pod from the CIA balloon shot down by Capitan Todor Trifonov on 16 January 1956, containing high-tech photographic equipment.

a reconnaissance balloon had been detected in Bulgarian airspace, but the prevailing bad weather was precluding landing at any airfield except for Gabrovnitsa in the north-western part of the country. Zhelyazkov told Trifonov that he could not order a launch so the scramble would be at Trifinov's own discretion and risk in these very bad weather conditions.

Capitan Trifinov eventually decided to launch for the mission, taking-off towards the airfield's non-directional beacon in order to keep the right heading in instrument flying conditions. While airborne, he got a sudden order to abort the mission, because the GCI officer lost the target. He got instructions to fly towards to Gabrovnitsa, but the radar guidance to reach the airfield was not accurate. The pilot had difficulties in flying the approach and also experienced a problem with the MiG-17PF's nose undercarriage leg, but eventually landed safely.

The most difficult sortie in Capitan Trifinov's career followed on 23 September 1956. On this day, the 1/19 IAE CO was a responsible duty officer in the 19th IAP's CP. In the afternoon he got a command to quit the CP duty and scramble for intercepting a balloon floating in the central northern part of Bulgaria, next to the city of Oryakhovo. Trifonov was ordered to take-off without wing drop tanks, leaving his jet with 40 per cent less fuel for the otherwise long-range combat sortie.

Capitan Trifinov recalled that he had no difficulties in visually detecting the target flying at about 14,500m (47,560ft) altitude, and at a distance of 30 to 40km (16.3 to 21.6nm) noticed that it had a strange shape, with pointed rear and upper ends, about 45m (148ft) tall and 35m (115ft) wide. This time he used the MiG-17PF's RP-1 radar for aiming, commencing the attack run from 15,500m (50,840ft) altitude. His first burst of 23mm rounds was unleashed from a 500m (1,600ft) distance. The projectiles hit the balloon in the middle, but without any effect. He got into attack position for a second run, from an altitude

500m (1,600ft) higher than that of the target, unleashing another long burst from a longer distance, in order to fire more rounds, scoring good hits, but without any effect once again. Then he went on into the third attack, this time performing a tight turn and firing the guns in a slight climb from a point-blank distance, aiming in the balloon's lower end. Before the attack he noticed that the emergency fuel warning light in the cockpit was on, prompting the pilot that it was the time to recover. Furthermore, the aircraft stalled after firing the guns and Capitan Trifonov entered into a dive to 12,000m (39,360ft) altitude in an effort to regain speed before continuing in level flight.

He was not far away from the city of Pleven but the CP banned the emergency landing at the nearby Kamenets airfield and instead ordered him to recover to Graf Ignatievo. Capitan Trifonov entered into a shallow dive at minimum engine rpm to get home with the minimum fuel remaining. After landing with the last litres of fuel at the home airfield, he went on to report to the 19th IAP CO, Major Sava Netosv that the mission had been a failure. He did not know, however, that after his third attack the balloon eventually collapsed and its payload fell to the ground, right into a stadium in the city of Pleven, in the middle of a football game there.

According to Trifinov, this time his target was a multi-chamber balloon, resistant to combat damage, which proved a rather tough target, impossible to be shot down in a single attack pass. In fact, it was a balloon filled with helium, which, in contrast to the balloons filled with hydrogen and encountered in January that year, would not explode when hit by 23mm shells. By that time, however, Operation Genetrix had been terminated (its termination had already been ordered during February 1956), and most likely this particular balloon with a different design had been used in another CIA covert operation in the Eastern Bloc airspace.

Another Bulgarian fighter pilot, Capitan Dimitar Dimitrov – Dimitry from the 18th IAP at Dobroslavtsi, said that he was also successful in shooting down a balloon. When attacked, it was at about 15,000m (49,200ft) altitude, southwest of Sofia, well-visible from Dobroslavtsi. In that particular sortie (believed to date back to 1958 or 1959) Capitan Dimitorv flew a MiG-17F without wing drop tanks. In the first attack pass he fired only one of the guns from 500-600m (1,640 to 1,968ft), but without any effect. The next pass, from 14,000m (45,920ft) altitude, saw the use of all three guns from about 600m (1,968ft) distance, this time with success. The balloon exploded, while Capitan Dimitrov was sharply manoeuvring his MiG-17F to avoid collision with the balloon's remains. This sharp turn caused a spin at high altitude and the pilot recovered his aircraft at about 11,000m (36,080ft). The remains of the balloon and its mission equipment were found near the village of Pancharevo in proximity to the northern outskirts of Sofia.

The research of the authors showed, however, that there is no documentary confirmation of a balloon ever downed by then Capitan Dimitrov, which he had described in his memoire book. There is a different version of the story, recalled by General Major Todor Trifinov, who maintained that Dimitrov had been scrambled, but when in a ready to attack position, the balloon had already been shot down, with its mission equipment descending by parachute. The most likely cause of the shooting down of this particular balloon would be the fire unleashed by AAA batteries deployed around the Bulgarian capital.

The Yak-23 pilots also reported a balloon victory — this time carrying a case with propaganda literature dispatched from the other size of the Iron Curtain. The pilot, Starshi Leitenant Georgy Gradinarov from the 43rd IAP home-based at Dobroslavtsi, recalled that he was scrambled twice in 1956 to counter balloons. During the second scramble, in pair with Starshi Leitenant Yordan Andreev, his colleague unintentionally rammed a balloon with the wing of his Yak-23 and the damaged balloon fell to the ground.

There is unconfirmed information, unveiled by Polkovnik (retired) Ivan Petkov, who served at the time with the 11th IAP at Gabrovnitsa, that Major Dzhanko Dzhankov, Deputy CO of the regiment, had also downed a balloon in the second half of the 1950s, but no further details are known about this case.

New Organisational Changes

The first round of the Bulgarian air arm reorganisation began in June 1956 when the Air Force Department (VVS) and Air Defence Department (PVO) were merged and after 30 June 1956 formed a new structure. Known after the merge as the PVO i VVS Command (*Komandvane na VVS i PVO*), it was headed by the Deputy Minister of People's Defence, General Leitenant Zakhary Zakhariev.

The recapitalisation and downsizing of the fleet continued at a rapid pace and two years after the merge the last propeller-driven combat aircraft were retired, including the entire Il-2/Il-10 and Tu-2T fleets. In turn, the vast majority of the Bulgarian-made Laz-7 and Laz-7M training and light bomber aircraft were transferred to the pseudo-civil aeroclub organisation under the Bulgarian MoD's control.

The air defence component was reinforced with the introduction of the new Soviet-made P-20 long-range air surveillance radars, used for ground-controlled intercepts.

Todor Trifonov, now Podpolkovnik, seen here in the MiG-17F cockpit in the early 1960s.

Yak-23 pilot, Starshi Leitenant Yordan Andreev, serving with the 43rd IAP at Dobroslavtsi, is reported to have downed a balloon, mostly likely carrying agitation leaflets, by hitting it with the wing of its aircraft.

The next round of re-organisation of the Bulgarian air arm, undertaken in February 1961, saw the service's name changed once again, this time as the PVO and VVS Command (*Komandvane na PVO i VVS*), headed by the new Commander-in-Chief, General Leitenant Dobrin Dobrev. It had three main front-line units — the 1st and the 2nd Air Defence Corps (1st and 2nd cPVO) and the 10th Fighter-Bomber Aviation Division (10th IBAD). The directly-reported units included the 26th ORAE (Independent Aviation Reconnaissance Squadron), 16th TRAP (Transport Aviation Regiment), 1st OPLAE (Independent Anti-Submarine Squadron) and the Higher People's Air Force School.

This new organisational structure incorporated all Bulgarian military aviation assets, heavy-calibre anti-aircraft artillery, air surveillance radars and the newly-established Surface-to-Air Missile Troops, equipped at the time with the SA-75 Dvina (ASCC/NATO-codename 'SA-2 Guideline') high-altitude ground-based air defence system using surface-to-air missiles with radio-command guidance.

The 1st and 2nd cPVO were short-lived structures, disbanded during December 1961.

The abrupt downsizing of the fighter branch, undertaken between

The MiG-17F had the distinction of being the most successful and widely-used first-generation jet fighter in Bulgarian service, and also with a very good safety record.

1960 and 1963, saw no fewer than three fighter regiments having been disbanded, including the 43rd IAP at Dobroslavtsi, the 27th IAP at Balchik and the 11th IAP at Gabrovnista. The airfields at Gabrovnitsa and Balchik remained active and were used for permanent basing of single squadrons of other IAPs — 18th and 15th respectively.

In turn, the 22nd and the 25th IAPs, respectively, were reorganised as fighter-bomber aviation regiments, designated as the 22nd IBAP and the 25th IBAP. The 22nd IBAP remained based at Bezmer, while the 25th IBAP was moved from Graf Ignatievo to the newly constructed airfield at Cheshnigirovo (Sadovo) east of Plovdiv.

In September 1961, the 10th IBAD was re-structured as the 10th SAC (Composite Aviation Corps), which, in addition to the two fighter-bomber regiments (22nd and 25th IBAPs), also controlled one reconnaissance regiment, the 26th RAP, one transport regiment, the 16th TrAP, and one helicopter regiment, the 44th VAP.

The new fighter branch structure of the PVO i VVS after 1962 comprised two three-squadron regiments (15th and 18th IAPs) tasked with the country's air defence, directly reporting to the PVO i VVS HQ in Sofia, in addition to two more regiments (19th and 21st IAPs) within the 10th SAC structure, tasked with front-line missions in wartime, but in the peacetime these regiments also contributed to the country's air defence with QRA units.

There were several serious intrusions following the shoot down of Flight LY402, where the Bulgarian air defence system proved yet again unable to respond as required — in these cases when facing high-performance reconnaissance aircraft of a still unknown type.

On 2 July 1956, an unidentified jet aircraft violated Bulgarian airspace in daylight, reported as flying at between 12,000 and 14,000m (39,360 and 45,920ft). It entered the Bulgarian airspace from Romania, crossing the border near the city of Tolbukhin. Then it flew in a southerly direction over Balchik and Bourgas, turning into a westerly direction and passing over Plovdiv and Sofia before turning to the northerly direction to leave Bulgarian airspace near Oryakhovo at 10:34, re-entering Romanian airspace once. Two MiG-15s were scrambled against the high-flying intruder, but their pilots were not able to perform successful intercepts.

This was, in fact, Mission 2010 of the CIA-operated Lockheed U-2 spy aircraft, operating out of Wiesbaden in West Germany, which flew

In the early 1960s, the PVO I VVS service took on strength P-15 'Peperuda' mobile early warning radars, optimised for detection and tracking of low-level targets, with range of up to 60km (33nm) against targets flying at 500m (1,600ft) altitude.

over Poland, Czechoslovakia, Hungary, Romania and Bulgaria, at an altitude exceeding 17,000m (55,760ft). There is no information about the detection of another U-2, which flew Mission 2009 that same day, also crossing through the Bulgarian airspace, but in an anti-clockwise direction. It flew over Hungary, Yugoslavia, all the way across Bulgaria to the Black Sea then back to Wiesbaden.

Another deep violation into the Bulgarian airspace was reported on 10 December 1956. It involved two jets of unidentified nationality that at 13:16 crossed the border with Turkey south of the coastal city of Bourgas, flying at between 13,000 and 16,000m (42,640 and 52,480ft) altitude. Then the aircraft maintained a northerly and north-easterly

In 1960, the VVS took its first surface-to-air missile systems. The S-75 'Dvina' (ASCC/NATO reporting name SA-2 'Guideline') was the principal system fielded for defence against medium-to-high altitude air threats, and was deployed country-wide in the early and mid-1960s to replace the heavy-calibre AAA. This is one of the first public showings of surface-air-missiles at a military parade in Sofia in 1974.

A MiG-17F fighter seen undergoing pre-flight servicing at a grass-covered forward airfield, most likely at Sokolovo near Balchik.

The Il-28 twin-engine bomber, taken on strength in 1954, was used by the Bulgarian air arm as a long-range reconnaissance aircraft whilst also retaining the capability to be used in the bomber role.

direction, flying over Balchik and Rousse before splitting their routes. The first one turned into a southerly direction, flying over Sopot and Parazhdhik and entering into Greek territory south of Dospat. The second jet continued in the westerly direction and then also turned to a southerly direction, flying over Pleven, Sofia and Sandanski, and crossing the border with Greece near Petrich. No Bulgarian fighters were able to intercept the intruders, which flew at a speed of about 750km/h (405kt).

This was again an intrusion of CIA-operated U-2 – Mission 2029, launched from Incirlic in Turkey and the aircraft flew over Albania, Yugoslavia and Bulgaria, and back to Incirlik. That same day Mission 4018 saw another U-2 launched from Wiesbaden to fly over Albania, Bulgaria and Yugoslavia.

An unidentified jet fighter violated Bulgarian airspace on 29 September 1960, at 12:25, entering from Turkey and passing over the frontier city of Malko Tarnovo, then continuing to fly with a northerly heading until reaching a point over the sea 20km (11nm) southeast

of Bourgas and then exiting Bulgarian airspace at a point 20km southeast of the border village of Rezovo. Two MiG-17Fs from the 15th IAP at Ravnets were scrambled to intercept the intruder but they had reportedly failed to reach it.

The last known intentional and rather deep violation of Bulgarian airspace, apparently with reconnaissance or air defence probing purposes, was reported on 12 June 1961. The intruder entered from Greece at 04:06, crossing the border at 5,000m (16,400ft) altitude near Svilengrad and then proceeded in a north-westerly direction over Uzundzhovo and Kazanlak, turning to the west to overfly Karlovo before changing course once again to fly in the south-westerly direction, passing over Parardzhik and Razlog, re-entering Greek airspace at 04:43. Two MiG-17Fs from Balchik were scrambled to intercept the intruder, most likely a jet fighter travelling at about 550km/h (297kt), together with two MiG-19PMs from Graf Ignatievo, but the intercept efforts proved fruitless, most likely due to the late reaction of the air defence system.

8

LEITENANT SOLAKOV'S STRANGE ESCAPE TO ITALY

Leitenant Milush Solakov's daring escape to Italy with a jet fighter could be regarded as the last sharp event during the hot phase of the Cold War for the Bulgarian air arm between 1948 and 1962.

In the early autumn of 1961, the young graduate pilots from the People's Air Force School were divided into two groups and posted to fly MiG-17F fighters with the 11th IAP at Gabrovnitsa and the 27th IAP at Balchik. Among them was young Leitenant Milush Solakov. Together with 11 more colleagues he began a MiG-17F conversion course in October and was subsequently posted to service with the 2/11 IAE at Gabrovnitsa.

Solakov's friend, colleague, and classmate Kiril Radev shared how the service of the young pilot began at Gabrovnitsa with a disruption in his private life:

Solakov, in connection with his specific family status (he was an orphan), was allowed to travel to Plovdiv two or three times. It turned out that at these walks Solakov had met a girl in Plovdiv and

then she came to visit him in Gabrovnitsa. Over time, we learned from our classmates that Solakov had problems with that girl as she got pregnant and pressed him to marry.

Thus, the young pilot began to be pressured to marry his pregnant girlfriend. According to the traditions of the times, and in order to meet the norms of the so-called socialist morality, the 11th IAP Deputy CO, Political Affairs, Capitan Nedyalkov, began pressing the young pilot and even banned him from flying. This way in mid-January 1962, Solakov found himself in an unenviable situation. Yanko Prodanov, then Deputy CO of 2/11 IAE, recalled this moment:

As an acting CO of the 2/11 IAE, I banned Solakov from flying due to the issue with his allegedly pregnant girlfriend. In the event he went to [the] Political Affairs officer and told him that he will marry at last. The political officer, Nedyalkov, then came to the squadron room and asked me to schedule Solakov for the next flight shift as he had promised to marry. So, I scheduled him to fly a two-seater with the regiment's navigator officer, Kirilov.

On 20 January 1962, the young pilots at Gabrovnitsa flew MiG-15UTI two-seaters for refresher training. Leitenant Solakov did his refresher sortie in the two-seater and then the first solo flight after a prolonged interruption was to be made in a MiG-17F, wearing the serial 'Red 22'. As the flight was in the airfield landing circuit, no additional tanks were foreseen to be used; he also went on to fly without an oxygen mask. In this fateful sortie Solakov eventually decided to commit an escape from Bulgaria by turning into the westerly direction soon after take-off and crossing the border with Yugoslavia.

In the first minutes after the MiG-17F disappeared, the commanders and air traffic controllers at Gabrovnitsa airfield assumed that the young and inexperienced pilot had crashed, and an aircraft was immediately launched up to inspect the area. Then the Solakov's MiG-17F appeared on the radar briefly, but there was no time to organise a pursuit. Twenty minutes later, border posts provided information that an aircraft had just crossed the border. One of the best MiG-19 fighter pilots in the regiment, Major Metody Sandulov,

The busy flight line of the 11th IAP at Gabrovnista airfield in 1961.

Mulush Solakov seen here as a cadet in the People's Air Force School in 1960. He is to the right, while Kiril Radev is in the centre and Netso Likov is to the left. Radev retired as General Major and Likov as Polkovnik, after a long and productive service with the VVS. Both of them were COs of the 18th IAP at Dobroslavtsi, equipped with MiG-23 and MiG-21 fighter-interceptors.

proposed to launch and intercept the escapee, but he was forbidden to enter Yugoslavian airspace.

After crossing the border, the MiG-17F gradually climbed out to 12,000m (39,360ft) with a south-easterly heading. After crossing the territories of Yugoslavia and Albania, Solakov flew over the Adriatic Sea in complicated conditions at high altitude, with an iced canopy and lacking an oxygen mask.

At 13:30 the young pilot committed an emergency landing in the area of Acquaviva delle Fonti, near the Gioia del Colle military airfield in the area of Bari. With the engine flamed out due to fuel starvation, the MiG-17F glided and the pilot aimed to land on a small dirt road. Eventually, the aircraft touched down in a small olive grove and hit a stone wall. The pilot was discovered by a local villager — Solakov had a broken arm and head injuries caused by the aircraft's ASP-1N sight. The owner of the olive groove found the runaway Bulgarian pilot on the ground next to the aircraft and took him to the local hospital. The villager then notified Gioia del Colle of the emergency landing of a foreign aircraft. The Italian military and their US allies were caught by

surprise by the extraordinary event, as a warplane from a Warsaw Pact member country flew undisturbed and landed next to one of Italy's best-guarded military sites.

At the time, Solakov had not suspected that as he was seeking a suitable place to recover his unpowered jet, he inadvertently overflew the launch positions of PGM-19 Jupiter nuclear-tipped ballistic missiles, set up in the area of Acquaviva. In 1958, the US government decided to deploy ballistic missiles with nuclear warheads and to direct them against strategic military sites of the Warsaw Pact. Thor missiles were deployed in the UK while squadrons equipped with Jupiter missiles were planned for deployment in Italy and Turkey. In Italy, the area around Bari, and in particular Gioia del Colle airfield, had been chosen for stationing the nuclear-tipped US ballistic missiles. The airfield was the centre of a network of scattered launch sites, with about 60 per cent of the available missiles kept in constant combat readiness. There were two squadrons at Gioia del Colle, each equipped with 15 missiles, grouped by three in a total of ten sites. With an operational radius of 2,400km (1,296nm), Jupiter missiles launched

The MiG-17F 'Red 22', flown by Leitenant Solakov, seen here after its emergency landing in the olive grove near Acquaviva delle Fonti, just 1,800m (5,904ft) from the nearest site with Jupiter nuclear-tipped ballistic missiles.

After initially explaining the reasons for this rather strange flight, the Italian military and their NATO counterparts had to deal with the serious question of how the MiG-17F eventually managed to enter Italian airspace undisturbed and then overfly one of NATO's most secret military sites, without triggering the air defence system response.

Leitenant Solakov was more than lucky to avoid being intercepted on his route to Italy. He crossed the border between Bulgaria and Yugoslavia at a very low altitude. The outdated US-made radars were not able to detect and track his aircraft when he gradually climbed out to 12,000m (39,360ft) in Yugoslavian airspace. Then multiple MiG-15 fighters were scrambled in Albania in pursuit of the Bulgarian fighter, but the altitude and speed of the target rendered the intercepts impossible. At 13:30 the radars on the Italian coastline detected a formation of four to eight aircraft flying towards Italy at 40,000ft altitude. One of these separated from the formation and began descending, apparently in order to avoid radar tracking, and then overflew the missile site. On this course, Solakov made an emergency landing near Acquaviva delle Fonti, just 1,800m (5,904 ft) from the nearest missile site.

The MiG-17F flew the route from Gabrovnitsa to Bari, 605km (327nm) long, on only the fuel available in the internal tanks. According to the MiG-17F flight manual, the aircraft's maximum range is 1,080km (583nm) at an altitude of 12,000m (39,360ft), flying at 300 to 320km/h (162 to 173kt) speed. This, of course, could be valid for flying in ideal conditions only.

Many in Italy were wondering why the Bulgarian pilot did not land at the first airfield on his way to Bari. Nearby were also the air bases at Gioia del Colle and Brindisi but instead he elected to land in an olive grove. Some will say that he was intentionally searching for the missile bases and others that the aircraft made a crash landing. A possible explanation was provided by Nikolay Rinkov, a pilot from the 11th IAP and a friend of Solakov at the time:

from southern Italy were capable of reaching targets throughout the entire Balkan Peninsula and the Soviet Union's southern regions. Naturally, the interest of the socialist camp intelligence services in the launch sites of the US nuclear-tipped missiles was high and the area was heavily guarded.

In this situation on 20 January 1962 the unsuspecting Leitenant Solakov had the dubious luck to land his MiG-17F only a few kilometres away from the nearest missile site, having overflown it as he descended in the gliding MiG-17F with its engine inoperative. In the first hours of this extraordinary accident, no one in Italy wanted to believe that the Bulgarian runaway fighter had ended up next to a well-guarded missile site by accident. The young Bulgarian pilot had never realised that that he would be suspected of espionage in the coming hours and be portrayed as the Eastern Bloc equivalent of Francis Gary Powers (the US pilot of a U-2 reconnaissance aircraft, shot down on 1 May 1960 near the city of Sverdlovsk in the then Soviet Union).

At the highest level, the NATO system was activated to investigate the accident. The remains of the aircraft were transferred to Gioia del Colle to be cycled through detailed analysis. After the initial propaganda noise, it turned out that the only photo equipment on board was the gun camera, perfectly unfit for spy photos. However, many experts believed that the task of the young and unexperienced pilot was to probe the air defence system in this otherwise strategic area.

In his first interrogations, Solakov asked for political asylum in Italy. The Bulgarian Embassy staff in Rome was not allowed to attend. Meanwhile, the Bulgarian Military Attaché, Polkovnik Ivan Kanchev, stated the official Bulgarian position on the runaway pilot. According to him, the MiG-17F was used only for training flights as the Soviet Union already had much modern fighters such as the MiG-21 and was also developing the MiG-23. The Military Attaché simply explained that it was not necessary to send an aircraft from Bulgaria to photograph missiles sites in Italy, because Italian press was reporting on a daily basis about their location.

Later on, when Solakov returned to Bulgaria, he shared with me many details of his escape. I asked him how he managed to take off with a handful of fuel: "Well, like that. As I flew over Yugoslavia, I watched the contrails of the Yugoslavian fighter-interceptors [these were, in fact, the Albanian Air Force MiG-15s trying to take him down — author's note]. Reaching the sea, my engine flamed out and the aircraft began losing altitude. At one point, the canopy became covered by ice and nothing was visible outside. As the aircraft descended to lower altitude, the ice cover began disappearing. At one time I noticed that the coastline is approaching and began looking for a plain area and at one time saw a large green field below. It was an olive grove with low trees. I landed there and then I lost consciousness.

Later on, when they learned about this, the Bulgarian pilots tended to comment on the achievements of the young Bulgarian pilot in challenging the air defence systems of no fewer than four countries in a single daring mission. Vladimir Fesenko, a well-known pilot from the 18th IAP at Dobroslavtsi at the time, recalled:

We tended to joke then that Solakov had managed to challenge the Socialist air defence system (in Bulgaria), then the Revisionist one (in Yugoslavia), followed by the Dogmatic one (in Albania), and finally the Capitalist one (in Italy). And all of these air defence systems had failed to work as required. Finally, the Bulgarian pilot managed to overfly the largest American military base in Italy.

The Consequences

In Gabrovnitsa, Bulgarian pilots secretly listened to foreign radio stations on 20 January to learn the little-known details of their escaped colleague. On the very same day, a large number of military counterintelligence officers arrived at the airfield, together with officers from the Air Force HQ and various control bodies. A few days later, under the direction of the VVS Deputy CO, Political Affairs, a real auto-da-fe was committed. All officers who had any contact with the fugitive pilot had been put together, including his commanders in the People's Air Force School and the regimental COs of all fellow graduates. All of them were called to account for the unhealthy political environment, in an attempt, made by the Political Affairs authorities, to obscure the fact that the Deputy CO, Political Affairs of the 11th IAP, Major Nedyalkov, exercised a gross blackmail on the young pilot to marry his pregnant girlfriend by banning him from flying. Later on, it turned out that Solakov's girlfriend was not even pregnant, but she decided to force the young and promising pilot to marry her. However, the Political Affairs authorities declared them all guilty in a bid to justify themselves. This behaviour did not please the old and experienced instructor at the People's Air Force School, Polkovnik Semko Tsvetanov. Netso Likov, a colleague and co-graduate of Solakov, recalled his statement. Semko Tsvetanov, the School's Chief Inspector Pilot, then declared:

My job was to train these guys fly safely and reliably, and to be fighters. And it is a fact that this guy took off from Gabrovnitsa in a MiG-17 without additional tanks and landed in Italy. So, I accomplished my task. I trained him to fly while Polkovnik Benkin [the Deputy CO, Political Affairs of the People's Air Force School — author's note] in what Marxism threw him, and why he flew to the west instead to the east, he shall tell himself.

There was even a suggestion made at the highest command levels that all the pilots, who graduated in the 1961 pilot course together with Solakov, should be dismissed from the ranks of the military aviation as ideologically poisoned. In the event, the young pilots managed to convince the command authorities of their loyalty and the future proved that they were worthy defenders of the homeland. In the end, a number of commanders in Gabrovnitsa and Dolna Mitropolia were fired. Escaping in a jet fighter was an unprecedented act and the culprit and punishment had to be found in the military ranks. The 11th IAP CO, Major Georgi Bozhilov, was fired and replaced by Major Dimitar Medarski.

However, the 11th IAP was also set for disbandment not after long. On 27 June 1962, Capitan Rumen Nikolov was killed in a training sortie flying the MiG-19S in an unsuccessful ejection attempt. This was the drop that overflowed the glass and in an environment of massed cuts to the Bulgarian military, it was decided by the Ministry of People's Defence to close the 11th IAP and redistribute its personnel to other aviation units.

The Escapee's Fate

In Italy, initially, Bulgarian diplomats were denied access to the escapee. After several months of interrogations by the Italian authorities, it became clear that there were no political motives behind what had been committed by the Bulgarian pilot and it is almost certain that there was no intelligence task that had been conducted by him. On 15 June 1962, after a meeting with Solakov, Bulgarian diplomats reported:

Solakov began to talk about the reasons that led him to make this stupid decision. Without going into details, he said that his younger sister had gone the wrong way and he wanted to move to Plovdiv so that he could control her to preserve the honour of his family, but not only did his superiors not listen to him but did not accept him. Previously, he had no intention of escaping from Bulgaria. He decided not to flee to Greece or Turkey because he knew about the not so good relations between these two countries and Bulgaria.

Once again the Bulgarian diplomats promised the escapee that he would not be held responsible in the event that he would decide to return to Bulgaria. It was clear to Bulgarian officials that not allowing him to serve in Plovdiv and take care of his sister, as well as being blackmailed to marry, had been the chief reasons for his emotional collapse that eventually led to the decision to flee with his aircraft from Bulgaria.

On the other hand, Solakov himself renounced his claims for political asylum in Italy. Through Bulgarian diplomats in Rome, he was promised that he would not be tried for his desertion and to be forgiven if he behaved decently and did not slander Bulgaria. At this time the real reasons for the young lieutenant's adventurous act became clear at the highest levels in Bulgaria. His complex family status and the brutal pressure applied to him by the Political Affairs authorities in the 11th IAP were no secret to the military counter-intelligence service, and this eventually gave a less acute effect to the case. All this helped Solakov's escape be portrayed in accordance with the original Bulgarian version that the young and inexperienced pilot got lost — and he was so deceived that he flew across the Adriatic to Italy.

On 4 January 1963, almost a year after the dramatic flight to Italy, a court in Bari ruled that Solakov was innocent and removed all charges against him. On 17 January the prosecutor appealed the decision, but it remained final. Soon, all newspapers in Italy published photos of the happy and smiling Milush Solakov in front of his suitcases on his departure for Bulgaria.

And if, after a careful examination of the memories of the veterans of that time, the fate of the escapee could be restored, it still remains a mystery as to what happened to the remains of MiG-17F 'Red 22'. From the first day of contact between the Bulgarian Embassy in Rome and the Italian authorities, a demand had been raised for the return to Bulgaria of the ill-fated fighter. According to unconfirmed rumours among the pilots, the MiG-17F was eventually returned to Bulgaria, transported by ship. And due to the non-repairable damage inflicted during the emergency landing, and in an effort of leaving no trace of anything reminiscent of the recent escape flight of a Bulgarian aircraft abroad, it was eventually decided to dump the MiG-17F into the sea.

Upon his return to Bulgaria, Milush Solakov lived and worked in Plovdiv. He initially worked as a dispatcher in the local taxi department. In 1963, he was accepted to as a full-time student at the Faculty of Spanish Philology at Sofia University. He graduated with honours when his former colleagues heard again that he had committed a second attempt to illegally cross the border — this time on foot, bound for Yugoslavia. He was detained and sentenced to three years in prison. At the Sofia Central Prison, the double escapee was given the honorary position of librarian. From today's point of view, it seems strange that a person who was once acquitted of the death sentence got away with such a slight sentence after his second escape attempt.

Shortly after his release from prison, rumours circulated once again among pilots, soldiers and border guards that the tireless former pilot had committed the third escape attempt and was shot dead at the border line. The details were rather convincing at the time, among the border guards the case had been given as an example of successful action and even the number of the border outpost was quoted and exactly on which border mark the former pilot faced death, shot by the border guards. This legend was planted for years among all who had, in one way or another, contacts with Milush Solakov in the past. However, it proved that he was alive all the time, living and working in Canada for many years. In the 1970s and 1980s, his co-graduates, working at the Balkan Bulgarian Airlines, saw him at various airports around the world. Every time Solakov tended to tell them one thing: "I do not work against Bulgaria."

9
VVS IN THE SUPERSONIC ERA

The MiG-19 (NATO reporting name 'Farmer') firmly holds the title of the most controversial jet combat aircraft ever flown in Bulgaria and the twin-engine silver jet is still remembered with some heterogeneous emotions by those who flew and maintained it. It had never been used in anger by the Bulgarian air arm though the MiG-19-equipped squadrons maintained a constant high level of combat readiness during the Cold War era.

The type is known as the most important combat aircraft taken on strength in the second half of the 1950s and also had the distinction of launching the VVS into the supersonic club. A total of 84 aircraft in three different versions were taken on strength between 1957 and 1959, plus six more examples taken second-hand in 1966. The MiG-19 was seen by the Bulgarian military planners as a valuable air defence asset for reactive scrambles, able to climb rapidly to medium and high altitudes towards potential hostile intruders — either NATO tactical fighters or medium/strategic bombers carrying nuclear weapons.

At the same time, it was widely considered as hard-to-maintain, fastidious to fly and boasting pretty high — though often underused — combat capabilities in the air-to-air role. This could be especially true regarding the aircraft's low level climb and turning performance, which was much better than that of its predecessor the MiG-17; it

was even better is some aspects to the performance of its nominated successor, the MiG-21F-13 fielded in VVS service in 1963. All of these capabilities had rendered the MiG-19 the most important tactical fighter of the Bulgarian air arm in the late 1950s and early 1960s.

On the other side of the coin, the MiG-19, especially the most widely-used MiG-19S version optimised for VMC (visual meteorological conditions) operations, recorded an extraordinarily high attrition rate in peacetime training operations. And very few combat aircraft types in Bulgaria had ever received such differing appraisals — the MiG-19 is remembered by many in Bulgaria as a rather troubled type for both pilots and technicians, despite its impressive speed and manoeuvrability performance. It had remained consigned to the history books as just another jet fighter with a 20 year-ling lifespan, in most cases being used to complement but reportedly failing to fully replace the ubiquitous MiG-17F/PF in the air defence role. Many younger and inexperienced pilots paid for their handling mistakes with their lives.

In its general design, the MiG-19 resembled the earlier Mikoyan jet fighter line with main representatives being the MiG-15 and its improved derivative MiG-17. Their supersonic successor featured a longer fuselage and larger wing with a swept-back increased to 55° and

The MiG-19 offered a stable weapons platform with good manoeuvrability and in the hands of experienced pilots it might have been a formidable foe for any Western tactical fighter or bomber type of the 1950s and 1960s. This is an aircraft from the 21st IAP at Uzundzhovo, delivered in December 1957.

two large fences on the upper side. The MiG-19 was powered by a pair of RD-9B axial-flow turbojets installed side-by-side in the rear fuselage, each rated at 25.50kN (2,600kgf or 5,732lb st.) dry and 32.36kN (3,299kgf or 7,275lb st.) with afterburning. Indeed, the designers had been forced to use two engines installed side-by-side in the fuselage on the MiG-19 simply due to the unavailability of a suitable 63kN-class (6,422kgf or 14,000lb st.) turbojet in the Soviet Union in the mid-1950s.

The three powerful 30mm NR-30 cannons with a rate of fire of 900 rounds per minute each were provided with a total of 210 rounds. The NR-30 was considered as a highly effective weapon to be employed not only against aerial targets, but also for strafing soft and semi-hardened ground targets such as infantry fighting vehicles and light tanks. The trio of NR-30s provided between 3.7 and 4.9 seconds of non-stop firing. The NR-30, used in conjunction with the ASP-5N gunsight, had an effective range of fire of 2,000m (6,560ft) when employed above 8,000m (26,240ft).

The VVS took delivery of a total of 60 MiG-19S' built in mid and late 1957. The new fighters were initially delivered to Graf Ignatievo airfield, situated near the city of Plovdiv in central Bulgaria, in dismantled form by railroad in December 1957. There the crated 'Farmer-Cs' were quickly re-assembled by Soviet factory teams. The first MiG-19 flights by Bulgarian aircrews at Graf Ignatievo began in January 1958.

In the summer of 1957, four highly experienced pilots from the Graf Ignatievo-based 19th IAP (Iztrebitelen Aviopolk, fighter regiment) and a number of selected maintenance personnel underwent a short MiG-19 conversion-to-type course at the large Soviet Air Force training centre at Krasnodar in the southern part of Russia. The prominent VVS pilot Capitan Georgy Razsolkov from the 19th IAP was the first Bulgarian pilot to fly at supersonic speed.

The newly-delivered MiG-19S were initially used to equip five squadrons of two fighter regiments. Twenty-four aircraft were delivered to equip two of the three squadrons of the 19th IAP based at Graf Ignatievo — 2/19 IAE and 3/19 IAE — while 32 more went on to serve with the three squadrons of the Uzundzhovo-based 21st IAP. Another four aircraft were assigned to the HQ Flight of the 10th IAD, based at Graf Ignatievo, flown by a selected group of high-ranking

This MiG-19, originally delivered to the 21st IAP, is among the few that had a really good service record. Delivered in December 1957, it saw retirement in September 1977, logging 997 flight hours.

The radar-equipped MiG-19PMs, 12 new-built examples of which were delivered to Bulgaria in 1958, saw a brief service with the 19th IAP at Graf Ignatievo before being transferred to the 11th IAP in 1960 at Gabrovnitsa, while the survivors went on to serve in 1962 with the 18th IAP at Dobroslavtsi near Sofia. This particular aircraft was consumed by fire on the ground at Gabrovnitsa during engine checks in April 1962.

pilots with higher instructor qualification.

The aircrew conversion-to-type proved to be a major challenge, especially for pilots with little flying experience, due to a lack of a dedicated two-seat conversion and continuation trainer version of the MiG-19. The pilots, most of whom had logged no more than 300-400 hours on the MiG-15 and MiG-17, were required to undergo rigorous flight checks on the two-seat MiG-15UTI for checks of their handling abilities; then strict theoretical exams followed. The MiG-19S' cockpit was reported as being much more complex and crammed with instruments than that of the MiG-15 and MiG-17, and the difference required prolonged familiarisation during the ground-based training phase. Prominent Bulgarian pilot, General Major (Ret) Todor Trifonov, then Major serving as an inspector pilot with the staff of the 19th IAP, was among the first group of pilots to convert locally to the MiG-19S. He recalled the complexity of the process:

The MiG-19 conversion course was like to train one to drive a car and immediately afterwards putting him to drive a big truck that is rushing down busy city streets. However, such comparison would not be absolutely correct as the truck driver can stop his machine when and where he wants while the MiG-19's newly-converting pilots had only two valid choices on their disposal — either to land successfully or die!

The aircrew conversion phase at Graf Ignatievo was completed in a relatively short period, and without a single accident. In the spring and summer of 1958, the 19th IAP aircrews began practising formation flying and air combats, and soon afterwards they saw themselves standing on the QRA duty. Initially, gunnery practise was carried out against retired aircraft placed as targets on an improvised range located within airfield boundaries. Air-to-air gunnery against sleeve targets towed by MiG-15s was occasionally practised at mountain and sea ranges.

In contrast to the 19th IAP's outstanding safety achievement during the regiment's conversion-to-type phase, the process at the other 'Farmer'-equipped regiment, the Uzundjovo-based 21st IAP, proved to be much more problematic from the very beginning. On 22 February, 1958, Leitenant Gancho Ganchev, an inexperienced pilot who had less than 100 hours of total jet time in his pilot's logbook was killed during his first MiG-19 sortie near the airfield while flying into the landing circuit; the cause of the accident being a supposed aircraft control system malfunction. This first fatal accident involving the MiG-19 was followed not long after by many similar events that eventually turned the 21st IAP into the VVS unit with the worst safety record of the 1960s; the unit reported nearly half of the total MiG-19 accidents and aircrew fatalities in Bulgaria.

In January 1958, a dozen radar-equipped and gun-armed MiG-19P all-weather interceptors (NATO code 'Farmer-B'), also manufactured at the GAZ-21 factory, arrived in crates at Graf Ignatievo by railroad. The new fighters were quickly re-assembled, flight-checked and handed over to the 1/19 IAE. There the radar-equipped 'Farmer-Bs' replaced a dozen MiG-17PFs taken on strength three years earlier. The squadron's pilots, all of whom had amassed a considerable experience flying the radar-equipped MiG-17PFs rapidly mastered their new mount, practising intercepts in the most difficult weather conditions — in clouds and at night. The other two squadrons of the 1/19th IAP — the 2/19 IAE and the 3/19 IAE — continued operating the MiG-19S.

The MiG-19P (P-Perekhvatchik, interceptor) was equipped with the twin antennae RP-5 Izumrud-2 air intercept radar, similar to the MiG-17PF's RP-1. Its search antenna was housed under a prominent radome located in a lipped top to the intake, whilst the tracking antenna was housed in the intake centre-body. The weight penalty imposed by the heavyweight air intercept radar necessitated the removal of the nose cannon. The MiG-19P's lengthened nose housing the radar antennas and black boxes, combined with the large hood of the radar display in the cockpit, both contributed greatly to a severe restriction of the pilot's visibility, especially during the landing approach phase. A manoeuvring limitation of 3.5-G was imposed to the MiG-19P (and later on to the MiG-19PM) due to the radar operability and reliability concerns. That is why the pilots of the MiG-19P- and MiG-19PM-equipped squadrons used to maintain their high-G manoeuvring currency on the MiG-19S.

The RP-5 radar, developed on the base of the RP-2 used on the MiG-17P/PF had a scan capability of +/- 60° in the horizontal plane and +26°/-17° in the vertical plane relative to the aircraft's centreline. The detection range against a medium-size bomber target was about 8km (4.4nm) while tracking range was not exceeding 4km (2.2nm). In service, the bulky RP-5 proved to be a notoriously unreliable piece of kit, significantly reducing the MiG-19P's actual all-weather capability.

The MiG-19P's service with the 1/19 IAE was very brief as in the late summer of 1959 the dozen radar-equipped/gun-armed 'Farmers' were transferred to the 11th IAP based at Gabrovnitsa in the north-western corner of Bulgaria. There the MiG-19P equipped the 1/11 IAE, while the other two squadrons, the 2/11 and 3/11, continued flying the MiG-17F/PF.

In September that year, the 1/19 IAE, then known as the VVS' premier fighter-interceptor squadron, began its conversion to the MiG-19PM missile-carrying interceptor. Earlier on during the summer months of 1959, a group of 11 selected pilots from the 19th IAP was sent on a MiG-19PM conversion course at the Soviet Air Defence Forces' 148th Combat Training & Aircrew Conversion Centre at Savastleika near Moscow. Later on in the same summer they moved to Krasnovodsk range on the eastern shore of Caspian Sea where the Bulgarian aircrews had practised bad weather intercepts and live missile firings against high-speed target drones.

A dozen MiG-19PMs (NATO 'Farmer-E'), manufactured at the GAZ-153 factory at Novosibirsk were taken on strength by the 19th IAP in September 1959. This missile-only interceptor version featured the RP-5-U radar (a slightly improved RP-5 derivative), facilitating the search, acquisition and automatic tracking of air targets to achieve the solution for pursuit attack with guided missiles. The MiG-19PM lacked guns and was armed with four RS-2US (NATO code AA-1 'Alkali') beam-riding air-to-air missiles (AAMs). The RS-2US had a brochure effective range of between 2km and 5km (1.4 nm and 2.8 nm), extending to 6.5km (3.6nm) at high altitude, the launch weight was 85kg (185lb), with a warhead weight of 13kg (28.6lb), and a maximum speed of 1,650km/h (891kt).

Carried on APU-4 launch rails, the RS-2US was a first-generation AAM, very sensitive to the radar beam shape of the launch platform and its movements. The missile

This MiG-19PM missile-armed fighter-interceptor was delivered to the 1/19 IAE at Graf Ignatievo in September 1959 and soldiered on for 20 years with the all-weather fighter squadron, specialised in operations against non-manoeuvring bombers and reconnaissance aircraft. It was phased out on 5 September 1979, having amassed 1,394 flight hours.

required constant target tracking until scoring a hit and was prone to jamming and proved effective only against non-manoeuvring bombers and transport aircraft. Furthermore, the lack of cannons limited considerably the MiG-19PM's usefulness and the missile-carrying 'Farmer-E' was entirely unsuitable for combat against turning fighters or fighter-bombers.

The elite 1/19 IAE flying the MiG-19PM was the VVS' 'Farmer' unit, boasting the lowest attrition rate and the highest level of combat readiness in the 1960s and early 1970s. The squadron was an integral part of the Warsaw Pact's extensive air defence network spreading across Eastern Europe and was responsible for the daytime bad weather and night-time QRA (for both bad and clear weather conditions). Usually two aircraft were held at QRA at Graf Ignatievo — their number raising to four or even six during periods of tension between the superpowers, such as the Cuban Missile Crisis of 1962. The daytime VMC QRA was maintained by the two MiG-19S-equipped squadrons at Graf Ignatievo.

The 1/19 IAE's MiG-19PMs were often scrambled for practice intercepts against

From the pilot's point of view, the MiG-19 was a 'real beast' — a powerful fighter possessing a very high, then unused to a full extent, combat capability for the late 1950s and the early 1960s. This is a MiG-19P radar-equipped interceptor serving with the 1/11 IAE at Gabrovnitsa and then moving to the 1/18 IAE at Dobroslavtsi, responsible for the air defence of the western part of Bulgaria and the capital Sofia.

The MiG-19 was rapidly overshadowed by the newer, faster, much more reliable and maintainable MiG-21 after amassing only 10 to 13 years in Bulgarian air force service. Repeatedly plagued by a plethora of technical problems, the type hardly remained in mass service until the early/mid-1970s. This is a MiG-19P gun-armed fighter-interceptor which suffered from a serious attrition during its 20 years of service with the Bulgarian air arm.

'mock' air targets (or the so-called 'Warsaw Pact check targets'), in most if not all cases these being Soviet Air Force or Naval Aviation Tu-16 twin-engine jet bombers and reconnaissance aircraft dispatched on routine training missions over Bulgaria and the western part of Black Sea. In the early 1960s, a serious incident was recorded during such an intercept: a scrambled MiG-19PM from Graf Ignatievo is reported to have mistakenly launched a salvo of all its four RS-2US missiles against a Soviet Air Force Tu-16. There were no hits as the unmindful pilot promptly recognised the danger in time and halted the radar illumination of the launched missiles to miss the target. During another QRA incident, an 1/19 IAE pilot at Graf Ignatievo mistakenly launched all four missiles in salvo while checking his aircraft on the ground before the start of his night shift.

The Gabrovnitsa-based 11th IAP was the third VVS fighter regiment to convert to the 'Farmer', albeit partially. In the summer of 1958, its first squadron, the 1/11 IAE, was provided with a few MiG-19S previously operated by the 21st IAP, intended for conversion training of its pilots. Later on during the same year the dozen ex-1/19 IAE MiG-19Ps were taken on strength, replacing the MiG-17PFs, which were handed over to the 27th IAP. Interestingly, there were no MiG-19P aircrew conversion problems reported during the work-up phase as most of the squadron's pilots had plenty of experience amassed

on the MiG-17PF. However, the MiG-19P operated by the 11th IAP suffered from a relatively high number of accidents between 1958 and 1963. Four aircraft, representing some 30 per cent of the 'Farmer-B' fleet in Bulgaria by that time were written-off in flight and ground accidents during its four years of active operations at Gabrovnitsa.

In early 1963, the 11th IAP was disbanded during an abrupt rationalisation campaign of the VVS's strength. The surviving eight MiG-19Ps, together with a few MiG-19S', went on to serve with the 18th IAP at Dobroslavtsi airfield near the country's capital Sofia. There the 'Farmer-B/Cs' replaced the MiG-17F in the regiment's first squadron, the 1/18 IAE; in 1966, six ex-Soviet Air Force MiG-19Ps were acquired second-hand as attrition replacements.

The MiG-19P/S soldiered on with the 1/18 IAE until September 1975 when they were swiftly replaced by brand-new MiG-21MFs. The ten surviving MiG-19Ps and a few MiG-19S' were ferried to Graf Ignatievo to be stripped there for spare parts; however, some airframes remained in active use in the 1/19 IAE for three more years until November 1978.

The enormous MiG-19S attrition rate recorded by the 21st IAP at Uzundzhovo eventually caused serious pilot dissatisfaction as there were a lot of complains of low airframe/powerplant reliability. This had eventually caused an early end of 'Farmer-C' operations with the 21st IAP and in mid-1972 all its MiG-19S' were transferred to Graf Ignatievo. The powerful but notoriously unreliable 'Farmer-C' was replaced in the 21st IAP by a mixture of afterburner and non-afterburner MiG-17s.

The 1/19 IAE had the distinction to remain the last VVS squadron operating the MiG-19; the other two Graf Ignatievo-based squadrons of the 19th IAP having converted to the MiG-21F-13 (3/19 IAE) and MiG-21M (2/19 IAE), in 1963 and 1969 respectively. The 1/19 IAE continued to fly a mixture of MiG-19PMs and MiG-19S, a total, in round numbers, of about 40 airframes, until late 1978. The last regular flying operations of the 1/19 IAE's MiG-19s were carried out in November 1978. By the end of the same year the type was replaced by 14 MiG-21MF/UMs transferred from Dobroslavtsi.

The MiG-19 firmly heads the VVS jet accident statistics as the type amassed extraordinary attrition and loss rate figures. According to the authors' research using the available VVS service records, no fewer than 25 MiG-19s (which is nearly 30 per cent of the total number of the aircraft delivered) were lost in various flight accidents while at least ten more MiG-19s were damaged beyond economical repair in various landing and ground-servicing accidents. A total of 16 MiG-19 pilots were killed and eight more managed to ejected safely during the type's service in Bulgaria between 1957 and 1978.

Statistically, the 21st IAP heads the MiG-19's attrition list. The three squadrons of this unit are known to have suffered from eight fatal and at least five non-fatal MiG-19S flying accidents. In addition, four fatal and one non-fatal flying accidents were recorded by the 19th IAP; three and two respectively happened in the 18th IAP; one and one respectively by the 11th IAP.

Declassified Bulgarian service records maintain that human error was quoted as the main cause of some 60 per cent of the VVS MiG-19 accidents. Lack of flying discipline, poor pre-flight preparation, handling errors and last but not least maintenance personnel errors had been quoted as the main cause for at least 13 flying accidents involving the MiG-19. A significant factor, which is said to have greatly contributed to the high rate of the human error-caused flight accidents, was the lack of a dedicated twin-seat conversion and continuation trainer. The MiG-15UTI, widely-used in this role, was deemed as being ill-suited to replicate fully the MiG-19's complex handling characteristics, especially on landing.

The dozen MiG-19PMs proved to be the most reliable 'Farmers' in Bulgarian service thanks to the combination of the high manufacturing standards, well-trained pilots and skilled maintenance personnel. Only two aircraft were lost in operational accidents, this resulting in one loss per approximately 7,200 flight hours and an accident rate of 13.8 losses per 100,000 flight hours. In contrast, the MiG-19P recorded much worse safety figures as five aircraft were lost in flying accidents; this translates into one loss per 2,600 flight hours equating to an accident rate of about 39 loses per 100,000 flight hours. In addition, two more MiG-19Ps were burned-out due to engine fires when on routine maintenance while two more were damaged beyond economical repair in non-fatal landing accidents. The worst safety record, however, was recorded by the MiG-19S version, accounting for one loss per 2,200 flight hours (or even less as the lack of reliable data in the preserved MiG-19 service records makes it impossible to have a more precise calculation of the MiG-19S' total flying time in Bulgarian service), which equates to an accident rate of no fewer than 45 loses per 100,000 flight hours!

Table 2: Deliveries of Prop Trainers and Jet Fighters to the Bulgarian Air Force 1951-1962

Aircraft type	Delivered
Yak-11	45
Yak-17UTI	16
Yak-23	120
MiG-15	93
MiG-15bis	67
MiG-15Rbis	6
MiG-15UTI	61
MiG-17	138
MiG-17F	62
MiG-17PF	12
MiG-19S	60
MiG-19P	18 (including 6 second-hand examples, received in 1966)
MiG-19PM	12

Table 3: Deliveries of Prop Trainers and Jet Fighters to the Bulgarian Air Force, 1951-1962 (by Batches)

Aircraft type	No	Year of delivery	Source
Yak-11	10	12.1950	Soviet Union
Yak-23	40	1951	Soviet Union
Yak-17UTI	5	05.1951	Soviet Union
MiG-15	23	11-12.1951	Soviet Union
MiG-15UTI	3	12.1951	Soviet Union
Yak-23	80	1952	Soviet Union
MiG-15	34	1952	Soviet Union
Yak-17UTI	5	04.1952	Soviet Union
Yak-11	10	05.1952	Soviet Union
MiG-15UTI	3	05.1952	Soviet Union
MiG-15	6	1953	Soviet Union
Yak-17UTI	6	04.1953	Soviet Union
MiG-15bis	20	08.1953	Soviet Union
MiG-15	30	10.1953	Czechoslovakia
MiG-15UTI	8	01.1955	Soviet Union
Yak-11	4	03.1955	Soviet Union
MiG-15bis	5	04.1955	Czechoslovakia
MiG-15bis	10	05.1955	Czechoslovakia
MiG-17PF	6	04.1955	Soviet Union
MiG-15bis	22	05.1955	Soviet Union
MiG-15bis	10	06.1955	Soviet Union
MiG-15UTI	8	07.1955	Czechoslovakia
MiG-15UTI	12	08.1955	Czechoslovakia
Yak-11	6	08.1955	Soviet Union
MiG-17PF	6	11.1955	Soviet Union
MiG-15UTI	3	08.1956	Czechoslovakia
Yak-11	5	09.1956	Soviet Union
MiG-17F	12	02.1957	Soviet Union
Yak-11	10	03.1957	Soviet Union
MiG-19S	60	12.1957	Soviet Union
MiG-19P	12	01.1958	Soviet Union
MiG-15UTI	4	02.1958	Czechoslovakia
MiG-17F	20	03.1959	Poland
MiG-15UTI	4	04.1959	Soviet Union
MiG-19PM	12	09.1959	Soviet Union
MiG-15UTI	4	09.1959	Czechoslovakia
MiG-17F	12	02.1960	Poland
MiG-17F	18	03.1960	Czechoslovakia
MiG-15UTI	12	04.1960	Soviet Union
MiG-17	138	12.1961	Soviet Union
MiG-15Rbis	6	03.1962	Soviet Union

Table 4: VVS Order of Battle, December 1960[1]

Unit	Aircraft	Base
Front-line units		
1st Fighter Division		Yambol
15th IAP	MiG-15bis, MiG-17F, MiG-15UTI	Ravnets
22nd IAP	MiG-15bis, MiG-17, MiG-15UTI	Bezmer
27th IAP	MiG-17F/PF, MiG-15UTI	Balchik
4th Fighter Division		Dobroslavtsi
11th IAP	MiG-19P/S, MiG-17F, MiG-15UTI	Gabrovnitsa
18th IAP	MiG-15bis, MiG-17F, MiG-15UTI	Dobroslavtsi
43rd IAP	MiG-15, MiG-15UTI	Dobroslavtsi
10th Fighter Division		Plovdiv
19th IAP	MiG-19PM/S, MiG-15UTI	Graf Ignatievo
21st IAP	MiG-19S, MiG-15UTI	Uzundzhovo
25th IAP	MiG-17F, MiG-15bis, MiG-15UTI	Cheshnigirovo
16th TrAP		Vrazhdebna
1st TrAE	Il-14, Li-2, Mi-4, Mi-1	Vrazhdebna
2nd TrAE	Mi-4	Thcaika
Training Units		
People's Higher Air School		Dolna Mitropolia
1st UBAP	Yak-11, Laz-7M	Dolna Mitropolya
2nd UBAP	MiG-15, MiG-15UTI	Kamenets

Aircrews: a total of 574, including 74 with the 1st Class rating, 179 — 2nd Class rating, 208 — 3rd Class rating and 98 without class rating.

1   Source: Prof Col Dimitar Nedyalkov: Bulgarian Aviation in the Cold War, Military Publishing House, 2011

Bibliography

Books

Author's team, *Възхвала за летище Каменец – порталът към небето и звездите* [Praise for Kamenets Airfield – the portal to the skies and stars] (in Bulgarian), (Pleven, Ivko EOOD, 2013)

Author's team, *История на радиотехническите войски* [History of Radio-Technical Troops] (in Bulgarian), (Sofia, Air Group 2000, 2007; ISBN: 978-954-752-10-87)

Author's team, *Нашето летище Узунджово* [Our Uzundzhovo Airfield] (in Bulgarian), (Sofia, Propeller Publishing House, 2009; ISBN: 978-954-392-030-3)

Author's team, *Хората и летище Граф Игнатиево* [Graf Ignatievo's People and Airfield] (in Bulgarian), (Sofia, Air Group 2000, 2006; ISBN: 978-954-752-095-0)

Bakalov, Zelyu, *Животът на летеца – от земята до небето* [Flyer's life – From the Ground to the Skies] (in Bulgarian), (Sofia, Bulgarika, 2000)

Dimitrov, Dimitar, *Когато българската авиация беше на върха* [When the Bulgarian Aviation was on the Peak] (in Bulgarian), (Sofia, 2006)

Haas, Michael, *Apollo's Warriors: United States Air Force Special Operations during the Cold War* (Maxwell Air Force Base, Alabama, Air University Press, 1997)

Kodikov, Boris, *Българската щурмова авиация – първа част* [Bulgarian Attack Aviation: First Part] (in Bulgarian), (Plovdiv, Izdatelstvo Vion, 2011)

Mladenov, Alexander, *Soviet Cold War Fighters* (Fonthill Media Ltd., 2016; ISBN: 978-1781554968)

Mladenov, Alexander; Andonov, Evegeni; Gozev, Krasimir, *The Bulgarian Air Force in the Second Word War* (Solihull, Helion & Co. Ltd, 2018; ISBN: 978-1912390649)

Nedyalkov, Dimitar, *Българската авиация през Студената война* [The Bulgarian Aviation during the Cold War] (in Bulgarian), (Sofia, Military Publishing House, 2012; ISBN: 978-954-509-448-4)

Nedyalkov, Dimitar, *История на българската военна авиация* [History of Bulgarian Military Aviation] (in Bulgarian), (Sofia, Military Publishing House, 2011; ISBN: 978-954-509-47-12)

Pedlow, Gregory & Welzenbach, Donald, *The CIA and the U-2 Program, 1954-1974* (Diane Publishing CO, ASIN: B01182PLZC)

Petrov, Stoyan, *Жажда за небе – дневникът на един зам* [Thirst for the sky: The Diary of a Deputy] (in Bulgarian), (Sofia, Air Group 2000, 2004; ISBN: 978-752-070-09)

Trifonov, Todor, *Летешки преживелици* [Flyer's Experience] (in Bulgarian), (Sofia, Air Group 2000, 2004; ISBN: 954-752-06-52)

Journals and Magazines

Andonov, Evgeni, *Оръжието на българската авиация – част VII*, Armament of the Bulgarian Aviation – Part VII, *AERO Bulgarian Aerospace Magazine* (Issue 78, February 2015), pp.38-43.

Andonov, Evgeni & Grozev, Krassimir, *100 години българска военна авиация*, 100 Years of Bulgarian Military Aviation supplement, *AERO Bulgarian Aerospace Magazine* (Issue 50, October 2012), pp.4-37.

Andonov, Evgeni & Grozev, Krassimir, *Ме 109 в България – приложение*, Me 109 in Bulgaria supplement, *AERO Bulgarian Aerospace Magazine* (Issue 39, September 2011), pp.3-45.

Andonov, Evgeni, *Балонната епопея – част 2*, Balloons' Epic – part 2, *AERO Bulgarian Aerospace Magazine* (Issue 34, June 2011), pp.46-50.

Andonov, Evgeni, *Бягствата – част VI*, Escapes – Part VI, *AERO Bulgarian Aerospace Magazine* (Issue 59, July 2013), pp.45-51.

Andonov, Evgeni, *Граф Игнатиево на 60*, Graph Ignatievo at 60, *AERO Bulgarian Aerospace Magazine* (Issue 31, March 2011), pp.44-50.

Andonov, Evgeni, *Как нашите ме свалиха*, How I was downed by friendly fighters, *AERO Bulgarian Aerospace Magazine* (Issue 16, December 2009), pp.42-45.

Andonov, Evgeni, *Трагедията на полет LY402 – част I*, Tragedy of Flight LY402 – Part I, *AERO Bulgarian Aerospace Magazine* (Issue 82, June 2015), pp.40-45.

Andonov, Evgeni, *Трагедията на полет LY402 – част II*, Tragedy of Flight LY402 – Part II, *AERO Bulgarian Aerospace Magazine* (Issue 83, July 2015), pp.33-39.

Andonov, Evgeni, *Трагедията на полет LY402 – част III*, Tragedy of Flight LY402 – Part III, *AERO Bulgarian Aerospace Magazine* (Issue 86, October 2015), pp.26-31.

Andonov, Evgeni, *Трагедията на полет LY402 – част IV*, Tragedy of Flight LY402 – Part IV, *AERO Bulgarian Aerospace Magazine* (Issue 87, November 2015), pp.34-39.

Andonov, Evgeni, *Трагедията на полет LY402 – част V*, Tragedy of Flight LY402 – Part V, *AERO Bulgarian Aerospace Magazine* (Issue 88, December 2015), pp.38-43.

Andonov, Evgeni, *Трагедията на полет LY402 – част VI*, Tragedy of Flight LY402 – Part VI, *AERO Bulgarian Aerospace Magazine* (Issue 89, January 2016), pp.34-39.

Andonov, Evgeni, *Трагедията на полет LY402 – част VII*, Tragedy of Flight LY402 – Part VII, *AERO Bulgarian Aerospace Magazine* (Issue 90, February 2016), pp.35-39.

Israeli Report on Tragedy Over Bulgaria: El Al Plane Shot Down Without Warning, *Aviation Week*, December 26, 1955, pp.51-58.

Mladenov, Alexander, A Decade of Air Power – Bulgaria 1940-1949, *Wings of Fame* (Vol 13), pp.92-111.

Mladenov, Alexander, Bulgarian Air Power Analysis, *World Air Power Journal* (Vol 39, Spring 1999), pp.142-157.

Combat Logs

The authors also used information retrieved from the Central Military Archive at Veliko Tarnovo in this book, including the complete file of the investigation of the shoot down of the Israeli El AL Lockheed Constellation.

Interviews

The authors also used information retrieved from previously unpublished interviews they made with the following Bulgarian veteran pilots and officers serving between 1945 and 1960: Peter Manolev, Stefan Stoyanov, Mikhail Grigorov, Todor Trifonov, Vidyo Penev, Atanas Atanasov, Stoyan Petrov, Angel Mladenov, Khristo Ivanov, Ivan Stankov, Viktor Atanasov, Ivan Petkov, Ilya Penchev, Georgy Vukov, Georgy Todorov, Kiril Radev, Netso Likov, Stoil Stoilov.

ACKNOWLEDGEMENTS

The authors would like to thank the following for their kind assistance and support with work on the book: Krassimir Grozev, Vladimir Petrov, Nikolay Katsarov, Stefan Boshnyakov, Peter Penev, Ognyan Iliev, Stoyan Popov, Silvyia Zheleva, Sonya Simeonova, and Gancho Kamenarsky.

ABOUT THE AUTHORS

Alexander Mladenov, from Bulgaria, is an aerospace & defence author, journalist and photographer, based in Sofia, Bulgaria. A graduate of the Technical University of Sofia, he is also the author of a series of books on Soviet/Russian modern military aircraft and this is his third book for Helion.

Evgeni Andonov is an aviation journalist and historian based in Sofia, Bulgaria. He is a graduate of the Technical University of Sofia and his special interests include deep research into little-known moments of the history and operations of the Bulgarian Air Force, mostly from the 1920s to the 1980s. This is his second book for Helion.